HISTORICAL APPROACHES TO CRIME

Volume 57, Sage Library of Social Research

SAGE LIBRARY OF SOCIAL RESEARCH

HISTORICAL APPROACHES TO CRIME
Research Strategies and Issues

James A. Inciardi
Alan A. Block
Lyle A. Hallowell

Volume 57
SAGE LIBRARY OF
SOCIAL RESEARCH

 **SAGE PUBLICATIONS**　　Beverly Hills　　London

364.09
I37h

For information address:

SAGE PUBLICATIONS, INC.
275 South Beverly Drive
Beverly Hills, California 90212

SAGE PUBLICATIONS LTD
28 Banner Street
London EC1Y 8QE

Printed in the United States of America

Library of Congress Cataloging in Publication Data

Inciardi, James A
    Historical approaches to crime.

    (Sage library of social research ; v. 57)
    Bibliography: p. 179
    1. Crime and criminals—History. 2. Crime and criminals—Research—History. I. Block, Alan A., joint author. II. Hallowell, Lyle A., joint author. III. Title.
HV6021.I58   364'.07'22   77-21260
ISBN 0-8039-0887-3
ISBN 0-8039-0888-1 pbk.

FIRST PRINTING

CONTENTS

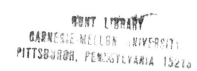

To our children . . .

Brooks
Craig
Dana
Glenn
Hallie
Kristin
Leslie
Michael

PREFACE

The data of human history have long had only limited priority in the substance and logic of social inquiry. The majority of contemporary sociologists have traditionally concerned themselves with the more general aspects of social behavior, while historians' interests have focused on the more unique aspects of particular personages and events. Yet for the sociologist, history can place social behavior within the frame of time. The longitudinal view offered by the observation and documentation of phenomena through time can provide for a more complete analysis and understanding of the emergence, scope, and persistence or change of given social organization and behavior, and as such, history becomes the very framework of detached inquiry.

The avoidance of history by many sociologists has been due, in part, to certain biases against this ancient discipline. For many millennia the partly scientific and partly literary form of narrative history predominated. Much of it offered objective and dispassionate views of individuals and events, but a significant portion also contained much that was mythical, allegorical, and historically false. Shortly before the turn of the century a more academic history emerged. It embarked on a search for new subjects, sources, interpretations, and relationships. It was concerned, as well, with scientific investigation and verification of data. Yet among sociologists, the conception of history as simplistic narrative reports of unique events has lingered, resulting in their disinterest in records of the past.

During recent decades, this bias against history has become less pronounced. Among sociologists, there has been an increasing interest in historical analysis, and this phenomenon has also become apparent within the discipline of criminology. A growing number of criminologists have come to realize the need for analyzing the past for a better understanding of the present, and for correcting many of the misconceptions about crime that have been entrenched in our consciousness for many decades.

Most recently, at the twenty-eighth Annual Meeting of the American Society of Criminology in 1976, the growing interest in the history of crime was especially evident. The response to a call for papers on the topic of historical approaches to crime was overwhelming. It was apparent that there was an additional group for whom the history of crime seemed challenging, yet somewhat threatening. These were researchers new to the discipline whose training had been of a more empirical nature and who were seeking information on the philosophy and method of historical inquiry as well as direction and guidance regarding appropriate historical sources. And it is within the context of these interests and concerns that this volume has been prepared. For those new to the area, it is hoped that our efforts can provide an understanding of history—its philosophy, scope, and rewards—as well as an introduction to some of the strategies employed in historical research. For the more seasoned observer, our intention is to reflect on problems we have encountered in our historical investigations and to share some of the data and source materials we have located through our inquiries.

During the preparation of this volume, as typically occurs with the writing of any manuscript, a number of debts were incurred. Our first acknowledgment must go to George McCune whose interest in the subject made this publication possible. In addition, for helpful criticism and suggestions, for the many hours of library and microfilm search, and for the almost endless days of typing, retyping, proofing, copying, and indexing of the final manuscript, acknowledgment is due to Marcia Block, Margaret Dobroski, Gary Fine, Carolyn J. Inciardi, Marie C. Inciardi, Sherryl Kleinman, Sandy Richardson, and Joanne Walter. And finally, to the small army of anonymous librarians across the country who endured our persistent groping and questioning, we thank you for your patience.

July 1977   *James A. Inciardi*
                                                              Glasgow, Delaware

                                                                 Alan A. Block
                                                               Newark, Delaware

                                                              Lyle A. Hallowell
                                                         Minneapolis, Minnesota

INTRODUCTION:

In Search of the Unicorn

Conceptions of crime and the history of ideas have many things in common. Both offer reflections of social behavior and interpretation; both provide insights as to the dynamics of human interaction and phenomenal relationships; yet in addition, they are often incomplete or beset with mystery and error generated by the frailties of constricted understanding and limited observation. Characteristic in this respect are the events surrounding the legend of the unicorn, which, to a large degree, parallel much of the dehistorization within the annals of crime.

The books of the Old Testament were originally written in Hebrew, but in ca. 250 B.C. a group of Hellenistic Jews translated the scriptures into Greek, producing a version of the Bible known as the *Septuagint*. A portion of the Old Testament is believed to have been written as early as the tenth century B.C. (Keller 1956: 415), and as historians, philologists, and paleographers well understand, the translation and interpretation of ancient documents is plagued with numerous difficulties. There are the problems of linguistics, typically in the form of idioms and words with special meanings, which can be altered or lost when transferred from one language to another. In the Book of Job 23:11, for example, there is an idiom that remained unknown until 1939 and a rare negated tense that was unanalyzed until 1968 (Gordon, 1974: 81-82). In addition, the authors of the original Hebrew texts manipulated their language so deftly that the scriptures included riddles subtle to a degree that even modern cryptanalysis finds difficult to unravel. Common in the Old Testament, for example, was encipherment by substitution known as *atbash,* in which the first letter of the Hebrew alphabet was substituted for the last, the second letter for the next-to-the-last, and so forth (Pritchard 1955; Stenring 1970). *Acrostics,* through which certain letters, usually the first in each line, formed a name or message, were also not uncommon. And finally, there was the issue of natural history. There were facts of local nature which were taken for granted by the original recorders of the Old Testament, and left undetailed for later translators (Ley 1959: 13). As such, the Hellenistic Jews who produced the Septuagint were not only confronted with the usual problems of translation, but with the difficulties of riddle, mystery, and undescribed phenomena.

In the original scriptures, the Hebrew writers had mentioned with some awe an animal they called *Re'em*. In Job 39:9-12 and Numbers 23:22, the *Re'em* was mentioned as having great strength; it was characterized as fleet, fierce, indomitable, and especially distinguished by the armor of its brow; but it was never actually described. Later studies indicated that *Re'em* was *Bos Primigenius* or the urus, a wild ox that is believed to be the ancestor of European domestic cattle (Shepard 1930: 44). But the urus, now extinct, had never been seen by the translators since it no longer existed where they lived. Yet the traits of the *Re'em* awakened dim recollections of another beast which was believed to be as fierce, mysterious, strange, and remote. They used the Greek word μον όκερως or *monokeros*.

The monokeros of the Greeks came from the writings of Ctesias, the Greek historian and one-time physician of the Persian King Artaxerxes II. Ctesias returned from Persia around the year 398 B.C. and prepared a volume on India, a place he himself had never seen. His book was a compilation of hearsay based on the tales of travelers and included the following comment:

> There are in India certain wild asses which are as large as horses, and larger. Their bodies are white, their heads dark red, and their eyes dark blue. They have a horn on the forehead which is about a foot and a half in length. The dust filed from this horn is administered in a potion as a protection against deadly drugs. The base of this horn, for some two hands-breadth above the brow, is pure white, the upper part is sharp and of a vivid crimson; and the remainder, or middle portion, is black. Those who drink out of these horns, made into drinking vessels, are not subject, they say, to convulsions or to the holy disease [epilepsy]. Indeed, they are immune even to poisons if, either before or after swallowing such, they drink wine, water, or anything else from these beakers. (Cited by Ley 1959: 15.)

Zoologists have determined that Ctesias' monokeros or "wild ass of India" was actually the Indian rhinoceros, with admixtures of features of some other animal. But in English, monokeros means *unicorn,* and

Ctesias suggested the existence of an animal with one horn that had mythical and magical qualities.

Re'em was translated into monokeros with one main result: for many centuries to come, the existence of the unicorn would be reiterated, and it could not be doubted, for it was repeatedly mentioned in the Bible. As such, the unicorn emerged through a classical error, and persisted in religious, cultural, and literary legends. Among medieval writers, the unicorn was depicted as representing many curiosities:

> The unicorn has but one horn in the middle of its forehead. It is the only animal that ventures to attack the elephant; and so sharp is the nail of its foot, that with one blow it can rip the belly of that beast. Hunters can catch the unicorn only by placing a young virgin in its haunts. No sooner does he see the damsel, than he runs toward her, and lies down at her feet, and so suffers himself to be captured by the hunters. The unicorn represents Jesus Christ, who took on Him our nature in the virgin's womb, was betrayed by the Jews, and delivered into the hands of Pontius Pilate. Its one horn signifies the Gospel of Truth.[1]

In recent years it has been demonstrated that unicorns might be "created" scientifically through the surgical manipulation of the horn buds of cattle (Dove 1936), but it was historical inquiry which documented that the unicorn was legend, and that the lore of the unicorn had been generated by civilized man.[2]

Our knowledge and conceptions of crime have much in common with the unicorn story. The history of crime contains many valid representations of past events, but in addition, it also includes much that has become clouded by legend and folklore and generational distortions unreclaimed by rigid historical analysis. Consider, for example, the explanation of the term "Mafia" in contemporary literature. In Ed Reid's The Grim Reapers (1969: 4-5), the initial use of the term is located at the outbreak of the Sicilian Vespers on March 30, 1282, and suggested to have come from the motto of the insurrection: "Morte Alla Francia Italia Anela!" (Death to the French is Italy's cry). Alternatively, author Andrew Varna (1957: 58) offers the notion that "Mafia" was created in 1860 by Sicilian gang leader Joseph Mazzini, who is alleged to have contracted the initials of his slogan, which read, translated into English, "Mazzini authorities theft, arson, and poisoning." And more recently, in journalist Gay Talese's bestseller Honor Thy Father (1971: 189-190), we returned to Easter Monday in 1282. Talese relates the rape of a young maiden on her wedding day and the an-

guished cries of her mother: *"ma fia, ma fia"* (my daughter, my daughter).
By contrast, Inciardi (1974: 368-369) contends that an analysis of the
Italian language during these earlier periods combined with an investigation into Sicilian history and literature would suggest that the tendered
explanations of "Mafia" are pure fiction. He states that

> more laudable comments on the origins of *Mafia* from Italian his-
> torical and literary works link the root and meaning of the term to
> elements prevailing within the Sicilian culture. *Mafia* is seemingly of
> Sicilian-Arabic content, descending from the etyma *hafa*—to pre-
> serve, protect, and act as guardian; from *mo'hafi*—friend or com-
> panion; from *mo'hafah*—to defend; and from *mo'hafiat*—preserva-
> tion, safety, power, integrity, strength, and a state which designates
> the remedy of damage and ill (DaAleppo & Calvaruso, 1910: 226-
> 29). That the Arabic *mo'hafiat* became *mafiat* by elision, and *mafia*
> by apocope, can be drawn from Pitre (1884, 1894, 1898, 1902),
> who described the latter as a dialect term common in pre-1860
> Palermo. It expressed "beauty and excellence," united with no-
> tions of "superiority" and "bravery"; and in reference to *man* it
> meant something more: "the consciousness of being a man," "assur-
> ance of the mind," "boldness" but never "defiance," and "arro-
> gance" but never "haughtiness." Thus, both Arabic-Sicilian linguistic
> referents and common *Palermitani* usages converged to generate
> *Mafia's* polycentric meanings: protection against the arrogance of
> the powerful, remedy to any damage, sturdiness of body, strength
> and serenity of spirit, the best and most exquisite part of every-
> thing.

And furthermore, it appears that the first use of "Mafia" in a criminal
context can be attributed to Guiseppe Rizzoto's dialect play *I Mafuisi
della Vicaria* (Barzini 1941: 327), an 1863 presentation dedicated to "the
handsome and daring men" of Palermo's jail.

Historical Approaches to Crime has been designed not only to discuss
the philosophy and method of history, but primarily to examine specific
areas of the history of crime for the purposes of documenting specific phenomena and demonstrating how ahistorical materials have intersected the
continuity of our knowledge base. In so doing, it will make manifest that
the historical approach to crime is not merely the uncovering of events
from disparate points in time, nor the simple collection of data from anti-
quarian reference works. Rather, it involves the fitting together of events,
personages, processes, and understandings drawn together from sources
deemed historically reliable through the careful location, selection, verification, and comparative analysis of appropriate data.

Part I of this volume, consisting of two chapters, deals with a variety of theoretical and methodological aspects of the historical approach to crime. In Chapter 1 the basic issues are briefly explored. First, what is history? Second, what methods are typically employed in historical research? Chapter 2 examines the relationship of folklore and history, specifically targeting (a) the nature and content of folklore; (b) folklore vs. history as an approach to defining and examining social phenomena; (c) the differences between the materials of folklore and historical data; and (d) the problems of evaluation raised by folklore with respect to the historical critical method.

Part II examines specific areas in the history of crime to demonstrate how the reliance on unreliable sources has generated any number of misconceptions. Chapter 3, in pursuit of this purpose, focuses on the American "Wild West." The history of our Western outlaws is reviewed followed by an inquiry as to the extent to which much of our understanding of this segment of Americana is based on folklore and legend. Finally, it is demonstrated how much of this ahistorical writing emerged and persisted. Chapter 4 is based on the notion that in the social scientific literature concerned with organized crime, historical claims, judgments, assumptions, and opinions are rampant; that some of these have even been worked into a history of sorts that is most notable for its reliance on undocumented popular sources and the unsubstantiated memoirs of celebrated informers. The most telling features of this history are its naiveté and devotion to the idea that an alien conspiracy has run organized crime for the last five decades. Additionally, it is assumed that organized crime's development has been part of an inexorable march toward centralization and bureaucratization. Among the consequences of this haphazard reconstruction, preoccupied with a *mafia mystique,* has been the stifling of serious work on the social world of organized crime. To examine these issues the chapter deals, first, with the contemporary arguments and claims which promote the notion of organized crime as a rigidly structured bureaucracy, somewhat reminiscent of Max Weber's "Iron Cage." After establishing the frame of the contemporary arguments, we inquire into the historicity of the claims. Through an examination of the historical sources used to support the contemporary sociologies, we argue that the historical foundations are exceptionally weak if not absolutely deficient. Next, the chapter addresses a series of reasons for the biased and warped histories of organized crime through an examination of sexual segregation in its alleged social world. An examination of what proper historical research can illuminate is provided, focusing on the roles of women in organized crime primarily on the Lower East Side of New York City during the Progressive Era. In conclusion, it is argued that our misconceptions about organized crime are ideologically caused.

In Part III, as an epilogue to our discussions, three issues are explored. First, the commentary suggests the seriousness of history by investigating its relationship to concepts of time and the western world's perception of reality. Through a discussion, based on the philosophy of Karl Jaspers, of the manner in which time has been conceptualized since the Old Testament, it is argued that all western thought is historical. History, therefore, is at the very foundation of what we conceive to be the knowable world. The second issue discussed is the instrumental use of history. This includes a critique of meta-histories and an acknowledgment of the ways in which history *is, can be,* and *should be* exploited by social scientists. Here consideration is given to the perils of historical naiveté as well as the dilemmas of the ahistorical social sciences. Finally, the Epilogue focuses on the new histories of crime as examples of the methodological sophistication found in those aspects of contemporary social history which merge social science techniques with explanations of lower-class life.

Part IV offers two appendices of use to the student and researcher in historical criminology. Appendix A is an extended presentation and discussion of source materials for research into the history of crime, and Appendix B is a full reference of the works cited or suggested throughout the volume.

NOTES

1. This passage was written during the thirteenth century by *Le Bestiaire Divin de Guillaume, Clerc de Normandie,* and cited in *Brewer's Dictionary of Phrase and Fable* (n.d.: 930). For additional information on the unicorn legend, see, Shepard (1930), Mercatante (1974), and Huneker (1921).

2. It might be noted here that the story of the unicorn represents but one of the many classical errors that have emerged in biblical translation. Another example is apparent in Michelangelo's sculpture of Moses in Rome's Basilica of San Pietro in Vincoli, which shows two small horns on the head of the Hebrew lawgiver. This addition resulted from the translational confusion between the Hebrew *karnay hashamesh* (rays of the sun) and *karniam* (horns).

PART I

ON THEORY AND METHOD

Chapter 1

IN PURSUIT OF THE PAST:

Some Perspectives

Of what use is history? Can we derive from history any illumination of our present condition? Does it offer us any guidance for our judgment and policies? Can we find through history such regularities in the sequence of past events that we can predict the future actions of humankind or the fate of states? Or does history make no sense? Is it essentially no more than the amusement of recounting the rise and fall of nations, men, and ideas? Does the history of ideas simply march sullenly forward into some unimagined future, its eyes cast resolutely back over its shoulder at useless but perhaps reassuring guideposts of the past? Or as the Durants (1968: 11) have asked, is it possible that history teaches us nothing, that the immense past was only the weary rehearsal of the mistakes that the future is destined to make on a larger stage and scale?

These questions may be raised because we do not know the whole of history, we operate with only partial knowledge, and the conclusions of history represent at best, probabilities. History can indeed offer us some guideposts of the past, but before pondering the use of history, the more enduring questions involve the nature of history, the substance of history, and the methods utilized by historians in "collecting" history. This, then, represents the substance of our initial discussion—a brief examination of the nature and method of history, which will lead us ultimately to perhaps the more relevant question: *why the history of crime*?

The Nature of History

"What is history?" must surely be one of the more fascinating and, indeed, necessary questions in the intellectual world. This nagging question has been posed decade after decade and passed from one generation of scholars to another. But it is such a small, seemingly common sense question that it is difficult to imagine it not having been decisively answered long ago. In fact, not only does it appear to be a slight issue, but at first glance, it also seems to be quite banal. Certainly it is not as complex or ponderous a question as "how does electricity work?"

The problem is, of course, that it is not a trifling question at all. In addition, it is not the case that it has never been answered. Quite the opposite, it has received enough answers to fill many volumes. The apparent banality of "what is history?" masks what is a tricky and subtle series of questions which reach into the very foundation of intellectual life. In whatever fashion it is answered, the respondent is caught in a web of further related questions all growing from the implications of his initial answer. For instance, among the many answers to "what is history?" are: history is a story, nothing more, nothing less; history is the story of the experiences of men; history is the story of the experiences of men living in civilized societies; history is the custodian of the collective memory and as such performs the important function of nourishing the collective ego; history is the study of the past as a systematic discipline. Following from these and other answers, however, are such questions as (1) what is an historical fact? (2) is history objective? (3) what are the boundaries between the past and present? (4) what is historical evidence? (5) what sorts of explanations do historians make? (6) what is the relation of history to other disciplines? And these six questions are by no means exhaustive of the implications flowing from any answer to "what is history?"

Let us begin our discussion with at least one commonly accepted agreement: the term history is itself ambiguous. In different contexts it can mean the whole of the past or all past human actions, and the narrative, study, or account of the past. It is the second meaning which is to be discussed. Probably the most common notion about history (narrative, study, or account) is that the historian has the task of finding out what happened; the discovery of past facts which are then used by scholars from other disciplines for other intellectual pursuits. But historians themselves are more than fact-seekers; they desire to explain why something happened with as much fervor as other intellectuals. History for the historian is not merely the record of past events, but is instead a "significant" record of past events which are connected (Walsh 1960: 16). Historians claim, in fact, to offer explanations of the course of past occurrences at the same time as they relate them in detail.

The process by which historians explain past events starts with their tracing connections between one event and others with which it stands in inner relationship. The assumption underlying this activity is that different past events constitute parts of a single process and that they are bound together in a special and intimate manner. The primary aim of the historian, then, is to view discrete aspects of the past as part of a process, to locate them in their special context by describing those other events with which they may be related. All this suggests something unique about the manner and method of historical study. Often this area has been analyzed under the heading of historical objectivity. Walsh (1960: 21), for example, notes the similarity of historical and artistic expression. Even more to the point, Hexter (1971: 19) comments that historians "sacrifice exactness for evocative force." He adds that this sacrifice is only justified when it "serves to increase knowledge of the past," which is the task of the historian. An evocative rhetoric, to use Hexter's term, will almost always be the mode of historical expression as long as history incorporates empathetic knowledge within that of the past. Because historians wish their readers to . . .

> follow the movement and to sense the tempo of events; to grasp and do justice to the motives and actions of men; to discern the imperatives that move men to action; and to distinguish those imperatives that move men to action; and to distinguish those imperatives from the pseudo imperatives that have become mere exercises in pious ejaculations; to recognize the impact on the course of events of an accident, a catastrophe, or a bit of luck; and to be aware of what the participants in a struggle conceived the stakes to be (p. 25).

. . . they must be willing to sacrifice exactness for the power of suggestive prose.

Along with uniqueness of expression there is the possibility that historical thinking is a form of cognition which is coordinate with but not wholly reducible to scientific thinking. In the "what is history?" literature this represents one of the recurring debates. One of the most interesting and fruitful answers can be found in the essay "The Problem of Uniqueness in

History" (Joynt and Rescher 1965). Its point of analysis is the differences between history and what is called the historical sciences—biology, anthropology, sociology, and philology. Initially, Joynt and Rescher suggest that history "has no monopoly on the study of the past" (p. 4), since representatives of these other disciplines also study the past. Furthermore, they insist that there are no real distinctions between history and the historical sciences in research methodologies. The essential difference appears only in the interplay of data and theory, of fact and law in history and the historical sciences.

In the historical sciences as well as in chemistry and physics, the aim of the endeavor is to analyze fact in order to discover generalizations and what would be ideal, universal laws. This means that the status of individual facts is instrumental in the sciences. The facts are a means to an end. It is this relationship, they contend, which is different in history:

> The historian in effect reverses the means-end relationship between fact and theory that we find in science. For the historian is interested in generalizations, and does so not because generalizations constitute the aim and objective of his discipline, but because they help him to illuminate the particular facts with which he deals. History seeks to provide an understanding of specific occurrences, and has recourse to such laws and generalizations—largely borrowed from the sciences, but also drawn from ordinary human experience—which can be of service in this enterprise. But here the role of generalizations is strictly instrumental: they provide aid towards understanding particular events (Joynt and Rescher 1965: 6-7).

Clearly, the historian must develop and borrow generalizations in order to move beyond chronology to the understanding of past events. And as the historian aims to clarify the past for its own sake he becomes a "consumer" of general laws, not a "producer" of them. What is unique about history, therefore, is not the method or the subject matter, but the research objectives.

It is surely proper to ask in light of the above what is so compelling and important about understanding the past. Are we, after all, only dealing with the personal pleasure of individuals? The question is, does knowledge of the past for its own sake have a social role to perform beyond something equivalent of *l'art pour l'art*? David Landes and Charles Tilly in *History as Social Science* (1971) maintain that it does. They hold that in all societies history is a "primary vehicle of the socialization of the young, teaching them the past so that they may know who they are and behave appropriately in the present" (p. 5). The concern with doing history right, in freeing it from error and myth is, therefore, attributable to history's significant psychological, educational, and social functions. It is important to get it right because it is critical to know the truth of the past. It is as simple as that. And this concern, this endeavor to know the realities of the past, depends heavily upon the way the historian approaches the past, the way he collects his evidence, and the logic with which he interprets his historical facts.

The Methods of History

Historical inquiry, one might argue, is characterized by no unique methodological frame of reference; or stated more directly, there is no specific research or investigative strategy we might call an historical method; historical endeavors simply follow the prescriptions and proscriptions of scholarly common sense. At first glance, these statements may appear as reflections of intellectual biases against history, suggesting after all, that history is only an art and not a science. But history is both an art *and* a science. It is an art to the extent that it is a reproduction of the past:

> Written in narrative form [history] is an art in the same sense that good literature is an art. History, as Sir Lewis Namier notes, is more like a painting than it is a photograph of the past. Since the past has already occurred, it cannot be recaptured exactly as it happened, or even if it were totally recaptured, as in a photograph, we would not know it because we have no way of determining that it is an exact and precise picture (Stephens 1974: 12-13).

As such, in recapturing the past, or in constructing that portrait of past events, the historian must do so as accurately as possible, and it is at that point that history also becomes a science.

The methods of history, then, are the methods of science. The historian seeks to establish tentative generalizations about the past, and in doing so, he must subject all facts to tests of validity, all hypotheses to the most careful and searching examinations, and ultimately, all generalizations to systematic and thorough criticism. Or as historian Allan Nevins (1962: 29) has noted:

> [The historian] collects his data fairly, observes it systematically, organizes it logically, and tests its parts thoroughly. Then by induc-

tive logic and the use of hypothesis he reaches provisional generalizations, and only when he has carried out a final search for new data,
and made fresh tests, does he commit final conclusions to paper.

The scientific method as it relates to history begins with the perception
of some problem. The historical "problem" may emerge in the form of
something that is unknown about the past, an interpretation that can be
seriously questioned, or an incomplete or perhaps unsatisfactory explanation of some historical event. And too, the structure of history necessarily
changes with the perspective of the historian; all history is contemporary
in the sense that its presentation reflects the circumstances and attitudes
and perspectives of those who write it (Hughes 1964). As such, each generation necessarily writes history anew, and there is no definitive work of
historical scholarship.

Historian James F. Richardson's (1970) examination of the police in
early New York City emerged from this very issue. Prior works on the New
York City police were either wholly descriptive in nature (Sutton 1873;
Costello 1884) or they viewed the police as an emerging bureaucracy in
conflict with components of the political organization of the city (McAdoo
1906). Richardson's effort analyzed New York's police force against a
narrative of the growth of the city itself, reflecting how it changed to
meet the shifting needs of the metropolis and how those who governed
the city and the state influenced police administration and activities.
Richardson did not "rewrite" the history of the New York police per se,
for his perception of a problem was not one of "incorrect" history. Rather,
he produced a "new" history, one which examined the police within a
changing social context. By contrast, W. Eugene Hollon's (1974) *Frontier
Violence: Another Look* posed an alternative problem. He argued against
the prevailing conceptions that the violence and lawlessness on the American frontier hold primary responsibility for our violent society today. On
the contrary, he maintained that frontier lawlessness was the result, rather
than the cause, of our violent society. As such, Hollon's approach to history, his perception of a "problem," emerged from what he felt was a
questionable interpretation of historical data.

Given the perception of the historical problem, what follows is the
interaction of logic and hypothesizing, both grounded on the more crucial
historical endeavor—the search for evidence. And as is addressed throughout this volume, the reliability of historical accounts stands or falls on the
accuracy of the historical data.

The historian first locates his source documents, followed by a substantiation of the accuracy of his evidence. The steps by which he makes this assessment constitute historical verification:

> Verification is required of the researcher on a multitude of points— from getting an author's first name correct to proving that a document is both genuine and authentic. Verification is accordingly conducted on many planes, and its technique is not fixed. It relies on attention to detail, on common-sense reasoning, on a developed "feel" for history and chronology, on familiarity with human behavior, and on ever enlarging stores of information (Barzun and Graff 1962: 90-91).

The historical researcher must discriminate between what may be valid or false, and truth is reached through *probability*—that balance of chances, given certain evidence, that the event a document records did indeed happen in a specific way. The indicators of the accuracy of a document and the reliability of data *as fact* reinforce one another to increase total probability. And in case where direct signs may not be available, "a concurrence of indirect signs will establish proof" (Barzun and Graff 1962: 97).

The pursuit of increased probability leads the historical researcher to any variety of inquiries regarding each source:

- What is the source?
- What does it state?
- Who is its author?
- What do we know about the author?
- What is his credibility?
- How do his statements compare with others on the same point?
- Is what he says both logical and possible?
- What is the relationship in time and space between the author and his statements?

There are all levels of testimony, but the value of testimony typically increases in proportion to the nearness of time and place of the witnesses and the events about which they testify. Thus, primary sources—the original repositories of historical data, would reflect fewer distortions than those secondary sources one or more steps removed from the historical event. And further, while single witnesses may be quite accurate, the combination of additional witnesses, if independent, increases the probability of eliminating error. Finally, *proof demands decisive evidence!* Proof demands evidence that confirms one view while denying that of others (see, Garraghan 1946; Gustavson 1955; Hockett 1955; Barzun and Graff 1962).

In all the discussion about the problems and pitballs of historical data, there has been one concern often left unexpressed. This deals not with determining what is fraudulent or distorted evidence, but with commenting on the breakdown of historical prose. By this it is not meant simply poor style, but rather what Jacques Barzun and Henry F. Graff (1962) called "Historians' Fallacies." Barzun and Graff were primarily concerned with fallacies regarding "bad" or "overextended" generalizations, and placed their discussion within a chapter whose theme was the interplay of ideas and historians' language.

A much more ambitious work, one dealing totally with historians' fallacies, was prepared by David Hackett Fischer (1970). Fischer's purpose was to raise the issue of logic in historical prose and thought, and his method, which delighted many graduate students in the early 1970s, was to show, by example, logical mistakes committed by many of the most distinguished historians. In what emerged as a dramatic call for reason, Fischer identified eleven major areas of fallacious thinking: question framing; factual verification; factual significance; generalization; narration; causation; motivation; composition; false analogy; semantic distortion; and substantive distraction. Each of these major areas was further broken down under such headings as "the fallacy of division," "the fallacy of ethnomorphism," "the fallacy of cross grouping," and so on. Example follows example of shoddy, banal, and queer thinking by an enormous number of historians. Unfortunately for Professor Fischer, his book, which was seemingly written with both serious intent and intellectual rigor, has been received as an amusing index of the foibles of historians. As the blurb on the back of this work indicates, the effect of *Historians' Fallacies* was at best serio-comic:

> The wisdom is expressed with a certain ruthlessness. Scarcely a major historian escapes unscathed. Ten thousand members of the American Historical Association will rush to the index and breathe a little easier to find their names absent.

But the issues raised by Fischer were crucial ones, for it is not uncommon among historians to generalize beyond his facts, to shrink diversity to unity, or to otherwise misinterpret the data from his sources. As such, the historian's search for data must include safeguards against logical error.

And finally, the testing of hypotheses and search for evidence can also be contaminated by the unwarranted interaction of data and theory. All too often, in many of the social sciences there have been numerous attempts to "force" one's data to conform with hypotheses and theories. And the same phenomenon can emerge in historical research. Beyond any deliberate attempts to perjure historical truth, the historian can often be misled. The search for evidence must go beyond that which tends to substantiate a hypothesis; it must seek out the possibility of disparate historical facts that might preclude erroneous conclusions.

The Uses of History and the History of Crime

Philosopher George Santayana once maintained that "those who cannot remember the past are condemned to repeat it" (1905: 284). Taking "history" as synonymous with "the past" in Santayana's statement, he was suggesting that history does indeed contain certain lessons, and if that be true, can we deny the value of historical study? History indeed can offer us many lessons, but they are not as easy to discern as Santayana would have us believe. Historian Lester D. Stephens (1974: 113) argues that there are many who believe and maintain that the lessons of history are quite clear, and he notes journalist Thurman Sensing's indictment of the U.S. secretary of defense over the *Pueblo* incident in 1968:

> The lesson of history is that victory goes to the bold and daring. If the free world fails to use its scientific and technological know-how to stop the armed hordes of communism, it may be bled to death by the modern guerrilla war version of the old oriental torture death of a thousand cuts (Sensing 1968: 4).

Stephens, in refuting the assumed clarity of history's "lessons," commented:

> How nice it would be if the lessons of history were so simple and clear-cut. Unhappily, the writer conveniently forgets that Hitler was bold and daring but hardly achieved any real victory; Japan bodly and daringly attacked a major power and instead of victory reaped disaster for its effort—the story could go on with repeated examples refuting the writer's "lesson of history" (p. 113).

Indeed, while the lessons of history may not be fully clear, this should not suggest that history is of no value. History can indicate the possibility that certain consequences can issue from events which are comparable to other events of the past; history, as something more than a simple compilation of facts, can generate an understanding of the processes of social change and demonstrate how a multitude of factors have served to shape the present. And history also has an existential function. It tells us who we are, that we are links that connect the past with the present and future.

Within this context, what then is the role or roles of history in the study of crime? Of what value is an historical approach to crime? Does history have some practical value for criminological inquiry? To answer any of these questions one must first have at least a working definition of criminology. Surely one of the most acceptable is that provided by Sutherland and Cressey in the ninth edition of their famous text (1974). Criminology, they write, "is the body of knowledge regarding delinquency and crime as social phenomena." The range of criminology includes "the processes of making laws, of breaking laws, and of reacting toward the breaking of laws." Sutherland and Cressey continue:

> These processes are three aspects of a somewhat unified sequence of interactions. Certain acts which are regarded as undesirable are defined by the political society as crimes. In spite of this definition some people persist in the behavior and thus commit crimes; the political society reacts by punishment, treatment, or prevention. This sequence of interactions is the subject matter of criminology.
>
> Criminology consists of three principal divisions, as follows: (a) the sociology of law, which is an attempt at systematic analysis of the conditions under which criminal laws develop and also an explanation of variations in the policies and procedures used in administration of criminal justice; (b) criminal etiology, which is an attempt at scientific analysis of the causes of crime; and (c) penology, which is concerned with control of crime (p. 3).

The question then is in what fashion(s) historical research can further any or all of the above tasks. Put in this manner the answer is obviously affirmative. It is certainly the job of the historian to trace the changes in the overall interactive sequence; to provide interpretations of which "certain acts . . . are regarded as undesirable" in different eras, and so on. Clearly the sociology of law as described by Sutherland and Cressey is historical—"analysis of the conditions under which criminal laws develop." And just as clearly, both criminal etiology and penology are historical as well as sociological phenomena. Historical research is, therefore, one of the intellectual processes which in combination with others constitutes "the body of knowledge regarding delinquency and crime as social phenomena."

Consider in this regard two quite recent works in criminology: Sellin's study of the effects of slavery on the development of corrections (1976); and the Gurr, Grabosky, and Hula inquiry into crime and public order in London, Stockholm, Sydney, and Calcutta during the nineteenth and twentieth centuries (1977). Sellin's theoretical starting point is two "notable historical works" both completed in 1938. The first is the Rusche and Kirshheimer study (1939) which argues that there is a correspondence between types of punishments and stages of economic development. The second is Gustav Radbruch's essay (1950) which argues that with changes in the structure of Germanic society punishments originally inflicted on slaves became, as it were, democratized. Sellin traces in his work "the influence of the social institution of chattel slavery on the evolution of penal practices in Europe and the United States from ancient time to the present" (1976: viii).

Unlike the Sellin study which sets out to substantiate or refute a particular hypothesis, the Gurr, Grabosky, and Hula work is much more broadly based. They are concerned "specifically with *public disorder,* that is, manifestations of social disorder that are the objects of concerted public efforts at control" (p. 9). Besides the analysis of crime and disorder in the four cities for its own important sake, they are concerned with testing a common historical generalization: the notion "that crime and civil strife regularly declined in the nineteenth century in Western cities, then increased on some relative scale in mid-twentieth century" (p. 5). Another of their objectives is to indicate the "relative importance of political and institutional factors in the creation and maintenance of public order" (p. 5). And finally, these researchers have had to create their study from whole cloth noting that "there has been virtually no comparative historical research on the trends and politics of public order, urban or otherwise" (p. 8). Testimony of the historical needs and failures of contemporary criminology.

James A. Inciardi's (1975) *Careers in Crime* uses the historical approach to examine how the social organization and occupational structure of the professional thief persisted relatively unchanged for centuries, and then suddenly declined. He found through historical research, for example, that professional thieves—safe burglars, pickpockets, sneak thieves, and counterfeiters, among others—had evolved a "functional superstructure," a set of integrated phenomena and cooperative understandings that combined to offer the thieves immunity from sanction:

Professional criminal behavior is often of a low risk nature, for example, where victims act in collusion with the offenders. In addition, professional offenders often develop a political power base that enables them to "fix" cases. These immunities perpetuate contacts among members of the profession, strengthening the unique subcultural organization that has been structured to insure further the preservation of the profession. Codes of ethics, argot, self-segregation, and a complex communication system combine to form the functional components of the superstructure (Inciardi 1975: 132).

For some four hundred years professional thieves maintained this posture. Since the beginning of the current century, however, the professional underworld was found to be declining, seemingly the result of changes in science, technology, law, fashion, social structure, and mechanisms of social control which combined to erode the foundations of the professionals' protective superstructure.

There is another point about the roles of historical research in criminology which must be mentioned. It concerns the public's perception of crime and violence which has a direct influence on policy decisions. In the "special introduction" to the report on *Violence in America* (1969) John Herbers reports that "many writers of history, the schools and the disciplines of the overall society have denied or deemphasized the role of violence from the Colonial period to the present." Herbers is accounting for the pervasive fear during the 1960s that America was engulfed in a wave of crime and violence unprecedented in its history. That fear is explicable primarily, Herbers claims, because Americans presumed a pacific past:

> Nothing they learned in their schools, in their homes, and among their associates prepared them for the view that the domestic violence the nation has witnessed in the 1960s is not an aberration of United States history or a sign of the disintegration of American institutions but the usual type of behavior displayed in this country when there is a large division of purpose or when some group is trying to cast off some great wrong.

It is a peculiarity of Americans, he goes on to state, to revel in a kind of historical amnesia which obliterates past crime and violence. It is the job of both history and criminology to overcome this tendency toward amnesia which can only be culturally disastrous.

Chapter 2

HISTORY, FOLKLORE, AND CRIME

In one of the latest renditions of a time-honored and persistent social tradition, the Associated Press recently reported from Stockholm, Sweden that in "a deep yearning for a little disorder in affluent and law-abiding society, Sweden has turned a bank robber into a kind of folk hero" (Minneapolis *Tribune,* September 7, 1976: 2B). Though more sensational than analytical, the press report describes the typical disagreement that attends the interpretation of the latest folk hero, Clark Olafsson, whose bank robbery, hostage holding, and repeated prison escapes are offset by alternative interpretations of societal responsibility for his crimes, chivalry to hostages, nonviolence, bravado, and persistence in flouting authority.

Denounced as a "media creation," Olafsson is celebrated on film, television, and in commercial products, a situation which has brought strong reprimands from a Soviet youth publication for turning a thief into a "superman with romantic accents." While some Swedes are supportive of, or ambivalent about their new folk hero, local officials decry a "loss in perspective." For as Swedish criminologist Knut Sveri explained, "Clark is a criminal and it's wrong to make him look good and make him a hero for our youth."

Whether it be a "loss in perspective" or simply a *different* perspective, the interpretation of the outlaw or bandit as folk hero has captured the imaginations of disparate cultures and nations in a tradition that spans some eight centuries. The bandit-hero, as such, has been typified as a noble robber—a victim of injustice who attempts to right the wrongs of alien or unjust law, who takes only from the rich to give to the poor, who kills only in self-defense or just revenge, and who in so doing, is admired and supported by his people. The bandit-hero and noble robber was first depicted in fourteenth-century English ballads and poetry which spoke of the free life in the great forests, and described the adventures and valiant struggles for public liberties by such outlaws as Robin Hood and Fulk FitzWaren. And while Robin Hood is considered a "mythical" hero created by minstrels, poets, and story-tellers, his characterization reflected the prototype from which later outlaws were understood as folk heroes—Jack Shepherd and Dick Turpin of England; Angelo Duca of Italy, Diego Corrientes of Spain; Pancho Villa of Mexico; and in America, Jesse James, Sam Bass, Joaquín Murieta, Billy the Kid, Clyde Barrow, and Bonnie Parker.

This conception of the outlaw or "noble robber" as folk hero has been detailed by historian Eric Hobsbawm as *social banditry,* which he described as

> little more than endemic protest against oppression and poverty; a cry for vengence on the rich and the oppressors, a vague dream of some curb upon them, a righting of individual wrongs. Its ambitions are modest: a traditional world in which men are justly dealt with, not a new and perfect world (Hobsbawm, 1959: 5).

Hobsbawm insisted that while social banditry was a universal and unchanging phenomenon, it was also a specialized phenomenon. For although social banditry fell within the arena of robbery and violence, the bandits themselves were viewed within a unique perspective:

> [T]hey are peasant outlaws whom the lord and state regard as criminals, but who remain within peasant society, and are considered by their people as heroes, as champions, avengers, fighters for justice, perhaps even leaders of liberation, and in any case as men to be admired, helped and supported (Hobsbawm 1969: 13).

Just as popular culture and traditional folklore have ostensibly defined some banditry as noble rebellion, others have, with equal fervor, denounced this conception as false, misleading, and dangerous to society (Adams 1964: 4), or historically misleading (Inciardi 1975: 168-170; Steckmesser

1966). Anton Blok, historian and critic of Hobsbawm's treatment of social banditry, suggested that many studies of the outlaw indeed rest on poor evidence, which leads Blok to seriously question their accuracy (Blok 1972: 500). Hobsbawm (1969: 12) clearly admitted that in his *Bandits,* he relied heavily on what he called "a rather tricky historical source, namely poems and ballads." These folklore sources generally elicit negative evaluations by historians and in some cases have been rejected a priori as having virtually no historical merit. These notions are paralleled by some popular conceptions that folklore is synonymous with error or false belief.

The problems of selection and interpretation of evidence are complicated in such areas of study since, unlike the historian of ancient times, the scholar in pursuit of more contemporary events is virtually inundated with evidence. Ranging across all facets of verbal and material culture, the quantity of evidence requires selectivity, and this selectivity often produces a bias. This bias follows from the increased likelihood that sources of evidence determined as most reliable by the accepted "rules of precedence" of historical criticism, are written documents produced by only a small segment of the population. Hence methodological canons may serve as rationales for a limited historical account if they eliminate or diminish the credibility of alternative data sources. The alternative data sources of interest here—folklore and popular culture—add traditionally neglected dimensions to the historical record—the actions and perspectives of nonelites.

Hopwood commented on the use of popular culture as evidence, and, while he acknowledged an increased interest, he observed that historians

> fled from the popular culture, characterized those who continued to rely on it as "unscientific," and retired behind our famed "sieve of history," a nebulous, largely unarticulated tool which allowed us to separate arbitrarily the important from the "trivial" evidence (1971: 1027-1028).

Folklore, being an oral rather than a written mode of communication, fared even less well, and rather than providing evidence to support, supplement, or reject orthodox sources, is more likely to be ignored altogether.

The past and present controversy over the interpretation of the bandit or outlaw as a folk hero exemplifies the limitations of selectivity and the problems of nontraditional sources. Within this context, this essay examines the phenomenon of social banditry as a test case for the utility of folklore data in the historical study of crime and deviance. In pursuit of this task, a variety of themes are necessarily addressed: (a) the nature and content of folklore; (b) folklore vs. history as an approach to defining and examining social phenomena; (c) the problems of the evaluation of folklore with the historical critical method; and (d) the historical utility of folklore materials.

The Nature and Content of Folklore

A contemporary American folklorist, Alan Dundes, recently expressed with some disdain that "The public at large tends to think of folklore as a synonym for error, fallacy, or historical inaccuracy. One hears, for example, the phrase "That's folklore," meaning "That is not true" (Dundes 1975: 12).

Folklorist and historian Richard Dorson (1972a: 1) has echoed these sentiments, further suggesting that nonfolklorist academicians generally share this "folk concept" of folklore. And while folklorists would no doubt the unanimous in their distaste for this conception, they have also tended to disagree with one another's attempts to define in a scholarly way the subject of their discipline. This has necessarily led some to reject the need for a definition of folklore and others to fervently demand consensus as a critical feature of a social science striving for linkages to other disciplines (Abrahams 1969; Bauman 1969; Brunvand 1970; Welsch 1968).

Two alternative struggles have aggravated attempts to define folklore. The first is a heightened academic "imperialism" in which folklorists from anthropological, historical, and literary backgrounds have occasionally battled for control of a folklore society or university department (Ben-Amos 1973: 121-123). Although this problem may be of lesser importance since folklore has become an independent discipline, its definitional disputes emerged in response to the other academic interests of diverse students of folklore. The second and more critical problem attends the lack of a distinction between *folklore* as process and product in society, and *folkloristics* as the discipline studying folklore (Ben-Amos 1973; Dundes 1975). This latter distinction cannot be a fully pure one, but it does enable the nonfolklorist to evaluate definitions more easily.

The folklorist's approach to defining the phenomenon uses three strategies: emphasis on folklore skills and research techniques; emphasis on folklore materials; and emphasis on folklore purposes. The first two strategies elicit critical comment from some folklorists—the emphasis on skill is criticized for its lack of attention to folklore as it exists in the "real" world as an empirical entity, the emphasis on materials for being overly empirical and having no clear theoretical referent. The emphasis on purposes bears some relationship to theory but appears to more closely resemble the interests of the nonfolklore scholar. Dorson (1972a) identifies a variety of approaches in this latter category, ranging from the ideological manipulations of Soviet folklorists and the needs of historical reconstructionists for historical evidence to the geographical study of diffusion and change of folklore materials.

Efforts to define folklore per se relate not only to the foregoing taxonomies of materials and purposes, but go beyond them to identify and clarify key dimensions of folklore in society. These efforts focus on one of the following: (1) the definition of the folk; (2) the definition of the lore, and its form and mode of transmission; (3) the delineation of function and meaning; and (4) the study of folklore in context—an approach that combines all other approaches in an eclectic but comprehensive endeavor.

Early folklorists defined the "folk" as rural or peasant enclaves existing in, but not of, a civilized region. This emphasis produced a view of folklore as survivals from an old and rapidly dying culture with no recognition of the possibility for contemporary lore (Dundes 1975). Recent research by Dorson (1971a), however, has demonstrated that urban settings provide a viable context for folklore, including maintenance of immigrant traditions *and* the development of indigenous urban traditions. This has led to a more inclusive definition of *folk* as in Degh (1971a: 54-55):

[A] group of people united permanently or temporarily by shared common experiences, attitudes, interests, skills, ideas, knowledge, and aims. Those shared attitudes are elaborated, sanctioned, and stabilized by the group over a period of time.

Folklorists' willingness to shift the definition of *folk* to correspond with an urbanizing society have not been paralleled by an equivalent shift in the definition of *lore*. Disagreement over this facet has arisen from assessments of the importance of oral transmission as the most common feature, but many folklorists dispute its primacy. Dundes and Patger (1975), for example, offer a collection of printed materials that meet other folklore criteria and bolster their polar position in this respect. Furthermore, Ben-Amos (1972) has suggested that less concern for oral transmission is crucial to the continued vitality of folklore and more compatible with the generally recognized interaction between the written and

spoken aspects of literate societies. The current status of an item in relation to the artistic processes of small groups determines its relevance to
folklore more so than its traditional origin or mode of transmission.

Despite a rejection of definitions based merely on the delineation of
specific genres (types or forms of folklore such as legend or proverb),
some current scholars retain the requirement of artistic form. Bauman's
definition is concerned with artistic verbal performance. He claims that
folklore rests on

> language usage which takes on special significance above and beyond
> its referential, informational dimension through the systematic elab-
> oration of any component of verbal behavior in such a way that this
> component calls attention to itself and is perceived as uncommon or
> special in a particular context (Bauman 1972a: 39).

General agreement on this aspect seems unlikely to be sustained, as
signaled by Dundes' (1972) suggestion that folklorists study *folk ideas,*
that is, "traditional notions that a group of people have about the nature
of man, of the world, and of man's life in the world" (1972: 95). Dundes,
hailed by Bauman (1972b: xiv) as an "extender and rearranger of the conceptual boundaries of the field," thus offered an interpretation that broke
free from tradition genre classifications, but he negated the artistic cri-
terion declaring that folk ideas were not likely to appear consistently in
any fixed-phrase form (Dundes 1972: 95-96).

Dundes' *folk ideas* are not necessarily artistic in form but they are traditional in nature. Ben-Amos (1972: 13-14), who proffered a definition of
folklore as "artistic communication in small groups," argued that the requirement of tradition is not essential to folklore. He supported his thesis
by presenting examples of folklore for which newness rather than tradition
is crucial, such as riddles; by declaring the traditional nature to be an analytical construct established by research and often unknown to those using
it; by pointing to the significance of new folklore; and by noting a methodological bias favorable to tradition through its emphasis on surviving materials and the neglect of the principles of forgetting. He concluded that
"some traditions are folklore, but not all folklore is traditional." Dundes
(1975: 13) suggested that the change in emphasis among anthropological
folklorists from folklore as a reflection of the present was central to a
functionalist viewpoint. Their contribution, he argued, minimized the importance of tradition and thus opened the way for contemporary studies
of folklore emphasizing present-day functions of a living, dynamic folklore.
As such, the definition of lore remains in flux, if not in conflict.

Anthropological writings centering on function and meaning also solicit criticism for failing to capture the uniqueness factor required by folklorists. Bascom (1965a: 26) identified folklore as a cultural universal, and outlined the general functions it fulfilled: (1) validation of culture; (2) socialization and education; (3) social control; and (4) release of repressed desires and ideas (1965b: 290-298). The notion that folklore has function and meaning is well accepted, but critics point out that certain tendencies of the functionalist approach reduce its overall value. The claim that folklore is a collective representation is attacked as a reification that ignores folklore as action, overemphasizing homogeneous, within-group aspects (see Bauman 1972a: 33). Similarly, the functionalist view is berated for its failure to account for folklore performance as a persuasive attempt to change rather than to support the status quo of the group (see Abrahams 1972: 27-29).

The current critics of folklore definition were grouped by Dorson (1972a: 45-47) in an approach he labeled "contextual." The central feature of that orientation is the eclecticism found in social science—a focus on the performance or event as a unit of analysis; the examination of all aspects of the folklore context or environment in addition to previous study of the form and content of the folklore item; and an emphasis on communicative processes. In the introduction to the American Folklore Society's *Toward New Perspectives in Folklore,* Richard Bauman stated:

> The present collection attains what may be its principal significance, that of representing a new generation of folklorists who are decidedly not content to remain within the confines of inherited intellectual pigeonholes, but who combine freely and as a matter of course features of all these approaches in a common commitment to illuminating the expressive behavior of man (1972b: xv).

In summary, although Bauman's commentary clearly demonstrates a continuing lack of consensus over the definition of folklore, several factors seemingly remain constant and pertinent: (1) folklore pertains to any socially defined group; (2) folklore is most frequently found in oral transmission, artistic form, and with traditional meanings; (3) folklore has meaning to both individuals and their group; (4) folklore includes objects, ideas, and artistic devices; and (5) folklore is a communicative process. Combining these consistent features, folklore might be defined as *a communicative process that abides in a socially defined group, and produces and utilizes objects, ideas, and expressive devices that have meaning for the group and its individual members; these objects, ideas, and devices are*

*most frequently characterized and identified by oral transmission, artistic
form, and traditional meaning.*

The foregoing definition serves more to summarize the definitional
battles of academic folklorists than to aid in the identification of the folklore product or the separation of it from other communicative processes.
The "identification" task requires knowledge of folklore genres and motifs, while the "separation" task suggests discussion of the relationship of
folklore to popular culture.

FOLKLORE GENRES AND MOTIFS

Brunvand (1976) characterized the process of folklore scholarship as
involving collection, classification, and interpretation stages. The central
tasks of the classification stage typically include the identification of the
genre—literary type or form; and the identification of *motifs*—recurrent
themes such as stock plots, episodes, character traits or other elements
that show continuity or similarity across genres. Recognition and knowledge of genre and motif classifications are essential to folklorists since they
are the basis of information retrieval and basic elements for comparison of
variants of a particular item or text. In addition, the artistic form or genre
that makes the story more memorable also affects its content; and determining the historical value of any folklore item requires some knowledge
of the characteristics of the genre in which the item is found.

Paredes (1958) included an analysis of the ballad per se as part of his
study of the folklore and history of the Mexican border hero Gregorio
Cortez. He showed that the story changed according to the history of the
ballad, its geographical setting and audience, the traditional themes and
the artistic conventions (e.g., stock lines, images), and forms (e.g., rhyming, meter); but that in contrast with the legend, which was characterized
by free wording, the ballad remained relatively fixed.

This comparison reveals the importance of studying the genre form
itself, and though all genre forms have specific defects, knowledge of each
aids in interpreting distortion. Although these are not of direct interest to
the historian, acquaintance with them is important since published and
archival collections are arranged by genre, and since analysis of items often
includes motif discussion.

Folklore genres of most interest to the historical criminologist are often
classified under the general heading of "folk literature" and include the
folktale, legend, myth, folksong, ballad, folkpoetry, and jokes. A discussion of each of these genres is presented in Appendix A, and core references are listed along with suggestions on definition, social function, and
significance for historical criminology.

In additon to a working knowledge of folklore and literary genre, the researcher interested in folklore should be conversant with the concept of motif. According to Brunvand (1968), a motif is an unusual and recurrent narrative element that may be an object, a concept, an action, a character, a character-type, an unusual animal, or a structural quality. Many of these are listed and referenced in the *Motif-Index of Folk Literature* (Thompson 1955-58) and are cross-cultural and transhistorical elements ascribed to numerous particular cases. It is necessary for the historian to identify and extract these motifs from any account. In relation to banditry, motifs provide catchy episodes that illustrate an ascribed outlaw trait in a dramatic way. In this tradition, Jesse James, like Robin Hood and numerous other outlaws, is credited with the widow's mortgage story, an episode that demonstrates the cleverness trait of the hero and his generosity toward the poor and tells how the hero lends the poor widow money to pay the mortgage, later stealing it back from the evil banker.

MODES OF COMMUNICATION: FOLKLORE AND POPULAR CULTURE

The chain of transmission of folklore in a literate society exists in inter-action with other modes of communication and raises the problem that Dorson (1971d) called "fakelore." The relationship between written and unwritten modes and products is a complex one, and Dorson's discussion focused on the invention of legends and other genre items by literary craftsmen, inventions later circulated as genuine folklore. These difficulties raised by the interplay of oral and written modes are complicated further by the diverse forms that oral traditional communication may take.

For example, Paredes (1958) compared the ballad accounts of Gregorio Cortez that originated in small communities with those versions performed in Mexico City. The city oral tradition survives only through professional entertainers whereas the border tradition remains part of the entertain-ment institution of the local, homogeneous, nonliterate community. The difference influences the dominant themes and the historical specificity of the ballad and reveals a more general difference between the two traditions in interpreting the outlaw:

> The proletarian ballad's concept of the hero as an outlaw who robs the rich to give to the poor does not gain acceptance, though Greater Mexican ballads containing it are sung and enjoyed. Nor does the border outlaw repent. [T]he outlaw is either seen frankly as an out-law, without sentimentalizing, or he is made an actor in border con-

flict. The hero, however, is not the highwayman or the smuggler, but the peaceful man who defends his right (Paredes 1958: 150).

This demonstration that folklore or oral communication systems differ but overlap brings into focus Adams' (1969: 10) suggestion that the historian must distinguish between legend that "is in the order of conscious artifice, not of accident in an oral or unwritten tradition." Of the latter he claimed: "If the study of human institutions and conventions teaches us anything, it is that an oral tradition has a singular purity, even among the most primitive."

Adams' distinction is important but incomplete and obscure. Before interpreting it, the historian acquainted with the oral process of transmission would realize that oral tradition does not have a singular "anything," but changes its nature and form as it diffuses geographically and across time. It is not a question of conscious artifice versus accidental-but-honest-legend, but of origin and acceptance. It is likely that oral traditions owe their origin primarily to the interpretations of individual performers all along the chain of transmission, and that legend as a *social* phenomenon depends not so much on what the performers suggest as on what the audience accepts and repeats. Although this distillation of opinion undoubtedly differs from the performances of individual actors, the final product is somewhat shaped by their interpretations as well as their artistic improvements. This distinction between origin and acceptance offers a clue to the difficult problem of the relationship between oral and writen modes of communication that is especially prominent in Western bandit lore.

This problem entails a recognition that many forms of media contribute to outlaw legends in both origin and acceptance aspects. In what way does oral traditional influence written communication and vice versa? Steckmesser's study of Billy the Kid (1965) and Settle's study of Jesse James (1966) both suggested that a variety of media including histories, dime novels, news articles, biographies, and juvenile books interacted with oral tradition during the outlaws' lifetime and later joined with the electronic media in keeping the legends alive. This interaction produced a "recirculation effect," which formed the legend in a particular direction and created a consensus. Steckmesser discussed how newspapers copied from one another: Local papers would suggest an interpretation, which was subsequently copied by nonlocal papers, whereupon local papers would recopy the nonlocal papers and take their accounts as independent confirmation of local speculation. Other media, especially the dime novels, would copy these new accounts and present the legends to a wider audience.

Another important force in "myth-making" is the literary legend. In Dorson's view (1971e: 159), this is only one type of legend. He criticized Steckmesser's definition of legend in the study of Billy the Kid as being ambiguous and overemphasizing "the manipulation, selection and distortion of historical data, mainly by writers addressing a national audience, to arrive at or reinforce a stereotype." In his analysis, Steckmesser (1965) claimed that the literary legend not only took precedence, but was eventually accepted by local oral tradition. Jones held a similar view, emphasizing the role of the author in originating and disseminating a particular legend or a general point of view about outlaws:

> [A]lthough originally formulated as a means of fashioning fictional outlaws, conventional persecution and revenge also played a profound role in the development and popularization of legends about actual Western badmen (1973: 663).

With legendary material circulating in both oral and written modes of communication, it is not difficult to accept Adams' (1969) suggestion that the latter-day memoirs of oldtimers were influenced by them and strengthen many questionable episodes and interpretations.

Rediscovering the "singular purity" of legend may be a difficult process in a literate society, but it is, nevertheless, essential for determining the historical facts of outlawry. These facts are undoubtedly lost, reworked, or embroidered in many ways by both literary and oral performers, but regardless of the "dehistoricizing" features of both modes of communication,

> The professional hero makers must bear only part of the responsibility for the persistence of the legends. They have simply supplied what the people have demanded. Beauty and truth are both aspects of the human experience, but beauty is preferred. There is something cold and abstract about truth. Attachment to it presupposes a certain cynism about human nature and conduct. Romance and legend, on the other hand, are warm and colorful, representing the ideal in human aspirations. Hence it is not surprising that each legend involves a highly selective process by which the beautiful eclipses the true (Steckmesser 1965: 249).

But beauty and truth depend upon the audience. The legendary Billy the Kid has been shown to diverge from the historical person, but in two opposite ways. During his lifetime and for several decades after his death,

Billy the Kid was portrayed as totally evil in literary accounts. Later, in the 1920s, a "saintly" image was advanced and corroborated by oral traditions collected shortly thereafter. Steckmesser's (1965) interpretation emphasized the literary genre as influencing the oral traditions, but other sources indicated that the Kid was already popular among many groups during his life. This would suggest the possibility that the later literary interpretations did not change oral tradition but corresponded with an already prevalent folklore depiction of the Kid as "saintly." This is even more convincing when one learns that these favorable folk versions were held by Mexicans, an audience with the kind of grievances that make outlaws into heroes, and an audience that was unlikely to be greatly affected by the literature of the eastern United States.

These problems show that it is necessary to know the interrelationships between the intertwining of modes of communication and their corresponding "levels" of culture. Although the requirement of oral transmission remains widely held among folklorists, many accept the possibility that there is a type of folklore disseminated by the mass media (Dorson 1976a), and that folklore and other modes of culture communication draw on one another (Brunvand 1972). Browne (1972) differentiated between elite, folk, popular, and mass culture in regard to distribution and motivation of originators. He stressed that

> all elements in our culture (or cultures) are closely related and are not mutually exclusive one from another. They constitute one long continuum. Perhaps the best metaphorical figure for all is that of a flattened ellipsis, or a lens. In the center, largest in bulk and easiest seen through is Popular Culture, which includes Mass Culture.
>
> On either end of the lens are High and Folk Cultures, both looking fundamentally alike in many respects and both having a great deal in common. . . . All four derive in many ways and to many degrees from one another, and the lines of demarcations between any two are indistinct and mobile (Browne 1972: 10).

The important point is that, in spite of academic jurisdictional disputes, modes and products of communication do overlap and trade material, *but* they also have unique features and characteristic audiences that influence the historical quality of information provided. The student of any one would do well to be conversant with other modes as well.

In sum, attention to all sources of evidence is crucial to establish the origin of an interpretation or theme, to identify its audiences, to account for and correct for intertwining and recirculation effects, to differentiate meanings and functions for disparate audiences, and to make the most accurate determination of the "facts," keeping in mind the continuous potential for change in folklore accounts. Toward these ends, knowledge of the key dimensions of folklore definition, its central genres and motifs, and relationships with other media is instrumental.

Folklore and History

Dorson (1971c: 129) noted that such standard manuals for the United States as Homer C. Hockett's *Introduction to Research in American History* and J. Franklin Jameson's *The American Historian's Raw Material* warn the serious scholar against legend, tradition, and folklore. This kind of a priori rejection, which characterized folklore and oral tradition as fallacious and without historical merit, and which typified historical thinking for many decades, has finally begun to pass. Vansina's (1965: 1-18) review of approaches to this issue concluded that the determination of historical value cannot be made in advance, and that such determination must involve an exploration of the unique nature of oral tradition and the application of historical criticism. Bynum (1973: 10-11) went further to suggest that while oral tradition may raise special problems in arriving at evidentiary value, both written and oral sources can be equally perjured and must be equally scrutinized.

Widely-held conceptions of historical evidence corroborate these views and though some historians are quick to point to the written document as the dominant source, others such as Gottschalk (1969: 57) accept a broader definition of the historical document including the orally transmitted document. Bloch's view is most amenable: "The variety of historcal evidence is almost infinite. Everything that man says or writes, everything that he makes, everything he touches can and ought to teach us about him" (1953: 66).

Rather than discounting specific types of evidence, historians are satisfied to establish "rules of precedence" as key aspects of historical cirticism aimed at determining the value of any document. Establishing historical evidence involves *external criticism* for assessing authenticity and *internal criticism* for mining the content of the document. Before reaching the *internal criticism* stage, the aforementioned "rules" are applied, including the closeness in time of the documentation to the event, the existence and direction of intent in the documentation, the credibility of the witness regarding the event, and the likely effects of an audience (Gottschalk 1969: 90-91). Acceptance of these general rules bodes poorly for folklore or tradition at the outset since the "chain of testimony" obscures the initial witness, is subject to shifting audience and performer intent with each change in the social order, and changes regardless of the original time-lapse between event and documentation.

Following Vansina's admonitions, folklorists have expressly evaluated the historical validity of traditional accounts in various societies. Pender-gast and Mieghan (1959) collected historical traditions from the Paiute Indians about an extinct tribe, the Mukwitch. On the basis of their data they claimed that the meager accounts were consistent with archaeological findings, indicating that traditional accounts might remain accurate for hundreds of years. Features of the oral tradition process were equally gratifying since the Paiutes consciously refused to embroider these tradi-tions with legendary motifs, and since they made distinctions between sacred and secular material (Meighan 1960). Pendergast and Mieghan's efforts ultimately suggested that oral traditions do retain some historical information, but with such minimal detail that its significance would be doubtful.

This problem of determining the overall significance of the bits and pieces of evidence was displayed graphically by Cohen (1972) in his com-parison of historical evidence with oral legends regarding the origin of a community of mountain people near the New York-New Jersey border. Four alternative stories circulated, yet none was corroborated by historical materials from genealogical records. The problem of overall significance was highlighted by the finding that each version was drawn from histori-cally accurate items, but that the items bore no relationship to the moun-tain people and their origin. One story, for example, began with Hessian deserters from the Revolutionary War, and while the Hessians and the Revolutionary War were quite real, they had nothing to do with the com-munity in question.

Robinson (1973) researched the impact of an Islam leader on a West African area, and in contrasting written with oral accounts, he found the latter less useful for history. This question of comparative value led to two additional studies. Louis Dupree (1967) engaged in a unique research ef-fort in gathering oral tradition while retracing the route of a British army retreat in Afghanistan. Comparing the written British versions with the oral folktales, he found that contemporary accounts from both sides sup-ported their respective social values and honor, but that later British writ-ten history became less distorted whereas oral accounts continued to change in a less historically accurate direction. Similarly, Gould (1966) contrasted Tolowa Indian and white settler versions of a massacre. His conclusion was that although the versions did not contradict each other, each side "selected the happenings and impressions which had meaning in the light of the values and attitudes of their respective cultures" (Gould 1966: 42).

In summary, the studies mentioned above suggest that while oral tradition and folklore may have some historical validity, they, as with written sources, require the application of critical methods to uncover possible distortion. Furthermore, these studies also point to the special problems involved in ascertaining historical fact in oral transmission—those of *historical significance and scope, external criticism,* and *internal criticism.*

SPECIAL PROBLEMS OF FOLKLORE DATA

The historical significance of oral tradition can obviously be questioned. When one deals primarily with nonliterate societies, the lack of written material for corroboration can lead to rejection of further investigation since it may be hard to determine the historical importance of events. This difficulty arises mainly in the absence of literacy and is not important when corroboration from other sources is possible. Yet any oral tradition does present certain "blind spots" that limit its usefulness. Among these are the obvious but damaging lack of quantitative data and the inability of oral sources to analyze and portray unconscious, gradual change in values, ideas, and institutions (Vansina 1971: 459). The diffusion and distillation of oral tradition over time cause this tradition not only to drift with major social changes but to lose detail both generally and in response to particular changes. Among the details often lost or distorted are those essential to the task of *external criticism.*

The need to determine author, time, and place for a historical document to ascertain its credibility is well accepted but impossible when it comes to oral tradition or folklore. In societies where the oral sources are considered valid historical documents, the sense of chronology is different from ours, and it is usually indicated by imprecise and easily distorted techniques, such as the genealogical list. In literate societies with a written tradition, folklore does not serve a conscious historical function, and attention to chronology is haphazard. Although individually authored documents often enter the folklore process, they are seldom communicated as individually authored, and in most cases authorship is indeterminate. Credibility could be approximated by external criticism declaring the "people" or the community to be author, but that would be less accurate since the "people" responsible often include an unknown number in a chain of testimony, which Vansina (1965: 21) schematized as involving an initial observer, a chain of transmission with numerous links, and a final informant and recorder. The characteristics of this chain raise some of the most difficult questions for internal criticism as well.

Major problems for internal criticism include the mode of transmission, the form of transmission, and the social-personal context of transmission. These categories are intertwined but are analytically separated for clarity. Vansina (1965), Finnegan (1970), and Dupree (1967) discussed the characteristics of the mode of transmission. Its distinctive feature is word-of-mouth transmission that is subject to distortion at any "link" in the transmission chain. Common results of this process are "telescoping," i.e., the collapsing of historical detail and loss of linkages; embroidery of the account by the addition of supernatural or legendary folklore motifs; mixing of the account by attaching several unrelated events, often creating a mosaic-like format; commentary on the later versions through which performers explain archaic words and customs; and straightforward but fatal failure of memory. However, Vansina cautioned the historian who would reject oral sources out of hand:

> All oral traditions are to a greater or lesser extent linked with the society and culture which produces them, therefore all are influenced by the culture and society concerned, upon which their very existence depends (1965: 164).

But the use of oral tradition can be improved with study of the oral tradition as a whole, determining its political-cultural-social sources of bias and its features and limitations as a medium of communication. Part of that task is the analysis of the specific types of oral tradition (e.g., poetry, folksong, ballad) and the characteristics and limitations of each as a historical source. Vansina's typology (1965: 142-164) is based on the idea that

> Each type has certain special features which affect the testimony and give each type of testimony a different kind of value as a historical source. These features are: the intentions or lack of intentions behind a testimony, the significance attached to it, its form and the literary category to which it belongs, the method of transmission used, and the manner in which the testimony is delivered (1965: 47).

Rules of form and meaning for oral expression also influence the overall value of a testimony. Many folklore or traditional genres have fixed-wording form or require certain stylistic conventions, such as rhyme, that affect the capability to express ideas clearly. This can be beneficial—for example, when fixed wording maintains an account unchanged through memorization; or it can be problematic when the rhyming conventions for a genre take precedence over clear and accurate communication. Commenting on this in relation to proverbs, Alagoa noted:

> Proverbs suffer particularly from their compressed and abbreviated rendition of historical fact. Fact and historical allusion are here distilled into the most compact record. It is, of course, the very fact of their rendition as formulas embodying a distillation of historical experience or of common sense that enable proverbs to be remembered from age to age (1968: 242).

This is the dilemma of all forms of oral transmission. The very feature that makes the item memorable or at least more easily remembered also provides a powerful motive for distortion. These pressures to replace obscure or ponderous detail with catchy, exciting, or awe-inspiring words, phrases, and episodes create one of the major sources of dissatisfaction with folklore's historical accuracy. Vansina (1965: 67) discussed the problems of separating literal meaning from intended meaning when the form of communication "imposes a style which affects the way thoughts are expressed, particularly if the style requires the use of symbolic expressions and poetic allusions, or of stereotypes" (1965: 67).

Looking at these issues from the perspective of banditry raises questions as to the interpretation of the stock phrase "robbing the rich to give to the poor," or to the interpretation of the heartwarming stories of the bandit who lent money to a grieving widow so as to prevent foreclosure of her mortgage, only to steal it back from the greedy banker after the mortgage was paid.

Aesthetic motives as these exert a powerful indirect force toward distortion of wording and meaning. Other forms of distortion, however, reflect a direct assault on historical meaning. Barbro Klein (1973) investigated the scholarly dispute over the death of King Charles XII of Sweden. In contrast with official history, which reports his death as a casualty of military action, the folk-oral version tells that Charles was assassinated by his war-weary soldiers. In this instance, the importance of distortion pressures was indicated in her observations that the disagreement between folk and official accounts had been repeated in subsequent scholarly endeavors, with the two debating intellectual leaders acting out the very conflict between aristocracy and folk that characterized the legends themselves (1973: 68). Furthermore, their debate became a national issue during the early days of World War II. Some commentators declared that the allegation that the king was assassinated from within was a threat to his image as the foremost folk hero of Sweden and personification of the newly stimulated sense of Aryan, aggressive national destiny (1973: 72-74).

Vansina (1965: 76-79) labeled every testimony "a mirage of reality" and pointed to the commonplace but crucial realization that perception is selective. He added that the very existence of oral tradition or folklore rests on the same motivations that distort it. Tradition requires an effort to maintain its use, and in serving personal, political, or cultural interests, it provides the motivation necessary to meet its objective. The personal interests of the performer or informant in pleasing the audience, explaining archaic passages, filling in gaps, and reworking and improving the artistic merit of the items are difficult to account for since the chain of testimony provides no checks on any participant other than the final informant. Personal falsification of tradition has limited effects if the group holds the tradition as important. These group features—socio-political interests and cultural values—produce the more profound and lasting distortion.

The importance of folklore in maintaining the status quo or in agitating for social change is manifest in recent definitions (Abrahams 1972; Bauman 1972a), and the importance of historical sanctification is so strong that recently the U.S. Army issued a report declaring that the label "massacre," in relation to the Wounded Knee incident at which 150 Indians were killed, is "unfair and inaccurate." Associated Press reports of the army's historical revisionism (Minneapolis *Star* 1975) quoted the report as stating that "individual excesses occurred," but that "contrary to the popular conception of the Wounded Knee episode, the civilian authorities and the army showed great restraint and compassion in the events leading up to the encounter. . . . Restraint and precautions were even observed during the battle." This particular revision was used in an army effort to stop government proposals to compensate survivors of the Sioux people killed in the "episode." In that light, it demonstrates modern interests in historical interpretation, but it also opens the way to consideration of the influence of group interests and cultural values in distortion.

In connection with the study of African traditions, Vansina (1965: 95-108) discussed three causes of distortion, including values determining historical significance of an event; assumptions determining the conception of historical time, truth, and development; and values embodied in cultural ideals. Earlier in this book we described several studies illustrating the importance of group values and interests in written and oral historical accounts. In a like manner, David Buchan (1968) contrasted ballad and historical versions of the Scottish Battle of Harlaw between highland and lowland Scots. The ballad shows the change in lowlanders' opinions of highlanders from a negative one regarding the battle, to a more neutral stance in later years. This shift in attitudes resulted in the addition and mixing of other events into the battle account to balance the no longer tenable negative viewpoint. Buchan stated that "the ballad's largest unhistoricity actually reflects the kind of historical truth that normally never finds its way into the documents, the nature and quality of the folk's emotional attitudes over a long span of years" (1968: 65).

Palavestra described a similar phenomenon among the Serbo-Croatians and labeled the process that transforms events *dehistorization*:

> The relationship between tradition and history, therefore, has depended upon a great number of factors which always were conditioned by the social, political, and cultural enrichment in which the given historical reality influenced national consciousness. When a certain historical event or personage, because of its importance for the fate of the people, prompted the creation of a given oral tradition, in the process of the evolution of that tradition dehistorization ensued to a greater or lesser extent, depending upon popular feeling, the influence of that event in the lives of the people, and external, artistic interventions. . . . In each age, the relationship between oral folk tradition and history takes on a new character, and is directly reflected in the intensity of national feeling (1966: 276).

But despite the evidence in favor of "dehistorization," he noted that some aspects of folk tradition are less conducive to continuous redefinition. In comparing folkpoetry to folksong, he stated that the former exists in such fixed form that it retains more of a reflection of the initial creation than free-form song, which changes more easily in response to social and cultural change.

All sources of evidence are subject to distortion, and the historical method is applied to separate fact from fiction and falsification. But the foregoing section describes folklore and oral tradition as uniquely susceptible to a process of "dehistorization" so that the oral document continually changes to reflect the values and interests of the times. Historians interested in using oral materials recognize these extra problems but have developed several techniques to increase the probability of accurate historical interpretation.

These approaches were discussed by Dorson (1973a: 110-112) and Vansina (1965, 1971). Analysis of the oral tradition or folklore system as a whole, within the social area under consideration, provides clues about sources of distortion, and knowledge of the characteristics of each type of folklore aids in determining validity. Once more and less likely distorted accounts have been identified, the comparison of variants can clarify the sources, directions, and causes of distortion. These variations are also a clue to psychological biases of informants that can be corroborated with other information on informant credibility. Knowledge of folklore motifs can aid in excising legendary embroidery from the materials, and corroboration by other sources—history, geography, material culture—can increase confidence. Finally, knowledge of other disciplines, such as anthropology, sociology, and linguistics, can help the process of historical criticism salvage valid historical information from the folklore process of dehistorization. As Vansina concluded his methodological treatise (1965: 186), history is not an ultimate truth but is a matter of probability, and the historian using oral sources is still doing valid history but with lower probabilities.

From the foregoing it appears that the historian who works hard and knows everything about his area from all disciplines and sources of information, can produce a reliable history from oral materials *but with a lower probability of accuracy*. That may bolster the historian in areas where written accounts are absent, but it seems to offer little solace or motivation to the historian of highly literate areas interested in folklore sources. On the other hand, folklore has a series of unique characteristics that makes it valuable as a data source in spite of its many shortcomings.

THE HISTORICAL UTILITY OF FOLKLORE

Folklore scholars interested in historical reconstruction have pointed to several contributions to the historical record for which folklore is an important if not the unique source of evidence. These include: (1) the identification and removal of folklore motifs from documents; (2) the determination of beliefs and stereotypes; (3) the determination of subcultural and cultural values; (4) insight into the nature and consequences of group conflict; (5) an indication of the central "myths" of subcultures and cultures; (6) inclusion of the historical record of groups usually neglected by orthodox historical research; and (7) the relationship of beliefs, values, and myths to later social action.

The first contribution of folklore research to historical study has already been cited but is somewhat peripheral to the purpose here. Still the task of "disentangling fact from fancy" is an important one, and knowledge of folklore genres and motifs can be of value in identifying and eliminating questionable episodes from historical documents (Dorson 1971c: 138-140).

The evaluation of folklore material as historical fact requires several distinctions among types of fact. If we consider historical facts to be only "barebones" statements such as "Jesse James was born on September 5, 1847," then folklore is nearly valueless since many of the facets of the dehistorization process eliminate or modify such information. However, historians refer to other kinds of "facts"—ideas, motives, beliefs, and stereotypes. In Dorson's words:

> There is, however, another class of facts, in a way more solid because they are not hypostasized, and these are the traditional beliefs of a group of people as to what happened. This shared belief is a fact which can be established by a folklorist or a local historian (1971f: 147).

Benson (1967) argued that historians need to begin the scientific study of past public opinion. This requires attention to numerous and varied data sources and techniques for establishing public opinion from them. Benson suggested that through this line of research historians would be able to make approximations of the influence or lack of influence of various publics on governmental decision-making. He did not explicitly mention folklore as a data source but it might be included in his general category of "works of art." Following Benson, folklore and other data sources on public beliefs can give the historian insight into public opinion and its impact on social action.

Even beyond beliefs about historical events, another class of facts can be established. As Bloch commented, "there are many errors that derive from a particular social climate. Such errors often assume a documentary value in their turn" (1953: 105-106). This is so since error or distortion does not really spread "unless it harmonizes with the prejudices of public opinion. It then becomes a mirror in which the collective consciousness surveys its own features." Along this line, comparison of folklore distortion with historical reality offers a powerful technique for determining group values and conflicts, and for establishing the central "myths" that give expression to the ideals or visions of the group.

An emphasis on cultural values has been the province of the scholar more oriented toward published literature as the dominant source of interpretations of banditry. For example, Jones (1973: 653) preferred to explain the widespread acceptance of the outlaw hero as a function of the theme's capabilities for vicariously resolving the culture conflicts inherent in industrialization, urbanization, class conflict, big business exploitation, moral collapse, and individual powerlessness. Perhaps, then, the modern-day counterpart of the original bandit legend serves as a generalized symbol of widely held values of justice and individualism and finds concrete expression in the outlaw's rebellion against an impersonal and constraining society.

Yet, the origins of the legends portray a less abstract and diffuse interpretation that highlights intergroup hostility and conflict. The disagreement over the correct interpretation of bandit activity and, consequently, the disagreement over the appropriate legal response, are reflected in the different accounts produced by the communicative outlets of conflicting groups. Comparison of disparate accounts provides insights into the nature and sources of conflict and the importance of group conflict for the process of defining deviance. The case of the James gang is instructive here. According to Settle (1966), the legend of the gang must be viewed in light of the Civil War and its aftermath. During the war, Missouri was wracked by the battle between the Union occupation forces and Confederate guerrilla bands, with the latter including the James brothers in their ranks. When many of the wartime Confederate marauders shifted to banditry, the initial public reaction was a typical call for swift and sure legal action. However, shortly after the Kansas State Fair robbery, a Missouri newspaper editor who had served in the Southern armies and held the guerrilla bands in high regard, began a campaign of glorifying the James brothers, depicting them as brave, chivalrous, and Robin Hood-like. Later themes included persecution, injustice, and revenge facets that merged with a "never robs Southerners" belief, and firmly implanted the gang's image among certain publics as heroic diehards of the Confederate cause. Of course this interpretation was hotly disputed by sources sympathetic to the North, but the legend remained forceful throughout the James' exploits and became an issue in postwar Missouri politics and a central theme at Frank James' trial and acquittal. Yet the Confederate cause was not the only force contributing to the James legend. Resentment toward banks and railroads was widespread and offered an inducement for non-Confederates to revel in the James' concentration on those institutions. Additionally, the diffusion of bandit stories in the press was accelerated by their use in rivalries between Chicago and Missouri economic interests and between the established East and the upstart West.

Thus, the interpretation of the bandit in folklore and other media may originate and spread along the lines of group conflict in the society. But disagreement over definition and interpretation is a ubiquitous feature of a complex society. What makes the bandit legend and its folklore sources of even greater interest is their utility in determining the central myths of the group.

As Rosa (1969) once stated, bandits or professional outlaw-killers were almost invariably drifters, antisocial misfits who were unable to solve their personal problems or achieve fame except through violence. Regardless, many are perceived as "social bandits." Their actions are seen as a form of individual or minority rebellion within peasant societies, and the bandits are considered by their people as heroes, champions of liberty, avengers, fighters for justice, or, perhaps, even leaders of liberation (Hobsbawm 1959; 1969).

Whether the setting is a peasant society or the frontier of the Western outlaw, the image of the "noble robber" seems to emerge.

First, the noble robber begins his career of outlawry not by crime, but as a victim of injustice, or through being persecuted by the authorities for some act which they, but not the custom of his people, consider as criminal.

Second, he "rights wrongs."

Third, he "takes from the rich to give to the poor."

Fourth, he "never kills but in self-defense or just revenge."

Fifth, if he survives, he returns to his people as an honorable citizen and member of the community.

Sixth, he is admired, helped and supported by his people.

Seventh, he dies invariably and only through treason, since no decent member of the community would help the authorities against him.

Eighth, he is—at least in theory—invisible and invulnerable.

Ninth, he is not the enemy of the king or emperor, who is the fount of justice, but only of the local gentry, clergy or other oppressors (Hobsbawm 1969: 35-36).

This image of the noble robber defines the parameters of what some scholars have called "the myth of the bandit," and its historicity has remained in dispute by folklorists analyzing the diffusion of bandit legends and by historians searching for clues to the reality of Robin Hood or the "facts" of Jesse James. The existence of the "myth" and its appearance in disparate times and places is accepted, but the historical meaning remains unclear. Two contemporary antagonists on the issue, Eric Hobsbawm and Anton Blok, exemplify its central points.

In Hobsbawm's (1959; 1969) notion of social banditry, the myth of the bandit becomes an historical fact in that it provides an interpretation of social and political relations from the otherwise ignored viewpoint of the peasant. But the bandit myth is not only a belief molded by collective imagination, it also bears some relationship to the actual behavior of the bandit (1969: 13-15). Blok (1974) criticized Hobsbawm's interpretation, basing the refutation on his work on mafia and bandits in Sicily:

> Though Hobsbawm describes the myths and legends about bandits, his two studies fail to penetrate them. Even when we admit that it is the urban middle class rather than the ordinary peasantry who idealize the bandit, we may well ask to whom or what the peasants refer when they glorify the bandit (Blok 1972: 500).

Blok's answer was straightforward: it is an idealized construct arising out of the people's aspirations and without behavioral validity. According to Blok, Hobsbawm's error was his narrow focus that concentrated on the bandit and on the peasant viewpoint and failed to link the phenomenon adequately to its social structural context. Seen in that context, the bandit was clearly antipeasant in behavior and the myth of the bandit was antipeasant in function. Rather than evoking rebellion, the bandit and his "myth" served to control the peasant population directly through terrorism and indirectly through deflecting frustration.

Hobsbawm is unmoved by most of Blok's criticism but he remains sensitive to the methodological problems of evidence and viewpoint and realizes that the bandit is also a symbol. Most individual bandits are forgotten by the short memory of oral culture or are transformed in agreement with the collective imagery of the group. That transformation negates behavioral detail but highlights the function and meaning of the myth for the bandit's supporters. These myths remain an important datum even though the ultimate impact of a particular myth may be to subjugate rather than uplift its believers.

The identification and analysis of beliefs, values, and myths can be undertaken without recourse to folklore data, but they are useful in providing information on the beliefs of usually neglected groups and thereby in offering an answer to Garraty's plaintive question (cited in Dorson 1972b: 239): "is the history of the inarticulate masses of the past lost simply because of their inarticulateness?" The folklorist replies no and offers a source that helps balance the historical record.

Folklore has another promising though controversial aspect that increases its utility as a record of group opinion—the debatable but intriguing possibility that folklore "is the composition rather of a folk than of an individual; it rose from the heart and lips of a whole people" (Nevins 1962: 79). Wilson's view of folklore creation is less magical:

Folklore, on the other hand, provides a sort of automatic random sampling. No matter what the origin of a folklore item, it will, if it is to survive, move from the individual expression of its originator to the communal expression of those who preserve it, sloughing off as it passes from person to person and through time and space the marks of individual invention, and in a short time reflecting quite accurately the consensus of the group (1973: 48).

This view is not entirely accurate since the degree of consensus is never known, but it might serve as a useful approximation of group opinion when other sources of evidence are unavailable.

Finally, folklore is important if we accept Barzun and Graff's (1970: 51-52) fourth meaning of history. This is the popular conception of history, the often inaccurate recollection of the past, which, despite its fallaciousness from the scholar's perspective, makes an impact on the present and the future. Roger Abrahams (1966) discussed heroes in America, and after recounting the familiar theme of the outlaw capturing public imagination as a heroic figure, he concluded: "American society, in its nostalgia for heroic manifestations of the past, sows the seeds of its own potential destruction." Abrahams' argument was extreme, but the popular conception of history is of great importance if, in fact, it is this kind of history that leads people to act.

Summarizing, folklore has utility for the historian in helping remove legendary material from sources; in helping to identify beliefs, attitudes, opinions, stereotypes, and values; specifying the nature and consequences of intergoup conflict; identifying the central myths of the group; studying usually neglected groups; and linking the popular historical beliefs of one era with the actions of the next.

FOLKLORE AND HISTORY: A FINAL NOTE

Distortion of any historical event is possible in both written and oral modes of communication, but to folklore are added the threatening features of continuous change in response to new pressures and the eventual dehistorization of any particular account. But folklorists and historians have suggested that these distortions have historical value! Outlaw stories, whether of Robin Hood or Jesse James, reveal much about social relations, values, and beliefs. The folklore account of the bandit gives useful information about beliefs and interpretations of crime. Taken as individual accounts, these folk legendary versions contribute to our knowledge about how some people viewed certain forms of crime. Taken a step further, variations in folklore accounts between groups and across areas and time, provide information to elaborate on the social dimensions underlying definitions of crime. The comparison of the folklore versions and official interpretations of bandits offers a clue to determining the outlines of group conflict and consensus and their impact on definitions. Similarly, the distortion of a folklore account often provides a vivid depiction of the myths of a group. Finally, as a folklore item diffuses, its function in exemplifying certain cultural values and aspirations for the entire society becomes clear. To make use of folklore data to study crime historically requires the collection of folklore accounts in many settings, the corroboration from other historical data, and the placing of both in a context that makes distortion clear and interpretable.

Though folklore is of limited utility in establishing the actual behavior of bandits or of any other historical group or individual, it has great potential in the study of definitions of crime and the social, political, and cultural contexts that shape those definitions. Using folklore successfully will require more attention to clarifying its distinct nature as a communicative mode, its relationship with other modes of communication, and the details of its genres—if the historical criminologist is to follow Nevin's suggestion that history involves "a spirit of critical inquiry for the whole truth" (1962: 39).

Pursuit of the whole truth precludes a priori judgments about evidence and demands that the historian recognize that the written document cannot provide the whole truth. Gaps in the historical record can be filled, historical facts of a different order obtained, and the future meaning and function of history clarified, if the historian recognizes the limitations of orthodox history and realizes, as Hobsbawm does,

> [that] the bandits belong to remembered history, as distinct from the history of books. They are part of the history which is not so much a record of events and those who shaped them, as of the symbols and theoretically controllable though actually uncontrolled factors which determine the world of the poor: of just kings and men who bring justice to the people. That is why the bandit legend still has power to move us (Hobsbawm 1969: 133).

Returning to Sweden and the saga of Clark Olafsson: if such legends retain their capacity to evoke admiration and action, exemplifying the popular meaning of history, then it is essential for the historically minded criminologist to dredge up the historical data that might illuminate this perplexing present-day phenomenon.

PART II

ON ISSUES IN RESEARCH

Chapter 3

OUTLAWS, BANDITS, AND THE LORE

OF THE AMERICAN "WILD WEST"

Reflections on the American West call forth any variety of images—of settlers and traders, trappers and buffalo, cavalry and Indian uprisings, homesteaders and range wars, cowboys and cattle drives, and of sheriffs, gunslingers, and outlaws. History, literature, and popular culture have sculptured these images into the notion of a "Wild West"—a land west of the Mississippi River comprising millions of square miles of rough prairie, desert wasteland, and mountain terrain, settled by only the hardiest and most strong-willed of men, and characterized by the violence of banditry and frontier justice. And perhaps most enduring among these images have been the somewhat magnificent demigods known as gunfighters and bandit-heros. Whether lawman or outlaw, the gunfighter was the embodiment of every hero of all time; he was a well-armed Galahad whose pistols made right all manner of injustices; the bandit, although depicted as an instrument of violence and destruction, was the personification of strength and purpose, and the object of worship. Such images emerged midway through the last century and have persisted for more than a dozen decades and on many continents.

   Much of what is currently descriptive of the gunfighter and bandit-hero descends from a curious mixture of history, folklore, and fiction; and our conceptions of law, order, and crime on the western frontier have rarely gone beyond the boundaries of these traditional ideas. By contrast, the history of crime in the American West is in many ways counterpoint to folklore, popular culture, or even traditional history. The history of crime in the American West represents one of the more striking examples of how social, cultural, and technological phenomena might generate a body of ideas and traditions which intersect the continuity of historical awareness to the degree that they are accepted as "fact" and are transmitted and maintained as such by both literature and history. Within this framework, the ensuing analysis reviews the data of western outlawry, examines their content, and demonstrates how history became jaded by fiction and legend.

The Emerging "Wild West"

The bandits, outlaws, and gunfighting lawmen of the American West who defined the territory from which legend could emerge were products of both violence and prosperity. Their skills and abilities as destructive predators or protagonists of swift justice were generated by conflicts in Texas, by the Kansas-Missouri border wars, by the guerrilla activities of the Civil War, and by the general dangers of frontier life; their emergence as gunfighters and outlaws was made possible by the prosperity of post-Civil War expansion, the growth of the railroad and cattle industries, and the discovery of gold in the far West.

Early in the progression of events which contributed to the legendary frontier character was the friction between Texas and the Mexican government during the first half of the nineteenth century. Texas was an area of rich and vast grazing lands, which drew migrants from east of the Mississippi seeking to establish settlements. And the migrants came, fully ignoring that Texas was under Mexican rule. Among them were politicians and agitators who were concerned with establishing the independence of the territory and bringing it within the jurisdiction or under the protection of the United States (Hawgood 1969: 140). Mexicans, resenting these efforts and attempting to drive the settlers from their lands, won a decided victory over a ragged Texas militia with the fall of the Alamo on March 6, 1836. Yet the heroic resistance by small groups of Americans at the Alamo and their massacre by superior Mexican forces hardened the opposition, inspired others to fight on, and won for "Texans" support from all parts of the United States. Under the leadership of Sam Houston, the Texas forces defeated the Mexican army at the Battle of San Jacinto less than two months later. The Mexican government conceded most of its Texas territory, but maintained that the western boundary would be the Nueces River rather than the Rio Grande. When the United States annexed Texas in 1845, including the territory beyond the Nueces River, trouble between the two nations again mounted. It continued until the Mexican War of 1846 to 1848, which forced Mexico to accept the independence of Texas (Moody 1963).

While these events were taking place, the legend of the Texas gunfighter was being nurtured—primarily in the image of the Texas Ranger. First equipped by Stephen Austin in 1823 as settlers' protection against Indians and later organized as a corps of irregular fighters at the outbreak of the Texas Revolution in the 1830s, the Rangers were a force that remained much in the public eye (Webb 1935; Castleman 1944). In addition to rifles, their armament included the newly developed Colt revolver, a .36-caliber model with a nine-inch barrel (Josserand and Stevenson 1972: 155-156). The Rangers had difficulty with the new weapons, but within a short period their revolvers made them more effective fighters than the musket-carrying Mexican soldiers or the bow-wielding Indians (Hughes 1964: 22-56). The Texas Rangers' success with the Colt revolver demonstrated that it was a weapon of choice. The significance of the revolver was quickly recognized throughout the West, and the Rangers had taken the first step toward the establishment of a "pistol-packing" tradition (Rosa 1969: 33).

On January 24, 1848, while the war was still being waged against Mexico, James W. Marshall discovered gold at Captain John A. Sutter's sawmill on California's American River (Lewis 1966: 103). It was an event that served to further shape the frontier West.

At first, Marshall's discovery was not taken seriously. Comments on the finding had not reached the East until later that year when it was briefly mentioned in a New York newspaper on September 16 (Chidsey 1968: 42). It was President James K. Polk who, in his message opening the second session of the thirtieth Congress on December 5, 1848, initiated the California gold rush:

It was known that mines of precious metals existed to a considerable extent in California at the time of its acquisition. Recent discoveries render it probable that these mines are more extensive and valuable than was anticipated. The accounts of the abundance of gold in that territory are of such an extraordinary character as would scarcely command belief were they not corroborated by the authentic reports of officers in the public service, who have visited the mineral district, and derived the facts which they detail from personal observation. Reluctant to credit the reports in general circulation as to the quantity of gold, the officer commanding our forces in California visited the mineral district in July last, for the purpose of obtaining accurate information on the subject. His report to the War Department of the result of the examination, and the facts obtained on the spot, is herewith laid before Congress. When he visited the country there were about four thousand persons engaged in collecting gold. There is every reason to believe that the number of persons so employed has since been augmented. The explorations already made warrant the belief that the supply is very large, and that gold is found at various places in an extensive district of country (Congressional Globe, 1848).

With Polk's announcement, "California" abrupty became a magic word. By the end of the following month, some ninety vessels had cleared Atlantic seaports bound for California, and with the spring of 1849, tens of thousands of overlanders had begun the trans-America journey. The *Gold Rush* had fully begun. At the end of 1848, some 6,000 miners had removed 10 million dollars worth of gold from Californian soil; in 1849, the amount of gold produced was two to three times as large with a miner population of 40,000; in 1852, the peak year, the gold output was estimated to be 80 million dollars, shared among more than 100,000 miners (Bean 1968: 122).

Within the gold fields, there was a great demand for revolvers (see, Shinn 1948). The gold seekers were largely self-reliant and few cared to be without personal protection. During January, 1850, .31-caliber pocket pistols arrived in California, and later that year, a new Colt .36-caliber Navy pistol became available (Edwards 1953: 259-261). It was of light weight and excellent balance, and its acceptance in California presaged its eventual demand in other parts of the West.

While the need for weapons in Texas was related to Mexicans and Indians and in California to gold, the issue in the Kansas Territory was slaves. The question of slavery was paramount in the minds of many Americans at midcentury, especially among Kansas settlers since they were to decide whether their state would be slave or free. The Missouri Compromise of 1820 had decreed that while Missouri would be admitted to the Union as a slave state, slavery would be prohibited in the territory of the United States north of Missouri's southern boundary, latitude 36° 30'. Yet this legislation was repealed in 1854 in favor of the Kansas-Nebraska Act with its "squatter's sovereignty"—self-determination in the matter of slavery. Missourians, fearing that their slaves would flee across their western border into Kansas if that state became free, crossed into this undecided territory to claim land. Their intention was not settlement, but only to retain land long enough to vote for slavery (Garwood 1948: 34-49). And the issue went far beyond the residents of Kansas and Missouri. Pro- and anti-slavery groups from other parts of the nation also moved to Kansas. The federal government opened a land office in the territory in July 1854, and the New England Emigrant Aid Society and other corporations financed emigration to Kansas (Howes 1952: 35). Anti-slavery efforts as these aroused the indignation of Missourians, who proceeded to blockade the Missouri River against immigrants from the Northeast. The result was open conflict between Missouri "Border Ruffians" and anti-slavery "Free Soilers" (Callahan 1926-1928). The Missouri factions invaded the Kansas territory, destroying homes and crops, murdering any one who resisted them. Allied against the "Border Ruffians" were the Kansas "Jayhawkers"—free staters who crossed into Missouri to avenge alleged attacks (see, Nichols 1954).

The Kansas-Missouri border raids reached their peak during the years 1855 through 1858, but ultimately continued to become part of the more intense Civil War. With the outbreak of the war between the states, both the "Ruffians" and "Jayhawkers" joined Union, southern, and independent guerrilla bands, which used the conflict as an opportunity to equalize harbored Kansas-Missouri differences and to otherwise plunder the countryside. These guerrilla bands contained many of the socially outcast, including bandits and soldiers of fortune who sought their share of war wealth through the violence of hit-and-run raids. They were heavily armed, employing the firepower of both rifles and revolvers, and they emerged from the war as a breed accustomed to violence and indifferent to human life (see, Connelley 1956; Castel 1962).

While the gold fields in California and the wars in Texas, along the Kansas-Missouri border, and between the Union and Confederate forces contributed to a culture of violence in the American West, the outlaw and gunfighter of history and legend did not become fully apparent until after the close of the Civil War. Bandits and highwaymen were not unknown to the West prior to this period, and the frequent robbery of gold-carrying stagecoaches was known throughout California and the Dakotas as early as 1852 (Loomis 1968: 142). But it was during the postwar decades that the legendary "heroes" first became prominent. They were drawn from the Union and Confederate veterans and the war-time guerrilla fighters who wandered the countryside searching for excitement and wealth after the surrender at Appomattox in 1865; from the dispirited easterners who went west in search of adventure and fortune; and from the miscreant soldiers of fortune, thieves, and other predators. All sought sanctuary in the seventy-four thousand square mile territory west of Fort Smith, Arkansas, where there was no formal law under which a fugitive could be extradited (see, Shirley 1957).

The violence of the outlaw West has been described in terms of cattle rustling, stagecoach theft, train robbery, horse stealing, and vigilante justice, but nothing has been more celebrated in legend and folklore than the activities of the train and bank robbers and the lawmen who were marshaled to oppose them. It would be difficult to specify which event marked the beginning of the outlaw era, but it is clear that it had certainly arrived when the Reno gang became known to America's railroad industry. On the evening of October 6, 1866, an Ohio & Mississippi passenger train had scarcely cleared the station at Seymour, Indiana, heading east, when two masked men entered the express car from the coach behind it, and removed some $13,000 from the railroad safe (Shields 1939). The thieves then pulled the bell cord to slow the train, pushed another unopened safe from the express car to track side, and promptly exited the vicinity. The robbery had been engineered by John and Simeon Reno, and Frank Sparks. The Renos were not the first train robbers, for the first railway holdup is believed to have occurred on May 5, 1865 when an Ohio & Mississippi train en route from St. Louis to Cincinnati was derailed and overturned, with its safe and passengers robbed by an unidentified gang of thieves (Harlow 1934: 331). But the Reno gang was reputed to represent the first organized band of train robbers who set the stage for an American institution, which was to endure for a half century. Following the efforts of the Renos, train robbery began in Missouri and Nevada, and during the 1870s it reached its peak throughout the West.

Perhaps the most celebrated of the train pirates was Jesse Woodson James, a product of the Kansas-Missouri border wars, who began his outlaw career in bank robbery along with his brother Frank, and the notorious Younger brothers—Cole, Jim, John, and Bob. The James gang first reached a national audience on July 21, 1873 with the holdup of a Chicago, Rock Island & Pacific train near Adair, Iowa. Their estimated $4,000 theft was decidedly small when contrasted with other efforts of the period, but the James-Younger technique of wrecking the train prior to its robbery represented a dramatic contribution to outlawry, which rapidly earned the attention of the railroad industry and the law throughout the West (see, Settle 1966).

In addition to the Renos and the James-Younger troupe, train robbery during the second half of the nineteenth century was mostly associated with such personages as Sam Bass, Bill Doolin, the Dalton brothers, and Black Jack Ketchum. The popularity of this form of robbery seemed to result from the minimal opposition to it during the 1870s and 1880s— a consequence of the security extended by the seclusion of country rail sidings, the limited number of law enforcement agents, and importantly, the widespread apathy toward the railroad industry. On this latter point, bitterness and hatred against the railroads solidified during the late 1860s because of the policies of the Southern Pacific (Block 1959: 9-12) combined with conflicts over the Kansas land grants, which endured from 1854 through 1890 (Gates 1966). The Southern Pacific and other railroad companies had in many ways plundered the West. Agents of the railroad industry had induced pioneer investment and development in areas proposed for track routing, later disclaiming these settlers' legal title to their lands. In addition, many railroads ultimately bypassed prosperous communities as a penalty for their not cooperating with the rail industry; federal land policies permitted many railroads to secure millions of acres of land which they then sold at exorbitant prices; and political and advertising patronage enabled railroads to engage in rate discrimination and monopolistic practices. In the end, much of the population of railroad territory felt cheated in land deals, freight rates, and wildcat stocks and bonds. As a consequence, they worried little when others preyed on the railroads; and criminals in the tradition of Jesse James, the Youngers, the Dalton brothers, and others operated for a time with what, in retrospect, might be viewed as comparative ease and safety.

Few lines of demarcation separated the train robbers from the bank robbers of the post-Civil War decades, for in many instances, the same individuals engaged in both kinds of theft. Characteristic in this respect immediately before the turn of the century were such notables as Robert Leroy Parker (Butch Cassidy), Harry Longbaugh (the Sundance Kid), Harvey Logan (Kid Curry), and Harry Tracy.

"Gunfighters" as we have come to call them, however, comprised a more heterogeneous collection of individuals, and included outlaws, gamblers, bounty hunters, and lawmen. These were attributed superhuman skill with weapons. They served as judge, jury, and executioner in matters they deemed devotion to law and order, just revenge, or survival of the fittest. The gunfighters of lore included such individuals as James Butler "Wild Bill" Hickok, Wyatt Earp, Charles Bolton (Black Bart), John H. "Doc" Holliday, William Barclay "Bat" Masterson, William H. Bonney (Billy the Kid), and John Wesley Hardin.

The Outlaw West in Legend and Folklore

The gunfighter and outlaw have become so firmly established in American folklore and legend that many historical treatments of our "Wild West" reflect a curious blend of fact and fiction. At one level, the outlaw has been depicted as a folk hero of the Robin Hood type, and both outlaw and gunfighter heroes have been characterized as champions of freedom and democracy, riding from one adventure to another righting the wrongs of evil and injustice. As heroes, they served only good causes, and they were physically strong, morally courageous, and the embodiment of cunning and cleverness—virtues which they drew upon in overcoming the tremendous odds pitted against them.

The outlaw as Robin Hood, as noted in Chapter 2, is a tradition which depicts the central character as the victim of injustice who becomes both hero and hunted in his attempts to serve a higher cause of justice. And this theme is clearly reflected in the legend and folklore of the life and times of Jesse James (see, for example, Dacus 1882; Buel 1881). In American folklore, Jesse, along with his brother Frank, return from Confederate guerrilla service in the Civil War only to find their home state of Missouri overrun with carpetbaggers and other Yankee oppressors. The story line states that these opportunists and Yankee persecutors attack Jesse's father, jail his mother, and savagely beat him, with the law serving the cause of the vindictive Unionists. To secure justice, Jesse James must live outside the law. He rights the wrongs inflicted by the economic aristocracy by preying upon the banking and railroad industries and by living a life devoted to opposing the established system.

By contrast, history suggests that Jesse James' entrance into a life outside the law was more of a conscious choice than the unjust decision of fate (Settle 1966). In 1863, Jesse joined the ranks of "Bloody" Bill Anderson's guerrillas, a segment of William Clarke Quantrill's raiders, who plundered, murdered, and raped during the war years in the name of the Confederacy. As a guerrilla fighter, Jesse James was a frequent party to the numerous incidents of burning, pillage, torture, and killing associated with the Quantrill and Anderson bands, including the massacre at Lawrence, Kansas on August 21, 1863 during which almost two hundred free soil "Jayhawkers" were gunned down or burned alive (see, Davis 1976). After the war Jesse formed his own bandit group, and progressed in a career of robbery and murder until shortly before his death in 1882.

The interpretation of Jesse Woodson James as folk hero makes manifest many of the "noble robber" characteristics outlined earlier, and interestingly, much of what appears in the Jesse James legend is also evident in the stories describing other outlaws of the American West. Initially, as Steckmesser (1966) demonstrated, some "persecution" of the innocent is a basic folk explanation of outlawry. Although historical search has been unable to unearth any verification, the attack on Jesse James and the mistreatment of his parents occupy a conspicuous position in the folk history of his life. In portraits of Billy the Kid, his lawless ventures were described as originating in retaliation for the assassination of his employer by a corrupt political machine (Burns 1925); "Bloody" Bill Anderson's joining of Quantrill's raiders was said to be the result of the hanging of Bill's father and uncle by Union troops (McLoughlin 1975: 16); and Joaquín Murieta, known as "the Robin Hood of El Dorado," turned outlaw to revenge the rape of his wife by miners and the hanging of his brother by vigilantes (Ridge 1854).

Folklore also offers a variety of anecdotes to exemplify the bandit-hero's generosity and sense of justice. Conspicuous in this respect is the well-known and already noted widow's mortgage story, which was originally attributed to Robin Hood, and appeared in Joseph Ritson's 1795 edition of *Robin Hood, A Collection of All the Ancient Poems, Songs and Ballads, now Extent, Relative to the Celebrated English Outlaw* (cited by Steckmesser 1966). In an early ballad, Robin Hood lends some four hundred pounds to Sir Richard of Lee, enabling him to pay his debts to the Abbot of St. Mary's. When the Abbot's clerk (and the Abbot himself in later versions) later rides through Sherwood Forest, Robin Hood holds him up and recovers the money.

In 1899, Jesse James, Jr., reflecting on an event that allegedly occurred some ten years before his birth, related the following about his father:

> A year of two after the close of the war my father and a companion who had been with him in Quantrill's command, were riding on horseback through the mountain districts of Tennessee. They stopped for dinner at a house along a country road, and while resting there learned that the woman of the house was a widow. . . . My father noticed that the widow was very despondent . . . and she told him that what worried her most just then was that her house and little farm was mortgaged for five hundred dollars, the loan fell due that very day, and she expected the sheriff and the money-lender to come that afternoon, and foreclose the mortgage and order her off the place (James 1889: 80-81).

Jesse James, Jr. continued his narrative with quotations from the actors, relating how his father offered the widow his last five hundred dollars, how the money was paid, and how it was later recovered. In a similar frame, James told how his father rescued a young black from a mob about to lynch him for wounding a white boy in self-defense (James 1889: 82-84). The ballad of outlaw Sam Bass, first sung by Texas cowboys almost a century ago, provides a further example of the almost identical mortgage story (see, Lomax 1947: 59), and it has also been offered regarding a member of Butch Cassidy's "Wild Bunch" (Baker 1965).

Finally, folklore depicts the outlaw-hero as one who kills only in self-defense or just revenge, and whose own death occurs through some betrayal—notions which have not withstood the test of historical analysis. Curious mitigations were now and then introduced to detract attention from any wanton killings attributed to the hero. Again consider the folklore of Jesse James. A noted biographer claimed that he never killed unless attacked or resisted, and that he had nothing in common with a murderer (Edwards 1877: 451). Similarly, Jesse James, Jr. (1889) put forth the notion of justifiable homicide, and regarding his father's participation in the Lawrence, Kansas Massacre by Quantrill's raiders, he simply stated: "Whether or not my father was in the Lawrence raid I am unable to say. I have heard some of his comrades say that he was there and some of them say he was not there" (p. 36).

But then consider the train robbery at Winston, Missouri on July 15, 1881. A passenger train on the Chicago, Rock Island & Pacific Railroad was held up and an unarmed conductor and a railway workman were mercilessly killed. In what represents perhaps the most reliable of the early books on Jesse James, written by an individual who was clearly sympathetic towards his subject, the robbery and killings were directly attributed to Jesse and his gang (Love 1926: 301-302). By contrast, a Jesse James protagonist emphatically denied any involvement by either of the James brothers:

> No matter what may be said to the contrary, neither Jesse nor Frank James were present at Winston; it was a venture of Dick Little, the Fords, and Jim Cummings. . . . The Jameses had never been unnecessarily cruel or brutal, and had they been present at Winston, there would have been no murder committed there (Triplett 1882: 195-199).

The gunfighter of legend presents both similar and alternative sets of characterizations:

> It is noon. The sun blazes down on a sun-baked, dusty street. Except for an occasional cow pony . . . no living thing can be seen. Suddenly

the street is no longer deserted. Two men have walked out from the shade of the buildings some fifty yards apart. Almost casually they step to the center of the street and stand facing each other. They begin to move forward slowly, but steadily. . . .

One of the men carries himself arrogantly erect, his lips drawn back in a sneer, aware that hidden along the street are people watching him with hate—a hatred born of fear. . . . The other man is tall, and his well-proportioned body moves with a panther-like grace as he paces down the street. Looking neither to the right nor to the left, he walks with deadly purpose toward his antagonist. . . .

Hands flash down, and the thunderous roar of heavy Colts fills the air. When the acrid blue smoke clears, our hero stands alone, guns in hand, his enemy dead in the dust. Once more good has triumphed over evil (Rosa 1969: 3-4).

Such was the portrait of the gunfight, and the hero—a big, sometimes cruel but magnificent demigod known as the "gunfighter." He manifested strength of purpose, his prowess was beyond reproach, his phenomenal reflexes enabled him to draw and fire a revolver with incredible speed and accuracy, in the service of those in trouble his dynamism brought death to wrongdoers, and his legendary nature was most typical in the personage of the great western paragon, James Butler "Wild Bill" Hickok.

Hickok was born in Illinois in 1837, and although little is known of his early life, he was reared in a God-fearing home of pronounced abolitionist views (Fielder 1965: 11-28). He emigrated to "Bleeding Kansas" in 1855 with the intention of becoming a farmer, but history also suggests that during 1856-1857 he rode with the Jim Lane Free State band of Jayhawkers against the Missouri Border Ruffians (Steckmesser 1965: 106). Early in 1858 Hickok became a constable in Johnson County, Kansas, but later that year he began a period of service as a teamster and station attendant with the Russel, Majors & Waddell freighting firm. And it was during this segment of his early career that his reputation as a gunfighter ultimately emerged.

As an assistant stock tender for the Russel, Majors & Waddell firm in 1861, he became involved in a shooting at a stage station in Rock Creek, Nebraska. The event occurred on July 12, 1861, and Hickok shot and killed one David McCanles and wounded two of McCanles' associates; the cause of the shootings had grown from strained relations between McCanles and the stage company. McCanles had been an aggressive sort, feared by many, and although the Rock Creek affair was soon forgotten in the greater excitement of the Civil War, it was later resurrected to serve as a basis for the Wild Bill Hickok gunfighter legend.

During the war years, Hickok was an army wagon master and scout, and in 1865 while earning his living as a gambler he killed a man over a disputed game of cards. During the period that followed, his reputation grew. He became a deputy U.S. marshall, a sheriff, a city marshall, and his legendary exploits were centered in Abilene and Hays City, Kansas, and Deadwood, South Dakota (see, Steckmesser 1965; Henry 1930; Rosa 1964; 1967).

The legendary Wild Bill Hickok is described as having killed as many as one hundred men (Fielder 1965: 11), and his abilities with a pistol were deemed miraculous. Hickok was reported to have put ten bullets through the letter "O" of a sign that was more than one hundred yards away, without even sighting his pistol (Lake 1931: 43); with one shot it was said that he cut a rooster's throat at thirty paces without touching the head or body, and with another he drove a cork into a bottle without breaking the neck (Buel 1880: 86-87); an 1884 *New York Sun* article stated that he could drop an apple from a tree by cutting the stem with a bullet and then put two more shots through it as it fell to the ground (cited by Steckmesser 1965: 134); and it was claimed that his marksmanship was equally as accurate when firing over his shoulder:

> Wild Bill, facing the desperate character who entered the front door, had shot him with a revolver in his left hand, while with his right hand he had thrown the other gun back over his shoulder and shot the man coming from the rear. History does not record a more daredevil act, a more astute piece of gun work, or a cleaner fight (Coursey 1924: 25).

The Hickok reputation and legend, as mentioned above, began with the events of the McCanles shooting at Rock Creek in 1861, but did not fully emerge until several years later. During the summer of 1865, Hickok had gained, at least locally, somewhat of a name for himself from having been an army scout and from his recent victory in a gun duel with gambler David Tutt. An eastern writer, George Ward Nichols, met Hickok and was taken not only by his reputation but also by his stature and appearance as an impressive physical specimen with long hair and clad in a deerskin suit. He selected Wild Bill for a local color story, and combined with both Nichols' and Hickok's embellishments of the McCanles affair, the publication of the events in the February 1867 issue of *Harper's Magazine* transformed Will Bill Hickok into a national hero. In the Nichols account, much of the incident was reported in Hickok's own words:

You see this M'Kandlas [sic] was the captain of a gang of desperadoes, horse-thieves, murderers, regular cut-throats, who were the
terror of everybody on the border, and who kept us in the mountains in hot water whenever they were around. I knew them all in
the mountains where they pretended to be trapping, but they were
hiding from the hangman. M'Kandlas was the biggest scoundrel and
bully of them all, and was allers a-braggin' of what he could do.

Hickok continued with a description of the events which transpired when
he visited the one-room cabin of his friend Mrs. Waltman:

The minute she saw me she turned as white as a sheet and screamed:
"Is it you, Bill? Oh, my God! They will kill you! Run! Run! They
will kill you!"

"Who's a-goin' to kill me?" said I. "There's two can play at that
game."

"It's M'Kandlas and his gang. There's ten of them and you have no
chance . . ."

Wild Bill then contemplated the fact that he had only one revolver, and
had to face ten men with only six bullets and one rifle-ball. His story tells
of how the McCanles (or M'Kandlas) gang rushed to the house, how he
shot David McCanles and six others with deadly accuracy, and how, out of
ammunition, he faced the three final killers:

The other three clutched and crowded me on to the bed. I fought
hard. I broke with my hand one man's arm. He had his fingers round
my throat. Before I could get to my feet I was struck across my
breast with the stock of a rifle and I feld the blood rushing out of
my nose and mouth. Then I got ugly and I remember that I got
hold of a knife, and then it was all cloudy-like and I was wild and
I struck savage blows, following the devils up from one side to the
other of the room and into the corners striking and slashing until I
knew that every one was dead (cited by Wilstach 1926: 44-50).

The Nichols-Hickok account of the Rock Creek affair which launched
the gunman's legendary portrait was not an exaggeration, it was an out-
right fabrication. In April 1861 the Russell, Majors & Waddell firm for
whom Hickok worked had purchased property at Rock Creek from David
McCanles, but was unable to fully meet its obligations due to financial difficulties. On numerous occasions McCanles attempted to secure his money
from one Horace Wellman, the station agent, which led to some bitterness

between the two. In addition, some reports indicate that there was considerable antagonism between McCanles and Hickok, whom McCanles is said to have called "Duck Bill" because of his rather prominent nose. Furthermore, it has been asserted that Hickok and McCanles were both rivals for the affection of one Kate Shull.

On July 12, the day of the shooting, McCanles, accompanied by his cousin James Woods, his twelve year old son W. Monroe McCanles, and hired hand James Gordon, appeared at the Rock Creek station seeking satisfaction. The three men were unarmed. As McCanles stood outside the station, Hickok shot him through the heart with a single rifle shell, firing from behind a curtain inside the station. After killing McCanles, Hickok fired on Woods and Gordon, only wounding them. Station agent Wellman then crushed Woods' skull with a hoe, and Gordon was hit with a close range shotgun blast offered by the station tender "Doc" Brink. Twelve year old Monroe escaped to the nearby McCanles ranch where he reported the events of the shooting. Hickok, Wellman, and Brink were arraigned for murder, but were acquitted on pleas of self-defense during a trial in which young McCanles was not permitted to testify (Hansen 1927; Henry 1930; Steckmesser 1965; Wilstach 1926).

The story of Wild Bill Hickok is but one example of the legend of the gunfighter that has been built more on fiction than of fact. Similar legendary phenomena can be found with respect to other western notables as Wyatt Earp, "Doc" Holliday, John Wesley Hardin, Luke Short, and Jack Slade. The legends often emerged during the lifetimes of the individuals portrayed, and they have endured through later generations. And furthermore, while the traditions and legends of the gunfighter are beset with misrepresentations of history, they are also confounded by historical error—falsehoods introduced by inaccurate reporting and transmission of historical events. What remains, and critical to this analysis, is an examination of the range of mechanisms through which both bandit and gunfighter folklore, legend, and ahistorical reporting emerged and persisted.

The "Wild West" Industry

The ahistorical character of much of the literature on the American West and the emergence and persistence of the legends descriptive of outlaws and gunslingers are rooted in both the cultural conditions of the early West and the development and growth of the mass media industry. The heroes of the West often sprang from the workings of the folk imagination, which attached superior qualities to selected individuals in local areas who represented symbols of justice or chivalry to a territorial audience. Thus, Jesse James became a hero to midwestern farmers because he typically limited his exploits to the robbery of banks and railroad—institutions hated by Jesse's worshipers; Billy the Kid was well admired by the southwest cowpunchers because he fought for the open range. Through literary elaboration, however, the deeds of the local heroes were expanded to epic proportions, new exploits and traits were added to their names, and the protagonists of the common man in local lore were transformed into legendary demigods before a more national audience. In addition, heroes of legend were fully created without the benefit of a preceding folklore base, or in the absence of some visible person to whom the fictional adventures and characteristics could be attached. Every legend, finally, passed through a cycle of portrayals beginning with folklore accounts in oral tradition or poems, in dime novels, and in biographies, followed by histories, novels, the movies, and television plays.

Oral Tradition

Much of what might be considered the original local folklore of bandit-heroes and gunfighters is buried in the past. The material first appeared in oral communication, only to be altered and embellished in subsequent transmission. Yet some has nevertheless been preserved in its original flavor, primarily in the words of the biographers who were both geographically and temporally local to the heroes, and in the early ballads which depicted events in the lives of outlaws.

The recollections of Jesse James, Jr. (1899), for example, offer much that was folklore during the life and shortly after the death of his father. What Jesse James, Jr. indicated was based on what little he remembered of his father, combined with what he learned from his mother, grandmother, and friends of his family. In the mode of the outlaw as Robin Hood, demigod, hero, and noble robber, what was portrayed depicted the exceptional skill and fairness of Jesse James, the man, and the betrayal and treachery which surrounded the death of Jesse James, the outlaw. For example:

> My father was a wonderful marksman. I have heard his old comrades tell that seated on horseback, with a revolver in each hand, he would ride at full speed between two telegraph poles, or two trees and begin firing at them when he was a few yards away, and before he was more than a few yards beyond them, he had emptied the chambers

of both revolvers, and the six bullets from the revolver in his left hand were buried in the pole to the left of him while the six bullets from the revolver in his right hand were in the pole to his right (James 1899: 15).

Or concerning the death of Jesse James:

> The Ford boys had the confidence of my father. Charlie Ford had been with him on and off for years, and father had befriended him and protected him and fed him when he was penniless. Father had not the slightest suspicion that the Fords meant to harm him. This is proven by the fact that after breakfast that morning father took off his belt and revolvers. . . . After my father put the revolvers upon the bed he noticed that a picture on the wall was awry. He placed a chair beneath the picture and stood upon it to straighten it . . . his back was turned to the Ford boys, who were in the room. . . . It was the first time they had seen him unarmed since they knew him. Bob Ford drew his revolver, aimed it at the back of my father's head . . . pulled the trigger and father fell backward dead (James 1899: 16-17).

Next to Robin Hood, Jesse James is likely the favorite of outlaw ballads—an alternative form of folklore transmission. Again, in the following *Ballad of Jesse James,* the treacherous death of "Mr. Howard" (the alias of Jesse James at the time of his death) was emphasized. And interestingly, although this ballad sprang from the people with its authorship unknown, an example of the ballad convention of "claim to authorship" appears in its eighth stanza (Larkin 1931: 158-159):

> Jesse James was a lad who killed many a man.
> He robbed the Glendale train.
> He stole from the rich and he gave to the poor,
> He'd a hand and a heart and a brain.
>
> *Chorus:*
>> Jesse had a wife to mourn for his life,
>> Three children, they were brave,
>> But that dirty little coward that shot Mister Howard,
>> Has laid Jesse James in his grave.
>
> It was Robert Ford, that dirty little coward,
> I wonder how he does feel,
> For he ate of Jesse's bread and he slept in Jesse's bed,
> Then he laid Jesse James in his grave.

Jesse was a man, a friend to the poor.
He'd never see a man suffer pain,
And with his brother Frank he robbed the Chicago bank,
And stopped the Glendale train.

It was on a Wednesday night, the moon was shining bright,
He stopped the Glendale train,
And the people all did say many miles away,
It was robbed by Frank and Jesse James.

It was on a Saturday night, Jesse was at home,
Talking to his family brave,
Robert Ford came along like a thief in the night,
And laid Jesse James in his grave.

The people held their breath when they heard of Jesse's death,
And wondered how he ever came to die,
It was one of the gang called little Robert Ford,
That shot Jesse James on the sly.

Jesse went to his rest with hand on his breast,
The devil will be upon his knee,
He was born one day in the county of Shea
And he came of a solitary race.

This song was made by Billy Gashade,
As soon as the news did arrive,
He said there was no man with the law in his hand
Could take Jesse James when alive.

Jesse had a wife to mourn for his life,
Three children, they were brave,
But that dirty little coward that shot Mister Howard,
Has laid Jesse James in his grave.

Jesse James died just after 8 a.m., April 3, 1882. He was buried on the grounds of his family's home at the outskirts of St. Joseph, Missouri. And fittingly in the folklore portrayal of the death of the noble robber, the inscription beneath his gravestone read:

> In Loving Remembrance of My Beloved Son,
> Jesse W. James.
> Died April 3, 1882.
> Aged 34 Years, 6 Months, 28 Days.
> Murdered by a Traitor and Coward Whose
> Name is Not Worthy to Appear Here.

The transmission of folkloric accounts also descended from many western "old-timers" whose "memoirs" were accepted as "facts" of local history. Invariably, without writing experience or fully reliable memories of their younger years, the authors' campfire stories evolved into established "facts" of personal experience. In the hands of eastern publishers who were fully ignorant of the language and history of the West, the "memoirs" were accepted as truth and distributed to an even more naive public.

Ramon F. Adams, perhaps the foremost bibliographer and lexicographer of the American West, pointed out that garbled memoirs have embroidered the lives of most western outlaws (1948, 1969). His carefully researched work on the life of Billy the Kid (1960), furthermore, suggested that this phenomenon of folkloric interpretation and dehistorization was especially evident in published recollections about this bandit-hero. Adams documented, for example, that the Kid's first killing occurred in 1877, some three years after his mother's death. He was approximately eighteen years of age at that time, and his victim was a blacksmith, one E. P. Cahill, who continually tried to humiliate the Kid. By contrast, the testimony of old-timers have alternatively indicated that this first killing involved a blacksmith who insulted his mother when he was twelve years of age (Moore 1935), a man named "Black Smith" (Hill, n.d.), a cook who threw hot grease in his face (Lord 1926), a sheepherder who abused him (Fridge 1927), and his stepfather who tormented his mother (Parker, n.d.). Adams (1970: 17-30) also demonstrated that only six killings could be fully attributed to Billy the Kid by the time of his death in 1881. Yet those who claimed to be familiar with the Kid during his life maintained that he killed a man for each of the years he lived–that he shot 21 men during his 21 years (Moore 1935), or 23 men during his 23 years (Callison 1914), or 24 men during his 24 years (Lord 1926).

Even more interestingly, one chronicler maintained that one Albert J. Fountain and his young son were murdered in New Mexico on January 31, 1896 (Hamilton 1932). The author stated that Billy the Kid warned Fountain of his impending assassination, saw the man and his son murdered by the Tate Gang, and ultimately shot each of the killers, one by one. The author insisted that the Kid told him this story personally, yet the reported incident of the Fountain murders occurred after the Kid had been officially dead for some fifteen years. Or similarly, cowboy, hunter, guide, scout, and ranchman James H. Cook (1923) maintained that Billy the Kid was not a product of the American West, but rather, a New York City tough who had read "yellow" novels of western bandits before he began his career in crime in New Mexico. Interestingly, Billy the Kid had been born in New York City, but he moved west with his parents at the age of three, and although dime novels had been published beginning in 1860 (Schick 1958: 50), their original covers had been orange in color, and the "yellow" journalism to which Cook may have been referring had not emerged until 1896 (Becker 1959).

The Dime Novel

On June 7, 1860, the New York *Tribune* printed the following advertisement which served to announce the birth of a major publishing phenomenon:

```
BOOKS FOR THE MILLION!

            ____

    A DOLLAR BOOK FOR A DIME!

            ____

 128 pages complete, only Ten Cents!!!

            ____

    BEADLE'S DIME NOVELS NO. 1.

            ____

       M A L A E S K A:
              THE
 INDIAN WIFE OF THE WHITE HUNTER
      By Mrs. Ann S. Stephens.
 128 pages. 12 mo.  Ready SATURDAY MORNING, June 9.
            RWIN P. BEADLE & CO. Publishers
              No. 141 William st., New York.
 ROSS & TOUSEY, General Agents.
```

Such was the birth of the dime novel, a publishing mechanism that ultimately created legends out of any variety of western characters. The first of the novels, *Malaeska: The Indian Wife of the White Hunter,* was not a new work, nor was it particularly sensational; it had appeared in the *Woman's Companion* magazine in 1839 (Bleiler 1974: vii). Furthermore, it was not the first of the inexpensive books, for low-budget paperbound publications were available in the American colonies as early as 1639

(Mott 1947: 149-150). The issue with the dime novel was its marketing, structured in a manner as to arouse the interests of a mass audience seeking cheap entertainment. Edward S. Ellis, for example, author of *Seth Jones, or The Captives of the Frontier*—a dime novel that sold some 400,000 copies—noted in his reminiscences that the initial advertising scheme for his book in October, 1860 had caused some disturbances among the residents of New York (cited by Bleiler 1974: vii):

> All of a sudden, all over the country, there broke out a rash of posters, dodgers and painted inscriptions demanding to know "Who is Seth Jones?" Everywhere you went this query met you. It glared at you in staring letters on the sidewalks. It came fluttering in to you on little dodgers thrust by the handful into the Broadway stages. . . . In the country the trees and rocks and the sides and roofs of barns all clamored with stentorian demands to know who Seth Jones was . . . and just when it had begun to be a weariness and one of the burdens of life . . . a new rush of decorations broke out all over the country. This was in the form of big and little posters bearing a lithographic portrait of a stalwart, heroic looking hunter. . . . And above or below this imposing figure in large type were the words, "I am Seth Jones."

The heyday of the dime novel endured from 1860 through 1910, and the giants in the industry included the publishing houses of Beadle and Adams and Street & Smith. Beadle and Adams, during its twenty-five years of publishing, mass-produced more than 7,500 different novels. These were essentially collections of fiction combined with the reprinted writings of classic literary figures (Johannsen 1950). Competition among the various publishers was severe, and marketing techniques included emphasis on a publisher's quantity and diversity of materials. Street & Smith, Publishers, of New York City, for example, released as many as ten new titles each week, and their operations were so prolific that their August 1902 catalog boasted some 1,300 different novels simultaneously in print (Street & Smith 1902). Street & Smith, Beadle and Adams, as well as such other houses as John W. Morrison, Frank Tousey, R. T. Dawley & Co., and Elliot, Thomes and Talbot not only prepared editions of the classical works, e.g., James Fenimore Cooper, Jules Verne, Charles Dickens, etc., but also purchased all copyrighted materials written by the most popular of the contemporary authors.

The dime novels that depicted events of the American outlaw West were highly sensationalized; few efforts at accurate reporting were undertaken, and many books were totally fictional accounts although accepted as historical and authentic by the reading public. Jesse and Frank James were still alive when their dime novel adventures began to appear, and no other outlaws so fully captured the attention and imagination of the readership. Street & Smith made somewhat of an industry out of the Jameses with their *The Jesse James Weekly* and *Jesse James Stories*. Little of the material had any factual basis, as exemplified in W. B. Lawson's (1902) *Jesse James's Diamond Deal, or Robbing the Red Hands*, in which Jesse destroyed a criminal secret society and hijacked their spoils. Similarly, an "Adventure Series" published by the Arthur Westbrook Company of Cleveland, Ohio, devoted thirty-six of its one hundred volumes to Jesse James. Typical here was *Jesse James' Ruse, or the Mystery of the Two Highwaymen* by William Ward (n.d.), in which Jesse James, determined to return to the cave of some mysterious hunchback, led his men across the plains of the West to the mountains of Colorado, pillaging and robbing stage coaches along the way, completely mystifying his pursuers by seemingly appearing in two places at the same time. The Westbrook "Adventure Series" was available from news and book dealers and through the mails, and was advertised as follows:

> The Most Thrilling, Exciting and Up-to-Date Stories of Adventure and the Far West Ever Published.
>
> The Absolutely True and Authentic History of the Lives and Exploits of America's Famous Bandits—All Profusely Illustrated.

Other western personalities as well were exploited by the dime novelists. On August 7, 1881 an account of Billy the Kid's career appeared in the Chicago *Tribune* in an article by P. Donan, and following its publication, Billy acquired dime novel infamy. The first three stories to appear were Don Jenardo's *The True Life of Billy the Kid*, Edmund Fable's *Billy the Kid: The New Mexican Outlaw; or the Bold Bandit of the West! A True and Impartial History of the Greatest of American Outlaws . . . Who Killed a Man For Every Year In His Life*, and the anonymously authored *The Cowboy's Career, or the Dare Devil Deeds of "Billy the Kid," the Noted New Mexico Desperado*. All were published in 1881, and were garbled accounts which relied heavily on the Donan *Tribune* article. And curiously, rather than a hero, the Kid was portrayed as a fiendish killer and was credited with theft, murder, and burning. Similarly, J. C. Cowdrick's *Silver Mask, the Man of Mystery* (1884), part of the Beadle and Adams library, also cast Billy the Kid as a common cut-throat.

As the popularity of the dime novel spread, outlaws of somewhat lesser renown were presented. The Younger Brothers, the Daltons, Harry Tracy,

and Rube Burrow appeared on the list of the Westbrook "Adventure Series," as well as in the offerings of Beadle and Adams, Street & Smith,
Frank Tousey, and John W. Morrison. In addition, the efforts of the publishers included the enlistment of other dime novel heroes to pursue the
outlaws. "Old King Brady" was a dime novel detective created by Francis
W. Doughty in 1885. He was not a superhuman sleuth nor a master of dis-
guise, but a soft-sell detective with the widest knowledge of crime and
human nature. Frank Tousey's publishing empire pit Old King Brady
against such outlaws as Frank and Jesse James, and Billy the Kid. In
Doughty's (1890) *Old King Brady and Billy the Kid; or, the Great Detective's Chase,* for example, Billy was again depicted as a contemptible
coward and villain, and the triumph of "good" over "evil" was a persistent
theme.

The gunfighters of the American "Wild West" were also drawn into the
fold of the dime novelists, and their exploits—like those of the outlaws—
were expanded, sensationalized, and often fully "created." Characteristic
in this respect was the saga of Col. Prentiss Ingraham and his endorsements
of both "Wild Bill" Hickok and William F. "Buffalo Bill" Cody. Ingraham
had a colorful life, and his own adventures often rivaled those later described in his dime novels. He attended Jefferson Medical College in Mississippi, but left school in 1861 to enlist in the Confederate army where he
acquired a taste for war and adventure. After the close of the Civil War,
Ingraham went to Mexico to fight against Maximilian under Benito Juarez;
he took part in the Austro-Prussian War and participated in martial exploits in Crete and Africa; and in the Cuban revolution in 1868 he held
the ranks of naval captain and cavalry colonel (Van Doren 1974: 532). In
1870 he settled in London and began mining his experiences and vivid
imagination for material for a long list of sensational novels of adventure
and romance. During his career as an author he produced more than 700
books, the majority of which were published by the Beadle and Adams
empire. Ingraham later settled in New York and then Chicago, where he
became acquainted with Buffalo Bill, became a publicity agent for *Buffalo
Bill's Wild West Show,* and produced some 200 dime novels of Buffalo
Bill's "adventures."

Ingraham was also a conspicuous contributor to the snowballing "Wild
Bill" Hickok legend, and was prominent in the exaggerations of the
Hickok-McCanles Rock Creek affair. In his *Wild Bill, the Pistol Dead Shot;
or, Dagger Dan's Double* (1882), he portrayed Hickok as a superhuman
engaging in exploits which had no basis in fact; in his other Hickok pro-
motions, written primarily for Beadle and Adams, he offered conflicting

accounts of the McCanles fight and continued with the fables and inventions characteristic of the dime novel genre (see, Ingraham 1884, 1899).

Edward Zane Carroll Judson, the author and adventurer more commonly known by his pseudonym "Ned Buntline," was also a prolific dime novelist who did much for the legendary careers of both Wild Bill Hickok and Buffalo Bill. While touring Nebraska in 1869, Buntline met William F. Cody, whom he immediately dubbed "Buffalo Bill" and cast as the hero of a long series of dime novels (Monaghan 1951: 3-19). As such, Buntline created "Buffalo Bill" and first introduced him in "Buffalo Bill, the King of the Bordermen," an 1869 serial appearing in *Street & Smith's New York Weekly*. Buntline's many writings about Cody (for example, Buntline 1886) were done in a theatrical style geared toward what the eastern markets expected of the West. His stories of Buffalo Bill were so inaccurate and contained so many falsehoods (for example, Buntline 1886), that William F. Cody admitted that many of the deeds had never occurred. Once Cody wrote to his publishers:

> I am sorry to have to lie so outrageiously in this yarn. My hero has killed more Indians on one war trail than I have killed all my life. But I understand this is what is expected of border tales. If you think the revolver and bowie knife are used too freely, you may cut out a fatal shot or stab whenever you deem it wise (cited by Adams 1969: 98).

For a time, Wild Bill Hickok was also a subject for Buntline, but again his dime novels about the noted gunslinger were based on hearsay and fabrication. Buntline wrote of the Hickok-McCanles fight, and having only minimal information, discussed the main operatives as "Wild Bill Hitchcock" and the "M'Kandlas Gang," and he described the older McCanles as having killed Buffalo Bill's father before the eyes of his entire family (Buntline 1886).

While the dime novelists created fictional accounts of real heroes and badmen—both living and dead—they also produced fictional heroes who were interpreted as real by the naive readership. Edward L. Wheeler's "Deadwood Dick," entering literary life in October 1877 as the first issue of *Beadle's Half-Dime Library*, was one example. In well over thirty Deadwood Dick adventures, beginning with *Deadwood Dick; or the Black Rider of the Black Hills* (Wheeler 1877), the settings included the Dakota gold camps, the trails which laced Wyoming, Nebraska, Colorado, and the Dakotas. The hero was a shotgun messenger assigned to guard the Deadwood treasure coach. The stories were heavily dramatic with a strong revenge plot and eventual justice for all. And there were many who claimed to be Deadwood Dick. Nat Love (1907), whose autobiography abounded in historical error regarding Pat Garrett and Billy the Kid, claimed that *he* was Deadwood Dick. At one time the fictional hero became the object of serious tourist search in Deadwood, South Dakota, and the local chamber of commerce selected a long-haired, loquacious old-timer named Dick Clarke to play the role. He proved to be as good a storyteller as Edward L. Wheeler; he sold locks of his hair to women tourists, rusty rifles and pistols to the men, and photographs of himself to all (Schmitt and Brown 1974: 100). But as Sabin (1929: 216) and others have noted, there was no Deadwood Dick:

> The "Deadwood Coach" dreams away its days in the Smithsonian Institution—a relic there, of the times of "Deadwood Dick," driver, messenger, express rider, bandit foiler and redskin slayer. But "Deadwood Dick" never was, and yet he was a legion. He was not one in all, but he was all in one; and transferred back from the pages of romance to the role of drivers and messengers of the "Deadwood Coach" he becomes, like it, only an example: a "Deadwood Dick" rather than the "Deadwood Dick."

In retrospect, the dime novel emerged during the second half of the nineteenth century as a significant factor in the creation of outlaw and hero legends. And it served as a medium for the portrayal of historical-fictional events which would be repeated for decades to come. Yet the impact of the dime novel was not simply an isolated publishing phenomenon, for its ultimate success was closely linked to existing cultural patterns and social change. Critical here was the element of American frontier spirit. The great heroic tradition of Daniel Boone leading American settlers westward had already become crystalized in the mind of the growing nation. At the base of the American ethos were the woodsmen and frontiersmen, strong and fearless, who overcame the perils of the mighty wilderness. This was followed by James Fenimore Cooper's *Leatherstocking Tales,* which dramatized the clash between the wilderness and the encroaching civilization, creating an arena within which the western hero might thrive.

To the easterner, the West was a distant land—uninhabitable, lawless, and beset with the perils of Indian attack. And the dime novel heroes, who emerged with the onset of mass culture in post-1860 America, were presented in the Leatherstocking tradition—fearless, cunning, and triumphant in the face of violence and injustice. A new mass audience was made possible by the population shifts from Europe to the United States, the concentration of people in cohesive urban and semiurban units with common social, economic, and cultural characteristics, combined with the spread of literacy, the expansion of leisure time, and the growth of a machine civilization. Both the tradition and the technology necessary for the mass dissemination of legend were suddenly available, and the dime novel served as the initial primary vehicle.

The Biographers and Historians of the "Wild West"

The dime novels were not alone in their publishing plunder of the American West, nor were they unique in their contributions to gunfighter and outlaw-hero legends. Significant also were the reporters, biographers, and historians who not only helped to create legend but were prominent in transmitting it through several generations.

The mass media promotion of the frontier was initially done by popular reporters whose works appeared in national magazines. Their style was essentially sensational and theatrical, and like the dime novelists, they considered the accuracy of their portrayals to be of minimal importance. This has already been noted in the George Ward Nichols treatment of the Hickok-McCanles altercation in *Harper's Magazine* and Ned Buntline's Buffalo Bill in *Street & Smith's New York Weekly*. Of interest here was the influence of the *Police Gazette,* a New York and California publication that offered biographies, adventure series, and "true-life" action stories of crime on the urban and western frontiers—all presented in the sensationalized manner of the dime novel (Every 1931). Much of the *Police Gazette* material was taken as fact, and was heavily relied upon by historians and biographers of the West. In 1881, for example, the *Gazette* presented a feature entitled *Billy LeRoy, the Colorado Bandit; or, the King of the American Highwaymen . . . A Complete and Authentic History of this Famous Young Desperado* (Daggett 1881). Exactly who the author was writing about was never clear. During the early part of the 1880s there was a bandit named Arthur Pond who operated in Colorado and often used the alias Billy LeRoy (Adams 1969: 164). However, the story also appeared to be the life of Billy the Kid, since the author used the names of individuals who were in fact members of the Kid's gang, as well as incidents in the Lincoln County War in which the Kid had had a prominent role. As to the life of Billy the Kid, the *Gazette* account was almost totally fictitious, yet it was drawn upon by later writers as a primary data source on the Kid. Marion Hughes' *Oklahoma Charley* (1910) related that the Kid was born in Illinois and was named Billy LeRoy (he was actually born in New York City as Henry McCarty and assumed the name William H. Bonney shortly after his mother's death in 1874), and presented a story reflecting a heavy reliance on the *Police Gazette* material. In 1943, some sixty years after the *Gazette* story, a Texas old-timer maintained that he knew Billy the Kid well, and that he went under the name of Billy LeRoy (Benton 1943).

Perhaps the most curious, far-reaching, and enduring example of the construction and transmission of fictitious western history had to do with Joaquín Murieta, California's greatest legend. During the 1850s, bandits flourished in California, and many of them were Mexicans. Of the numerous cattle thefts and robberies committed in various parts of the state, the most notorious were attributed to five men. All were known as "Joaquín," though they had different surnames—one of which was Murieta (Bean 1968: 188). In 1853, in response to an increasing level of highway robbery, the California legislature authorized Captain Henry Love, a former Texan, to recruit a band of rangers for the capture of any or all of the five Joaquíns (*Journal of the Assembly* 1853). In addition, California Governor John Bigler, considering reelection, personally offered a $1,000 reward for the capture of any of the five bandits. The rangers, returning from their Joaquín hunt, produced a hand pickled in alcohol as evidence of Joaquín Murieta's death and collected the reward. There was no other information or identification that could verify the bandit's death.

Perhaps the earliest book to mention Joaquín Murieta the outlaw appeared during the year of his death (Anonymous 1853), but the legend of Murieta did not appear until the following year with the publication of John Rollin Ridge's (1854) *The Life and Adventure of Joaquín Murieta, the Celebrated California Bandit.* Ridge was the son of a wealthy and educated Cherokee chief. At age twelve Ridge witnessed the knife murder of his father by a group of Cherokees who sought revenge for his signing the treaty under which they had given up their lands in Georgia. A decade later, Ridge appeared in gold rush San Francisco, where he was writing under the name of "Yellow Bird," a literal translation of his Indian name.

John Rollin Ridge can be credited with having fully invented the character and legend of Joaquín Murieta. The vague and dubious reports of Captain Nat Love's search for the five Joaquíns represented the background from which Ridge constructed his narrative; yet in his story, he went so far as to relate the bandit's conversations and inner thoughts. In Ridge's tale, Murieta witnesses the brutal murder of his wife (although in another version of the legend, he returned to his camp one evening to find her beaten and raped by a band of "Americanos.") Bitterly, he turned to a life of banditry, committing many acts of robbery and theft on his own and organizing other Mexicans into a predatory outlaw band. Through numerous guerrilla attacks upon *gringos,* Juaquín Murieta carried out his oath of revenge, always with a knife. He was a noble robber of the Robin Hood type who stole only from his enemies to distribute his spoils to poor Mexicans.

Not too long after the Murieta biography appeared, Ridge's publishers swindled him out of whatever money had been made on the volume, and the original edition was never widely circulated. Before Ridge could finance a second publication, his work was copied, reprinted, and translated into several languages with only slight changes. From September 3 through November 5, 1859, the *Police Gazette* presented an anonymous rewriting of John Rollin Ridge's work, in serial form, and many of the Murieta books which followed, especially the foreign and Latin American ones, relied on this version. In 1871, Ridge finally produced another edition of his narrative, and its content reflected much of the newer fiction that was added to the *Police Gazette* version a decade before.

During the next century, the Ridge and *Gazette* versions were constantly repeated by reporters and the writers of biographies and histories with the result that the legend of Joaquín Murieta emerged as a "fact" of California history. By the 1880s, a seaman had published his memoirs which included a description of his encounter with the noted bandit (Thomes 1872); the story was written as a poem in which the outlaw escaped death and returned to Mexico to live a happy life (Stewart 1882); in addition Joaquín Murieta became a dime novel hero (Badger 1881a, b). From the latter part of the nineteenth century through the 1970s, biographers and historians have continued to report the legend as part of the factual heritage of the American "Wild West" (see, for example, Savage 1892; Hall 1920; Bechdolt 1922; Ford 1926; Gollomb 1927; Chalfant 1928; Cossley-Batt 1928; Klette 1928; Burns 1932; Glasscock 1934; Cunningham 1938; Older 1940; Dane 1941; Corle 1949; Soito 1949; Florin 1962). In all, there have been hundreds of volumes written about Joaquín Murieta—all devoted to the character of a man created by John Rollin Ridge. Theodore H. Hittell's (1898) *History of California,* Book X, Chapter IV dealt entirely with Joaquín Murieta. The account was taken primarily from the 1871 edition of Ridge's book, and the acceptance of the legend by such a respected historian served to further strengthen public belief in it. Among the more recent entries into the Murieta library is the contribution of George Turner (1972), a writer for the *Amarillo Daily News*. His *George Turner's Book of Gun Fighters* offers a sloppy rehash of the Ridge story, with the added feature of an incorrect spelling of "Murietta" [sic]. What happened to Joaquín Murieta is by no means unique. The totally fictional or quasi-factual testimony of earlier writers about other events and people of the American West continue to be repeated, offering us a legacy of traditions based on incorrect history.

Conclusion: The Persistence of an American Tradition

While folklore, the dime novel, and the biographies and "histories" offered substance and enduring qualities to the bandit and gunfighter legends, the conception of an American "Wild West" and its heroes of lore became further solidified in the American mind by other forms of mass media promotion. Pulp fiction, for example, was an early variety of popular print that depicted the frontier West in a manner similar to that of the dime novel.

The pulpwood fiction magazine was invented by Frank Andrew Munsey on December 2, 1882 with the publication of *Golden Argosy, Freighted With Treasures for Boys and Girls* (Goulart 1972: 10). Later known as *Argosy,* the Munsey offering included science fiction, romance, jungle heroes, crime, detectives, *and westerns.* The presentation of the West in the pulp media was clearly fictional in terms of its characters, but its plots and story lines often provided unmistakable reflections of the bandit-heroes and unerring gunfighters who were simultaneously being described in other popular publications. Early entries in this field included the *Jesse James Weekly* and the *New Buffalo Bill Weekly.*

In 1919, the house of Street & Smith produced *Western Story Magazine* as a bi-weekly publication. Within a year, its circulation had reached three hundred thousand per issue, and it was made into a weekly—which it remained for the next quarter century. By the late 1920s, pulp magazines devoted exclusively to the West were numerous, and included *West* and *Frontier* published by Doubleday; *Cowboy Stories* and *Western Adventures* from Clayton House publishers; and *Triple-X Western* from the Fawcett library. And the Depression period saw the pulp westerns further expand into hundreds of varieties.

The significant impact of the pulps was their mass appeal. They bridged the years following the demise of the dime novel, and they provided tens of millions of readers with "spectacular" literature. Pulps were printed on the cheapest of paper, housed in lurid covers, and written by undignified and boisterous storytellers who were accused by moralists, mothers, and schoolmarms of endangering the pure thoughts of young America. For the Western hero, they served to extend his longevity; the notions of swift justice, violence against one's enemies, and just revenge were dominant themes; and noble robbers like Jesse James and Joaquín Murieta, and gunfighters reminiscent of Wild Bill Hickok were among the more prominent leading characters. By the 1950s the pulps had vanished from the American scene, forced into obscurity by post-World War II rising publication costs combined with a growing sophistication within the wider reading audience (Goulart 1972: 183-184).

In addition to the remnants of the dime novels, the persistence of the biographies and histories, and the rise and fall of pulp fiction, the current century has witnessed the growth of the even more spectacular media—film, radio, and television—which also served to further the legends of the "Wild West." The Hollywood version of the American West began in 1903 with Edwin S. Porter's *The Great Train Robbery* (Fenin and Everson 1977: 9). And it appeared at a time when the West was still "Wild." Only two years earlier, on July 3, 1901, the last exploit in the United States of Butch Cassidy and the Wild Bunch had taken place—the holdup of a Great Northern train in the vicinity of Wagner, Montana—and for most of the remaining years of the decade the adventures of Butch Cassidy and the Sundance Kid in South America were to be reported in the press as reminders of their outlaw raids on Western soil (Kelly 1958); Henry Starr, who claimed to have robbed more banks than any other man in America, had just been released from a penitentiary in Columbus, Ohio to return to his bandit trail (Shirley 1965: 145); and the more prominent Alexander Franklin "Frank" James and William F. "Buffalo Bill" Cody were still celebrities in circus and "wild west" shows. The result was that the new movie Western aroused popular fancy. With the traditional sympathy of the American masses for the underdog and noble thief and their worship of the gunfighter, fanned by a continuing procession of sensational newspaper reports of events on the frontier, the Western movie provided an ideal ground for the continued reinforcement of the hero legends.

The Great Train Robbery created the "Western" as a genre of the American cinema. The bandits and gunfighters were either depicted as they had been presented to the public in other media, or historical events were totally reconstructed for the sake of attractive scripts. By the late 1930s and early 1940s, the cinematic presentation of the outlaw as a sympathetic individual who had been forced into a life of crime by a combination of unfortunate circumstances had fully emerged as a trend in western movies, as evidenced by such films as *Jesse James, The Return of Frank James, When the Daltons Rode, Billy the Kid,* and *Badmen of Missouri* (which dealt with the Younger brothers). In productions by the larger Hollywood companies as Warner Brothers, MGM, Universal, and Twentieth Century Fox, the better known outlaws were presented to the public on a large scale basis in the heroic mold that had been common in folklore interpretations. Similarly, the gunfighters and others who were deemed champions of law and justice maintained their status as demigods in such films as *Buffalo Bill, Young Bill Hickok,* and *Wild Bill Hickok Rides.*

The gunfighters, more so than the outlaws, were often presented by twentieth century mass media in a manner that served to solidify their status as legend. For example, the Paramount production of Wild Bill Hickok from 1923 starring William S. Hart in the lead role offered a portrait of Hickok which reflected the image of the gunfighter as created earlier by *Harper's Magazine* author George Ward Nichols and dime novelist Ned Buntline. In later versions of the film, the gunman was again presented as a paragon of justice and was portrayed by the pleasing and popular actors Gary Cooper and Roy Rogers. Then on December 31, 1951, Wild Bill Hickok came to radio. Hickok, played by Guy Madison, rode through the West dusting off "badmen" with his fists and fancy gunplay, along with his sidekick, Jingles (Andy Devine). Sponsored by Kellogg, its success led to a television series during the 1950s which followed the same storyline and presented the same actors in the leading roles.

Wyatt Earp, a lawman of questionable character in the days of the "Wild West," was lifted to the status of legend during the twentieth century by a variety of mass media. Along with his brothers Morgan and Virgil, his colleague John H. "Doc" Holliday, Wyatt was well known in his day for his exploits in Dodge City, Kansas and Tombstone, Arizona, but having never been a dime novel hero, he had not achieved the status of legend. In 1931, however, the publication of Stuart N. Lake's *Wyatt Earp, Frontier Marshall* began the gunfighters path to glory. Lake's work claimed to be a biography of Earp, recorded at the instigation of the marshal's third wife. Many authors and other individuals who knew Earp personally maintained that he was quite unlike the character portrayed by Lake. The book omitted the many shady incidents in Earp's life while doing everything to glorify him. Further, the author reported many events that happened to other people as if they had happened to

Earp (Adams 1969: 380). But the character was presented and the mold created. In 1939 the Twentieth Century Fox production of *Frontier Marshall* starring Randolph Scott as Earp, which followed the plot prepared earlier by Lake, placed the marshal before a wider audience. Producer John Ford's retelling of the Wyatt Earp story in the extravagant Fox production *My Darling Clementine* starring Henry Fonda served to further solidify the heroic image. Finally, the John Sturges production of *Gunfight at the OK Corral* (Paramount) in 1957 with Burt Lancaster as Earp followed by the television series *The Life and Legend of Wyatt Earp* with actor Hugh O'Brian in the title role, finalized the marshal's elevation to legend.

In retrospect, the ahistorical nature of our image of crime in the American West evolved through an enduring process, one which was fortified by the cooperation of historians, biographers, the media, "legend-makers," and sometimes by the principal characters themselves. The biographers were concerned with the epic status of their subject, a preoccupation which led to many sins of omission. The dime novelists and other reporters were Easterners, concerned only with sensational material to offer a gullible readership. The historians, or rather, "armchair historians," who relied only on the more popular yet erroneous earlier works on their subject, repeated the misconceptions. Motion pictures and television perpetuated the Western hero tradition by personifying the legendary characters with the more popular actors of the day. Each of the media contributed to legend in a different way, yet all tended to favor the pseudobiographical format. More current works have attempted to correct the errors of the past, but legends are difficult to correct. Once they become embedded in a series of accounts, their reliability is measured by the number of times they are repeated. And finally, this arena of inquiry may have been lost to historians by default, for in years past the serious researcher seemed to almost totally neglect its study. Or as Walter Noble Burns (1925: 68-69) stated more than half a century ago regarding Billy the Kid:

> The history of Billy the Kid has already been clouded by legend. Less than fifty years after his death, it is not always easy to differentiate fact from myth. Historians have been afraid of him, as if this boy of six-shooter deadliness might fatally injure their reputations if they set themselves seriously to write of a career of such dime-novel luridness. As a consequence, history has neglected him.

Chapter 4

THE GODFATHER SYNDROME

In the social scientific literature concerned with organized crime, historical claims, judgments, assumptions, and opinions are rampant. Some of these have even been worked into a history of sorts that is most notable for its reliance on undocumented popular sources and the unsubstantiated memoirs of celebrated informers. The most telling features of this history are its naiveté and devotion to the idea that an alien (Italian-Sicilian) conspiracy has run organized crime for the last five decades. Additionally, it is assumed that organized crime's development has been part of an inexorable march toward centralization and bureaucratization. Among the consequences of this haphazard reconstruction, preoccupied with the "Mafia mystique," has been the stifling of serious work on the social world of organized crime. Within this context, this chapter will explore first, the components of the contemporary mainstream idea that organized crime is a monolith somewhat in the order of General Motors. This is followed by a testing of the historical accounts underpinning this claim, concentrating on the supposed key event in the origin of modern organized crime. It is argued, next, that the historical unreliability of these claims reveals that an ideology fueled by conspiracy doctrine is at the base of much of today's theorizing. The characteristics of this doctrine are rigid and exclusionary, holding responsible a single ethnic and *sexual* group for the evil of organized crime. The limitations if not folly of this approach are discussed by focusing on the manner in which women criminals have been systematically read out of the history and sociology of organized crime. Finally, suggestions are made concerning the manner in which organized crime studies could and should be refashioned.

The Iron Cage

The subject of organized crime has carried enormous weight in American culture as a handy vehicle for parables. Writing in 1948, for example, Robert Warshow (1970) suggested that the popularity of the fictional gangster was attributable to America's need to counter a shallow and optimistic creed with "a consistent and astonishing complete presentation of the modern sense of tragedy." According to Warshow, the gangster satisfied America's ambivalent attitude toward success by playing to the death a deeply held belief that "every attempt to succeed is an act of aggression" that will be punished. The gangster, therefore, embodied the American dilemma—"failure is a kind of death and success is evil and dangerous, is ultimately impossible." Real cities, for Warshow, produce "only criminals," while "the imaginary city produces the gangster."

Unlike Warshow, who was interested in the fictional gangster, social scientists have been intrigued precisely by the real city and the criminal. However, they too have located in crime, especially organized crime, a parable about success. Perhaps the classic statement of this is Daniel Bell's (1962) essay "Crime as an American Way of Life: A Queer Ladder of Social Mobility." In this famous work Bell suggested that being excluded from the political ladder and unable to find many open routes to wealth, the children of immigrants turned to illicit activities. The criminal, in this sense, hardly panders to an ambivalent and darkly conceived ethic of success, but is instead as business-oriented as a Rotarian. From the fictional world of the city as nightmare and the gangster as a metaphor of failure, we have moved to organized crime as the business of the underprivileged and the criminal as proof of the consensus on success. These assumptions have led to a definition of organized crime as simply a particular "form of the common economic drive to get rich quick" (Vold 1967: 395). Thorsten Sellin (1963) suggested that in whatever manner organized criminals operate, financial profit is the goal, and subscription to the tenets of American entrepreneurship, in a system of free enterprise, is the rationale. And as organized crime's nature is economic, so its function is supposedly knowable in business terms. Sellin held that the term "organized crime" came to be synonymous with economic enterprises organized for the purpose of conducting illegal activities and operating legal businesses illegally.

Certified as a rational, i.e., economic, endeavor, the mysteries of organized crime have been further reduced by criminologists through examinations of the forms of organized crime. The three broad categories which Marshall B. Clinard and Richard Quinney (1967: 389-390) claimed make up this criminal behavior system include the control of illegal enterprises, the control and often plunder of legitimate activities, and *racketeering,* which they defined as the systematic extortion of money from persons or organizations. Mark H. Haller (1970: 620-622), writing persuasively about organized crime in Chicago, offered a somewhat different framework, which consisted of business or labor racketeers, professional thieves, and participants in organized crime. Haller described the last category as the marketing and selling of "illegal goods and services such as gambling, prostitution, narcotics, and in the 1920s, booze."

Discussion of the forms of organized crime is essentially an argument about the social structure of organized crime. Until fairly recently, most social scientists identified a constant and common gang structure. For example, Martin R. Haskell and Lewis Yablonsky (1969: 135-136), with only slight changes by Clinard and Quinney, viewed the gang structure as hierarchical resembling the chain of command of a large corporation or the military and involving a system of specifically defined relationships with mutual obligations and privileges. However, neither Haskell, Yablonsky, Clinard, nor Quinney ever attempted to explain how and when criminal organizations developed into quasi-bureaucracies. Social scientists have long recognized that to understand the phenomenon of organized crime, it would be necessary to study the social and economic background of the criminal (Woetzel 1963: 3). In response they have developed a critical, often brilliant literature concentrating on the *origins* of criminal careers, yet few have moved beyond the background of the criminal to the historical study of careers in organized crime.

One exception to this posture has been sociologist Donald R. Cressey, who suggested that the basic framework of the current structure of American organized crime was established during the period 1930-1931 as a result of a gangland war, in which an alliance of Italians and Sicilians was victorious (Cressey, 1967a: 26). Using an analogy from legal business or corporate terminology, he maintained that organized crime syndicates all across America formed into monopolistic corporations in 1931. Following this development, these new entities aligned into a single monolithic cartel. Along with corporate organization went political confederation. Employing a political analogy, Cressey stated that the original criminal syndicates resembled feudal governments. These were overturned, however, when their rulers merged to form a national confederation which itself was a government (p. 31). As both a business and polity, the single most important social fact of organized crime since 1931, according to Cressey, has been its "division of labor," which is the *structure* of organized crime. Although not completely understood because of the inherent research difficulties, this division of labor is the cornerstone of Cressey's thinking. He maintained, for instance, that any crime committed by an individual who occupied a position or rank in an established division of labor was by definition a member of organized crime. And in addition, the organized criminal would be a person who held a position in an organization or social system which was rationally designed to maximize profits by performing illicit services and providing legally forbidden products demanded by the members of the wider society (p. 29).

Among the positions in criminal organizations is that of *enforcer.* The occupants of this rank arrange for the injuring or killing of other gangsters or outsiders (Cressey 1967b: 110). Analysis of this particular position, according to Cressey, allows a researcher to infer or develop information about complicated governing procedures as well as particular legal rules. The enforcer is accordingly one of a subset of positions existing within a broader division of labor whose function is to maximize organizational integration by means of just infliction of punishments on wrongdoers.

Moving from the area of structure to that of governance, Cressey stated that the mere fact of a position of enforcer in a division of labor is evidence that members of the organization must have created some functional equivalent of the criminal law, from which all government officials derive their authority and power. These rules, whatever their content, have been created to limit conflict while at the same time magnifying the degree of conformity among the members of the criminal cartel. To accomplish these tasks the rules must necessarily stress loyalty, honesty, rationality, respect for leaders, and patriotism; and, therefore, one might assume that such norms are stressed in the society of organized criminals (Cressey 1967b: 111).

The structure of organized crime, therefore, is characterized by a more of less "totalitarian organization" with "rigid discipline in a hierarchy of ranks" with "permanency and form," which extend beyond the lives of particular individuals and exist independently of any current incumbent

(Cressey 1967a: 58). Cressey stands as the most forceful exponent of the view of organized crime as bureaucracy, of syndicate criminals as bureaucrats, and as one of the few scholars interested in the history of organized crime.

Historical Reliability[1]

However, while Cressey recognized the importance of history, both his methods and conclusions are highly suspect. Consider the historicity of the origins of the *Cosa Nostra*. Cressey wrote, as we know, that the modern history of organized crime began with a gangland war. The culmination of this reputed war was the execution of Mafia boss Salvatore Maranzano, and an alleged purge of old-style Mafia leaders. The successful murder of Maranzano was the signal for the planned killing of some sixty Maranzano allies, called "Mustaches," a reference to their traditional Sicilian ways, according to another contemporary writer (Chandler 1975: 160). The historical source for the *Purge* of the Mafia, which is the key event in the construction of Cosa Nostra, "are the memoirs of one soldier, Joseph Valachi" (Cressey 1969: 36-37).

This brings us to the first major example of historical sloppiness, which is composed of two apparently contradictory parts. First is the almost total reliance on Valachi and second is the apparent disregard for Valachi's testimony before the Senate Committee Investigating Organized Crime and the Illicit Traffic in Narcotics (1963). Valachi was closely questioned by Chairman John L. McClellan on the very point of the purge. When asked by the chairman how many men were killed, Valachi responded, "four or five, Senator" (p. 232). The Committee was obviously concerned about the number of men killed that day, for almost immediately after Valachi's statement, the chairman asked New York City Police Sergeant Ralph Salerno to take the stand. Salerno, a recognized expert on organized crime, was asked if he had any information about other murders (besides Maranzano's and James Le Pore's, who was identified by Valachi as one of the four or five victims) that took place that day. Salerno replied no. Wanting to be sure, the Committee asked Salerno the same question once again. And again, Salerno answered that he had no record of any other murders occurring that day (p. 233).

While all the believers in *Purge Day* cite figures of from thirty to ninety men executed, and while all believers cite or refer to Valachi as evidence, Valachi only testified to about four or five murders. It should also be noted that Valachi's recollections about the murders were exceptionally hazy, undoubtedly because of the intervening three decades, but equally as significant because his knowledge was based on hearsay. Clearly, the popular story of Valachi (Maas 1968) was used as a primary source in the reconstruction of the history of organized crime.

There is another important and related question to be asked about the purge story. If Valachi did not testify about it, and if he is the major source for the history of organized crime, then how did the story evolve? Certainly, from the nature of their questions it seems obvious that the Senate committee had heard about the story. There really is no mystery, however. The story of the Mafia purge has been around since the late 1930s, when it first appeared in a series of articles written by J. Richard "Dixie" Davis (1939) and published in *Collier's* magazine. In the third installment of his life and times, Davis, who had been Dutch (Arthur Flegenheimer) Schultz's attorney, recounted a story told to him by Schultz mobster, Abraham "Bo" Weinberg. In an apparent moment of trust and confidentiality, according to Davis, Weinberg, who was supposedly one of the killers of Maranzano, confided that "at the very same hour when Maramanenza [sic] was knocked off . . . there was about ninety guineas knocked off all over the country. That was the time we Americanized the mobs" (Davis 1939: 44). Davis did add the caveat that he had been unable to check on the accuracy of Weinberg's claims about mass murder.

The unsubstantiated story of the *Purge* remained in limbo for approximately a decade. It resurfaced in one of the key books on organized crime published in 1951. *Murder, Inc.,* written by ex-Assistant District Attorney (Brooklyn) Burton B. Turkus and reporter Sid Feder, revitalized the story and transformed it into a major turning point in the history of organized crime. Turkus and Feder wrote: "The day Marrizano [sic] got it was the end of the line for the Greaser crowd in the Italian Society . . . a definite windup to Mafia as an entity and a power in national crime." They added that "some thirty to forty leaders of Mafia's older group all over the United States were murdered that day and in the next forty-eight hours" (p. 87). One of their primary sources for this part of their history was "Dixie" Davis' story of his conversation with Weinberg. Turkus and Feder also claimed that "even more irrefutable evidence was provided . . . by an eagle-beaked, one-eyed thug named, Ernest Rupolo" (p. 88). A convicted murderer turned informer, Rupolo supposedly divulged information about the background and modernization of the Italian society of crime. Turkus and Feder gave no details of the Rupolo story, implying that it was consistent with the Davis account and their particular notions about the history of organized crime. Even if they had supplied particulars, however, the Rupolo history would have been no more credible than the Davis one. Rupolo, who was a rather unsuccessful informer, was not a participant in either the "war" or its supposed culmination, the purge. In 1931 he was either fifteen or sixteen years old, and whatever knowledge he may have had about the inner workings of the underworld was at the very best based on rumor.[2]

There is one final personality or alleged source for the purge story. In 1971, reporter and crime writer Hank Messick published a biography of Meyer Lansky, one of America's more famous criminals. Messick recounted the story of the purge, but this time its accuracy was allegedly based on the supposed confessions of retired Mafia leader, Nicola Gentile. During the late 1920s and early 1930s, according to Messick, Gentile was something of a Mafia peacemaker. Messick noted that Gentile's account of the gangland war and purge was part of a long confession given to the FBI, which he, Messick, was fortunate enough to examine. "Thanks to Gentile," Messick wrote, "there exists a firsthand account never before published" (Messick 1971: 49). For those not so fortunate to have access to FBI files, however, the Gentile story can be read in an Italian paperback titled, *Vita di Capomafia* (Gentile 1963), which was published in the 1960s. Gentile's story is a vast history of the American Mafia overwhelmingly stuffed with the names of almost every leading gangster, the dates and places of innumerable meetings and conferences, and the trivia of gangland diplomacy and violence. Gentile's devotion to detail is followed through his description of the murder of Maranzano. But then, as if in an afterthought, Gentile stated that the death of Marazano was the signal for a massacre. But not a name, not a place, not a killing is described or given. As far as historical evidence is concerned, the Gentile account provides no more evidence for the purge than the earlier ones.

It is one thing to question or dismiss the historical sources for the story of the purge, it is something else to prove that it did not happen. That is, while the sources are incompetent, the event might still have taken place. In order to investigate that question, Block (1977a) surveyed newspapers in selected cities for the two week period before and after Maranzano's death. He searched for comments on gangland murders that might be connected with the Maranzano case. The cities chosen included New York, Los Angeles, Philadelphia, Detroit, New Orleans, Boston, Buffalo, and Newark. While several accounts of the Maranzano killing were located, Block found only three other related murders. Two of the killings were extensively reported in the Newark *Star Ledger.* The dead men were Louis Russo and Samuel Monaco, both New Jersey gangsters. Monaco and Russo were two of the men mentioned by Valachi in his testimony about the "four or five murders." The other was found in the Philadelphia *Inquirer* on September 14. Datelined Pittsburgh, September 13, an A.P. wire story told of the murder of Joseph Siragusa, whose death was "attributed to racketeers" who "fled in an automobile bearing New York license plates."

The killing of four or five men does not make a purge, and certainly the killing of three or four men in the New York metropolitan area and one in Pittsburgh does not make a national vendetta. It is also significant that all the names turned up in the survey of the historiography of the purge story—Maranzano, Monaco, Le Pore, and perhaps Siragusa—have been accounted for. Left out are only the fictional members of the Mafia's Legion of the Damned—those unnamed and more importantly, unfound gang leaders whose massacre signaled the end of one criminal era and the beginning of another.

Earlier we asked the question that if Valachi did not testify about the purge, and if he is the major source for this history of organized crime, then how did the story evolve. Having answered that question by discussing Davis (1939), Turkus and Feder (1951), and the other sources, we are, however, left with another puzzle. If all the accounts of the purge are unreliable, and if the newspaper survey is accurate, and finally, if the purge never really took place, then how and why did various people concoct it? Did Weinberg simply want to spice up his account of the murder of Maranzano with tales of ninety other dead Italians? Did Rupolo simply want to further ingratiate himself with the Brooklyn District Attorney's office, and, therefore, invent a story? The same question can be asked in relation to the other principals. The answer is no; we feel that they *believed* the story that they told.

All the commentators mentioned that the early 1930s was a time of intense confusion in the underworld compounded by the murders of such leaders as Joe Masseria in April 1931, and Salvatore Maranzano in September 1931. If not an actual war, there clearly were violence and division among Italian- and Sicilian-American gangsters. One can reasonably surmise that the death of Maranzano, especially to interested outsiders or principals such as Weinberg and Gentile and lower-level, young hoodlums like Rupolo, was a momentous event that both could have and should have signaled increased violence. Certainly, the level of anxiety along with the need for a comprehensible framework was high. When increased violence did not follow Maranzano's death, a comprehensible framework was established, not out of whole cloth, but out of the bits and pieces of events that were transformed as they were transmitted. The suggestion, therefore, is that the purge story performed the function of reducing anxiety by magically wiping out Maranzano's followers—those who would have been expected to revenge their leader's murder. Furthermore, there is evidence that suggests why criminals, especially in New York City, developed this particular story.

In the course of the newspaper search for purge victims, a number of stories were found about Maranzano and his presumably major racket: the importation of aliens. In the September 10 edition of the Newark *Star Ledger,* for example, there was a story headlined, "U.S. Hot on Trail of Ring Busy Smuggling Aliens." Datelined New York, the story noted that the federal government was seeking indictments "against more than a score of persons in the hope of breaking up an alien smuggling ring . . . believed responsible for importing 8,000 foreigners in this country." Reportedly, nineteen men had already been indicted. According to the press, headquarters were maintained in Montreal, while other administrative offices were established in New York, Chicago, and San Francisco. Other cities mentioned in the article included Detroit and Buffalo as transshipment points for the smugglers. On the following day, September 11, the *Star Ledger* headlined a story, "Murder in N.Y. Held Reprisal by Smugglers." The report noted that "authorities . . . were convinced that Salvatore Maranzano slashed and shot by three assassins . . . was the victim of the ring." The *Star Ledger* went on to say that the police were sure that members of the ring had murdered Maranzano for supposedly informing on them.

In the Los Angeles *Times* story of the Maranzano killing it was reported that detectives had "found immigration blank forms, and Department of Justice agents expressed the belief Maranzano had been engaged . . . in aiding aliens to enter the United States illegally." Finishing the Maranzano account, the Los Angeles *Times* wrote that "his slayers slashed a cross on his face—the sign of a traitor." Maranzano's link to alien smuggling was also reported by the New York *Herald Tribune,* which stated on September 12 that "among the theories engaging the attention of investigators is one that Maranzano was marked for death in the belief that he had given evidence or was about to do so against his fellow conspirators in the smuggling racket." The *Herald Tribune* pointed out that his death "came a week after the arrest of nineteen men . . . on charges of smuggling 8,000 aliens across the Canadian and Mexican borders, at a price ranging from $100 to $5,000 a head." And finally, the New York *Times* reported on the connection between Maranzano and alien smuggling. The New York *Times* story on September 11 noted that detectives were sent to Buffalo, Chicago, Poughkeepsie, New York, and Sea Isle, New Jersey, following Maranzano's murder. On September 12, the *Times* also stated that Murray W. Garrson, Assistant Secretary of the Department of Labor, admitted that Maranzano had been under surveillance for over six months.

In what way does this material on Maranzano contribute to the development of the purge story? First of all, it is significant to note that this particular racket was national, or rather international in scope. We have a number of reports that identify locales from at least Chicago to New York as crossing points for aliens and headquarters of the racket. In addition, there are stories which indicate that law enforcement agents were sent to a number of different cities for the purpose of investigating either the murder of Maranzano or the ramifications of the killing. It is possible, if not probable, that this kind of geographical activity accounted for the notion that the purge was national. Surely something was happening all over the country because of Maranzano's death. Second, the murder of Maranzano, if indeed connected to the investigation of the alien smuggling racket, could have caused the enterprise to cease, at least for an important period of time. If so, Maranzano's murder could be interpreted as resulting in the end of the traditional Mafia, which, if it existed, must have depended on the continuous importation of Sicilians. Third, it can easily be imagined how the deaths of four or five supposedly important racketeers could be transmuted through the mechanisms of rumor and hyperbole, standard fare in the secretive oral culture of the underworld.

It is possible to explain the belief in the purge on the part of various underworld figures. It is also clear how the story developed, and that Valachi was, in a sense, forced to bare witness to a story of which he was barely cognizant. But it is by no means clear why so many scholars have bought a story which so grossly violates historical respectability. It is important to note, therefore, that the scholarly attachment to the purge is a conspicuous example of the insensitivity to historical methods found all too often in work on organized crime. Unfortunately, it is not enough to point out examples of historical naivete and insensitivity with the admonishment for care and attention to historical methods. Much of the contemporary sociology of organized crime has been constructed from the interpretive framework of the popular histories as well as from their narratives. Academic sociology, especially that segment which has dealt with organized crime, has displayed a strong afinity with the ideological preconceptions of the creators of the popular works even when it shifts gears by focusing on different criminal personalities as the architects of organized crime. No matter which criminals are featured, the framework is the lawman's favorite: the ladder of conspiracy with each rung integrated in a series leading to the *Master Conspirator*.

Women and Organized Crime[3]

As must be obvious neither the master conspirator nor any of his alleged subordinates could ever be anything less than resolutely masculine. These are the possessors and intimidators of women. In fact, the social world of organized crime as traditionally described appears to be as persistently male as professional football. Women have no social roles to perform in either arena, it seems, except as commodities such as prostitutes or cheer leaders. Organized criminals, like professional athletes, are increasingly to be understood as members of criminal brotherhoods or male families—fraternal organizations in which young men typically swear some form of allegiance and devotion to other young men while promising to obey older men. One of the more remarkable aspects of this mono-sexual description of organized crime is how different it is from earlier studies of the urban underworld. For instance, Herbert Asbury's *Gangs of New York* (1927) presented a sexually integrated underworld, in which female criminals played a variety of important roles. Consider his discussion of Frederika Mandelbaum, "better known as Marm or Mother," who was reportedly "the greatest and most successful fence in the criminal annals of New York." Marm Mandelbaum, according to Asbury, "handled the loot and financed the operations of a majority of the great gangs of bank and store burglars." Asbury went on to note that Mandelbaum was both the patron and friend of such notorious female criminals as Black Lena Kleinschmidt, Ellen Clegg, Big Mary, Queen Liz, Little Annie, Kid Glove Rosey, and Old Mother Hubbard, all pickpockets, sneak thieves and blackmailers. In this same context was Sophie Lyons, "perhaps the most notorious confidence woman America has ever produced" (214-218).

The sexually diverse New York underworld of the nineteenth century was similar to other urban underworlds uncovered by Asbury in a series of "informal histories." Among the more interesting female criminals mentioned in his other work were Chicago's Kitty Adams "who for almost a dozen years was known as the Terror of State Street." During her reign which began in the mid-1880s, it was estimated by the Chicago police that she had taken part in over a hundred robberies and uncounted assaults (Asbury 1940: 96-98). Moving to San Francisco, Asbury recounted the stories of such criminals as the confidence woman, Big Bertha, and madams, Miss Piggott, Pigeon-Toed Sal, the Galloping Cow, and Mother Bronson. The illicit activities of these women were extensive and included procuring, fencing, and "shanghaiing." One final point about female criminality was Asbury's claim that "the membership of the early hoodlum gangs included girls, and several were captained by maladjusted representatives of the so-called gentler sex." And he added that these female gang leaders were "invariably more ferocious than their male companions," especially when it came to inventing methods of torture (Asbury 1933: 154, 212-225).

For the historian of organized crime, the discrepancies between the sexually segregated world of organized crime advanced by contemporary scholars raise a number of historical, ideological, and methodological questions. Among these are three that seem primary. Could it be that the women mentioned by Asbury were a tiny minority of "freaks" unrepresentative of the general composition of America's urban underworlds during the last century? Or perhaps contemporary commentators have seriously misrepresented the social world of organized crime in the twentieth century for ideological reasons, which have barred consideration of female organized criminals? And alternatively, could it be that the two opposed descriptions reflect historical changes in organized crime which have caused the exclusion of women from illicit activities?

Confirmation of Asbury's insights can be gained not only from such works as Alvin Harlow's *Old Bowery Days* (1931) and such primary sources as the Lexow Committee hearings (New York State, 1895), but also from modern studies of the London underworld in the nineteenth century, which furnish cross-cultural corroboration. In Kellow Chesney's *The Victorian Underworld* (1970), for example, female criminals play substantial roles. Chesney's discussion of organized thieves demonstrates that women "were among the commonest and most useful accomplices involved in almost every type of robbery." Among street thieves, women "most often played a leading part" with one particular variant of street stealing becoming a "feminine specialty." This was the systematic robbing of well-to-do children of their clothes and boots. Actually, there were any number of stealing specialties which were filled by women as they worked in conjunction with the full complement of urban male thieves (133-317).

Another social history of organized crime in nineteenth century England stated:

Women were well represented in the criminal class, and acted as accomplices in a number of ways. . . . They would carry a housebreaker's tools to and from the scene of operations . . . and would often be entrusted with the stolen property. Prostitutes would sometimes start a riot in a public house to draw the police away from the scene of an intended burglary, and were often in league with pickpockets.

The women of the criminal class did not, of course, restrict their activities to aiding the men; many of them were thieves themselves. The girls would beg or steal like the boys, with of course, the additional resort of prostitution when occasion served (Tobias 1967: 92).

Concerning the ferocity of women criminals, this study echoed Asbury's finding and noted that "though there were proportionately far fewer women criminals than men, they were said to be worse than most of the men" (p. 93). Clearly, there seems to be little reason to believe that organized crime in nineteenth century America as described by Asbury was either mistaken or unique.

What then of the possibility that today's interpreters have misread the contemporary social world of organized crime? Certainly there is a marked disparity of approach between the social historians of nineteenth century organized crime and most of today's scholars. Early writers such as Asbury, as well as modern historians like Tobias and Chesney, were interested in describing and analyzing urban underworlds—real tangible districts which provided a home and market for the entire range of criminals. Their studies of organized crime are grounded in the social life of San Francisco's Barbary Coast, New York's Five Points area and Lower East Side, New Orleans' Storyville vice section, and London's various criminal districts. Crucial to this approach is an understanding of the functions of such urban establishments as saloons, pool parlors, restaurants, hotels, ethnic market places, transportation terminals, political clubs, and gambling dens, within and around which criminal life was centered. Organized criminal activities were simply one of the features of the social life of impoverished districts, and miscreant females were part of this broad social panorama.

Contemporary discussions, on the other hand, have had little interest in the social context of organized crime. Today's sociology of organized crime is almost totally dominated by the question "how organized is organized crime?" Geographical considerations of criminal behavior have become, at the same time, the special province of those interested in the sociology of juvenile delinquency. Analyses of modern vice districts and the *urbaneness* of organized criminals play little part in today's sociologies. Organized crime, which was once a term to describe certain types of crime

which demanded coordination, but which could be carried out by a variety
of differently structured groups, is now merely a synonym for a single organization usually called, as we know, *La Cosa Nostra*. The identification
has tended to be complete: organized criminals are members of the Cosa
Nostra; organized crime is what Cosa Nostra members do. By removing the
analysis of organized crime from its urban historical context, organized
crime has become the exotic *Brotherhood*. How totally masculine a world
it is perceived to be can be seen in the following passage from Donald
Cressey's *Theft of the Nation* (1969):

> Membership in the Italian-Sicilian Mafia does not automatically
> make one a member of the American organization. This might not
> have been the case before World War II, but now, even a Sicilian
> Mafia member must be recommended for membership. In the old
> country, a *man* could not be a *soldier* (or a member of any rank) if
> his *father* were also a member. The idea was to avoid a blood line
> that would work to the disadvantage of *men* not in that line. Some
> American *"families"* follow this principle, some do not. Albert
> Anastasia, late boss of a New York *"family"* was the first of the
> American bosses to give up this taboo. Vito Genovese and Joseph
> Profaci followed it, but Thomas Lucchese and Joseph Bonanno
> did not. At least two current *"families"* both of New York, do not
> follow it. Although the *sons* of some bosses cannot be members of
> their *father's "family,"* they might be members of their *father-
> in-law's "family."* There are no restrictions on the membership of
> other *male* relatives. In one *"family" brothers* are boss and lieu-
> tenant (118-119: our emphasis added).

There are several things to be noted about this current analytic focus
which help explain its exceptionally exclusive sexual orientation. First,
it is important to remember that the historical underpinnings of the Cosa
Nostra sociologies are extremely suspect. The second point concerns the
ideological preconceptions (mentioned above) of at least part of academic
sociology. Clearly, there is a need and a desire to explain organized crime
by the device of the "Big Conspiracy of Alien Origin." There is, therefore,
an emotional if not intellectual affinity between that segment of contemporary sociology which consistently overlooks elementary historical
methods while chasing after the Mafia conspirators, and such nineteenth
century vagaries as the belief in the conspiratorial genius of the Catholic
Church and the Masons (Davis 1969). Naturally, the further along the
conspiracy road the contemporary writers travel, the less likely they are

to encounter the social reality of organized crime in this century or, indeed, in any century.

But the question still remains whether that social reality includes women criminals. That is, although it is clear that organized crime is not and has not been synonomous with Cosa Nostra and other masculine equivalents, is it then that women have been part of this century's social world of organized crime? The answer is that they have been very much a part of the organized underworlds, but have been effectively removed from the accounts both because of the belief in conspiracy as the engine of organized crime and because of a malign interpretation of female criminality, which reached its apotheosis during the Progressive Era, and which has remained an intellectual stumbling block ever since.

The only female criminal role discussed during the Progressive period is that of prostitute. And that literature, whether a study of the reformers who moved to eradicate the social evil, or of the enterprise itself, depicted women as passive victims of social disequilibrium and the venality and brutality of men. Equally as striking, the image of the prostitute, especially as developed by Progressive Era reformers, was of a lonely, detached, and confused female. Nowhere was it suggested that prostitutes or madams consciously and aggressively chose their activities as a positive adaptation to urban poverty (Woolston 1969; Seligman 1912; Benjamin and Masters 1964; Waterman 1932; King 1956; Pivar 1973; Lubove 1963; Feldman 1967; Kneeland 1913). Along with this particular view of the "dynamics" of prostitution, Progressive reformers concentrated their energies upon female deviance in the burgeoning immigrant neighborhoods of certain American cities. The controlling metaphor for prostitution during this period was "white slavery," and while there was compassion and concern for the rootless, uneducated, immigrant prostitute, there was only hatred and contempt for the white slavers. It was a Progressive discovery or invention that the slavers were also members of the immigrant communities—in New York, especially, it was claimed that the leaders of supposedly vast vice operations were Russian and Polish Jews. Undoubtedly Progressive moralists derived some solace from the fact that sexual slavery was an alien phenomenon in the same way that contemporary studies keep returning to the alien origins of organized crime.

Perhaps the classic example of this version of prostitution was broadcast by *McClure's Magazine* in a famous series of articles published in November 1909. One of the essays written by Editor S. S. McClure began with praise for the "Germanic races" as the architects of Western civilization. In contrast to this achievement, McClure held that the "great masses of primitive peoples from the farms of Europe, transported to this country as laborers, together with a considerable proportion of Negro slaves liberated by the Civil War, have struggled to degrade the standards and guarantees of civilization in America." For proof, McClure turned to a description of the white slave traffic in New York linking it to Tammany Hall and the East Side immigrant Jews. McClure wrote: "There has grown up, as an adjunct to this herd of female wretchedness, a fraternity of fetid male vermin (nearly all of them being Russian or Polish Jews), who are unmatchable for impudence and beastiality" (McClure 1901: 117-118).

Another of the essays was George Kibbe Turner's "The Daughters of the Poor." Turner' interest was the transfer of a vast empire of prostitution from its European base to the East Side of New York. He noted that around twenty-five years before, during the "third great flush of immigration," which consisted of Hungarian, Austrian, and Russian Jews, a very large number of criminals moved to New York. In fact, Turner wrote, it was the Jewish district which "opened the eyes of the minor politician of the slums to the tremendous enterprise, the business of procuring and the traffic in women offered him." It was also stated that the largest number of prostitutes came from immigrant Jewish families and that the East Side Jewish pimp was transferring his activities to other American cities (Turner 1909: 47, 49-52).

Clearly enough, as Arthur A. Goren (1970) has pointed out, these writers played upon the widely shared anxieties of the times: the fear of organized conspiracy by amoral business and political interests, and the degradation of the immigrants who now appeared to control a number of American cities (138-144). More explicitly, Egal Feldman reported in his excellent essay, "Prostitution, The Alien Woman and the Progressive Imagination, 1910-1915" (1967), that there were several distinct campaigns or approaches to the issue of immigrants and crime during those years. First was a "nativistic attack on prostitution with all its ugly xenophobic overtones"; this was "paralleled by an anti-nativist outburst." The nativists simply blamed the immigrant communities for prostitution, while the antinativists not only attempted to uncover the causes and devise cures for prostitution, but also tried at the same time to disassociate the reputation of the immigrant from commercialized vice (p. 197). For all its decency of purpose, however, the antinativist position was weak. It was logically unsound as the premise of immigrant innocence precluded discussion of immigrant venality. But more importantly, it subsumed female crime under the single heading of prostitution. And concomitantly, it undermined any consideration of female criminality outside the Progressive formula of weak women and brutal, exploitative men.

How wrong, misleading, and chauvinistic this view was and is, can be seen by an analysis of one of the finest primary sources for the history of organized crime during this century. The source is the reports of a unique organization known as the Bureau of Social Morals, which was part of a Jewish "self-defense" association called the New York *Kehillah*. The Kehillah's considerable influence was routed through its annual conventions and scientific bureaus, which by the late summer of 1912 included the Bureau of Social Morals, formed in the aftermath of the infamous Rosenthal murder (Logan 1972). More generally, the Kehillah and the bureau were part of the New York Jewish community's response to accusations of Jewish criminality—that part of the nativist outburst discussed above. The Kehillah maintained the anticrime Bureau of Social Morals for five years. Staffed by a number of private investigators, the Bureau focused on the First Inspection District, the six police precincts of New York City's Lower East Side. The Bureau's most important communal contribution was the supplying of detailed information that led to gambling raids, revocation of licenses, and the arraignment of individual criminals (Goren 1970: 159-170).

Unfortunately, there was no summary or final comprehensive report on organized crime, and there was no particular organizational scheme to the material. The investigators' function was to document Jewish involvement in crime and then to turn their evidence over to law enforcement agencies. But within the mass of material there are data concerning ethnicity, criminal occupations, kinship, past criminal records, the geography of illegal enterprises, and membership in particular gangs or vice rings for many of the *311* female criminals identified by the bureau.

Analysis of the data indicates that there were five fairly distinct groups of female criminals: those involved solely in prostitution; those who achieved a management position usually in a vice operation or displayed a special business skill such as fencing stolen goods or corrupt bail bonding; those whose criminal activities were exclusively some form of stealing; an exceptionally small group who were both prostitutes and thieves; and those who worked a combination of vice, gambling, and drug dealing. The 311 women criminals were divided into 149 prostitutes, 78 entrepeneurs, 56 thieves, four prostitute-thieves, and 24 vice, drug, and gambling operatives. Of course, the categories and numbers alone are telling indications of the varied female roles in organized crime. And it is sufficient for our purpose to point out that a computer analysis of the female criminals clearly shows that the traditional image of the female criminal was and is more representative of male psychology than of female criminality. Let a few examples stand for the extended inquiry (Block 1977c).

In contrast to the traditional image of the prostitute, consider the following report filed in August 1912, by the bureau's investigators. This extensive investigation was of a house of prostitution located at 7 East First Street on the East Side of Manhattan. The building was known as the Columbia Hotel and was owned by Rose Hertz, her husband, Jacob Hertz, and Max and David Rosenbach, brothers of Rosie Hertz. Also working there were two of Rosie Hertz's cousins, Hyman and Morris Goldman; the latter was the manager. They were Hungarian Jews and supposedly ran some of the more famous brothels in New York City. The Bureau noted that Rosie Hertz had accumulated great sums of money as a slum lord, and she was reportedly the first Jewish madam in New York, if not in the entire United States. To protect their interests in prostitution, the Hertz family contributed $1,000 every year to both the Democratic and Republican organizations. Their other interests included the fencing of stolen goods and a small bail bond business, and it is absolutely clear from the bureau's reports that the leader of the Hertz family was Rosie.

Stealing, like prostitution and other criminal activities, was also often a family affair dominated by women. For example, the bureau reported on the careers of two brothers, Sam and Meyer Solomon, and their wives, Tillie and Bessie. Sam, it was claimed, was notorious "for his propensities as a seducer . . . around Hamilton Fish Park from where he graduated a full fledged pickpocket and fagin." Meyer's wife, Bessie Solomon, was described as one of the "cleverest boosters—gun molls" in the world. She was supposedly responsible for training a large number of women, including Sam's wife, Tillie, as pickpockets and thieves. When their wives went to work, the brothers retired from active stealing and turned to other pursuits such as gambling, loan sharking, and the fencing of stolen goods.

It is apparent that sexually integrated mobs far removed from the master-slave model of the Progressive imagination abounded among thieves as well as in the other categories. Several more examples include Spanish Mary and her husband, Earle Williams, known as the "King of the Panhandlers" who worked ferry boats, elevated trains, and subways. In the same category were Sarah and Jacob Glucksman, May and Joe Hess and the picketpocket team of Taube and Aaron Goldsbard.

The subject of female involvement in organized crime was dominated by a series of sentimental conceptions dealing especially with prostitution and cast principally by Progressive reformers and their immediate forebears as they grappled with the enormity of urban culture (Davis 1957). Once firmly established, these notions left little room for any understanding of female criminality including prostitution as a rational method of adapting to urban opportunities and institutions. The sentimentality of the approach fixed concern upon the single question of cause—what could have led girls to so degrade themselves, to ultimately destroy themselves, was the reigning issue. This meant that female criminality would really become a part of the general field of juvenile delinquency (in much the same manner as social area analyses), that section of criminology devoted to seeking reasons for the transformation of young people from potential citizens to criminals.

Adult female criminality had seemingly been settled as a separate topic by that part of the Progressive formula which went inexorably from juvenile female crime to degration, disease, and death. Under this formulation, mobility in organized crime for females was an explicit one-way street, leading rapidly downward. As long as this viewpoint prevails, there is little sense in considering adult female criminals as more than the victims of brutal male criminals, used by them until they reach some disgusting level of disease which renders them criminally useless and after which they are abandoned. Naturally, within this traditional litany of causes and concerns there is no room for female independence and equality in this century's world of organized crime. Women such as Rosie Hertz and Bessie Solomon, therefore, make little sense. Indeed, the female criminal class composed of those women who achieved a management position or displayed special criminal business skills is either considered a gross misinterpretation or, at best, a historical oddity with no general significance according to both the Progressive and contemporary views.

The all-male world of organized crime is a product of a special kind of historical insensitivity partially supported by a naive belief in conspiracy and the remarkable staying power of Progressive imagery. This does not mean that female organized criminals, post-Progressivism, are never mentioned, however. They sometimes appear even in the popular works which so resolutely maintain a sexually exclusive underworld. But when female criminals are identified or described, their roles and functions are never analyzed—in a real sense, then, they are scenery. Consider the following examples from three of the popular works on the history of organized crime.

In the last chapter of informer Vincent Teresa's memoirs, *My Life in the Mafia* (1973), appear two "rare" women. "Years ago," Teresa stated, "there was Butsey Morelli's wife. She was a very, very smart woman, and she helped advise Butsey in the early part of his career as he took over the mob in Rhode Island and the New England area." Teresa added that "she was well thought of by all the old Mustache Petes and she had plenty of power." Besides Morelli's wife, Teresa remembered "a guy named Rusty—he's big today with the Bonanno mob—who had a wife called Connie." According to Teresa, Connie was a "real tough broad" having been a loan shark and bookmaker before she married. Connie's attributes were decidedly in the masculine mode as Teresa described her: "Guys would borrow money from her and figure that because she was just a broad they could make a mark out of her. But Connie fooled the hell out of them. She'd have their legs broken, or she'd go down and shoot them herself. Even after Rusty and Connie were married," Teresa continued, "she stayed in business and stayed tough. Once Rusty shot two guys and one of them survived, and he fingered Rusty to be killed." When Rusty went into hiding, "Connie decided to get the guy. . . . She had him set up and gunned down in a cemetery" (pp. 344-345). These rather remarkable women are used by Teresa as a counterpoint to the traditional roles of "mob" wives—silence and the nurturing of children.

Female organized criminals are also mentioned in Paul Sann's biography of Dutch Schultz, *Kill the Dutchman* (1971). In one of the early chapters appears racketeer Stephanie St. Clair, better known as "Madam Queen of Policy." Sann wrote that "this flamboyant figure, sometimes called the Tiger from Marseilles, truly had fought the Dutchman to his death." St. Clair had reportedly "refused to yield her numbers bank to Schultz when he was on his triumphal armed march through the Negro community." Her particular "piece of the policy racket in Harlem" was supposedly worth more than a million dollars a year (pp. 56-57). Also appearing in the Sann book is Polly Adler, who was one of New York's most notorious madams during the 1930s. With his eye fixed upon the development of the National Crime Syndicate, Sann had no time or interest in speculating on either woman or such issues as ethnicity and female criminal specialties.

Even *Murder, Inc.,* the one work that most clearly set the tone and categories for so much of the contemporary understanding of organized crime, contained several passing references to female organized criminals. The most notorious woman mentioned was Virginia Hill, who apparently consorted with the following infamous racketeers: the Fischetti brothers of Chicago, Joe Adonis, Charles "Lucky" Luciano, Frank Costello, Dandy Phil Kastel of New Orleans, Meyer Lansky, and Benjamin "Buggsy" Siegel. In addition to being the courtesan of so many racketeers, Hill was suspected of being the mob's cross-country "bagman," or money messenger (pp. 270-272). More interesting than Hill, however, was the "Red Rose of Williamsburg." In a chapter devoted to a somewhat sentimental and chauvinistic discussion of the wives and girl friends of various racketeers,

Turkus and Feder (1951: 193-194) noted that "Rose was established as a figure in the Larney gang, a mob of shylocks and killers." What is remarkable about Rose Pantiel and her membership in the Larney gang of gamblers and loan sharks is that neither she nor the gang can be fit into the schema of organized crime advanced by Turkus and Feder. This sexually integrated outfit operated independently of the National Crime Syndicate, a fact simply glossed over by Turkus and Feder (New York *Times,* August 26, 1940: 17). As far as they were concerned, Rose Pantiel's only importance was as the mother-in-law of racketeer Chippy Weiner.

There are two other women criminals mentioned by Turkus and Feder: Rose Gold, the owner of a candy store in Brownsville, Brooklyn, which became the "headquarters" of Abe Reles, Martin Goldstein, and Harry Strauss—prominent Brooklyn racketeers and the so-called contract killers employed by the Syndicate; and Lena Frosch, the leader of a family of bail bond racketeers. As might be expected, Turkus and Feder were unable to expand their approach by asking anything interesting about these women or to connect their particular activities to a wider context.

Fortunately, it is not necessary to rely on *Murder, Inc.* for information about Rose Gold and Lena Frosch. Both women were among the subjects of a four-year investigation into official corruption in Brooklyn carried out by Assistant Attorney General, John Harlan Amen, and summarized in *Report of the Kings County Investigation, 1938-1942.* The report stated that on May 4, 1939, Mrs. Rose Gold, "69 years of age, decrepit and unable to read or write English," was charged with seventeen counts of perjury stemming from her attempts to hide her relationship with Reles and his associates. Gold's involvement with the Brooklyn killers was complex, according to Amen. She made frequent court appearances in Brooklyn police stations to bail out men arrested for disorderly conduct or gambling where the games were operated or protected by Reles. Gold also provided bail for Reles and the others in several New York courts. After examining Gold's bank account, Amen found that $395,983.70 had been deposited and withdrawn from November 1937 to December 1938. Among the deposits was a check for $7,236 given Gold by Louis Capone, a notorious racketeer and associate of Albert Anastasia. Amen established that all the bank transactions were carried out by Gold's daughter, Shirley Herman, whose husband was an assistant research clerk to Irwin Steingut, the leader of the Democratic minority in the State Assembly and considered one of Brooklyn's most powerful politicians. Amen also found that part of Reles' loan shark racket was operated from her candy store and was managed by her son, Sam "The Dapper" Siegel (pp. 73-74).

Amen uncovered the criminal activities of the other woman alluded to by Turkus and Feder, Lena Frosch, while pursuing the links between corrupt bail bonding and Brooklyn racketeers. His major concern was with the current activities of a bail bond conspirator named Abraham Frosch, and in reviewing Frosch's history he was compelled to discuss his mother, Lena. Abraham Frosch, whose testimony resulted in the removal or forced retirement of twenty-five New York City police lieutenants and sergeants, had been in the bonding business since he was fourteen. He started out helping his mother, Lena, a licensed bondswoman, who had sent him after school either to the courts to check on the disposition of cases on which his mother had gone bond, or to the police stations to get from lieutenants cash deposited by his mother as bail for clients. In 1934 Lena Frosch was convicted of perjury and forgery on bail bonds, and her license was revoked. But this did not deter her from continuing the business, which, by then, consisted of getting her property-owning neighbors to offer their real estate as bail for a percentage of her fee. It became her son's job to shuttle the neighbors to either the courts or police stations, along with helping in the execution of the bonds (pp. 75-76).

At this point, we might suggest what a social historian interested in female organized criminals could do with the examples of Rose Gold and Lena Frosch. There appears to be a connection between women and corrupt bail bonding and an inquiry into the bail bonding business at that time would be in order. A check through police records, court records, and other primary material would reveal that women played a substantial role in this activity. Corrupt bail bonding was one of the areas investigated by the New York City Department of Investigation and Accounts in the mid-1930s. In a report distributed by the Department under the leadership of Commissioner Paul Blanshard, it is stated that criminal actions were taken against fifty-three bail-bond conspirators, twenty-one of whom were women. Female criminals in this case composed almost 40% of the total of convicted racketeers. The names of the women were reported, and it does not take much imagination to suggest ways for a social historian to explore any number of important questions from this starting point. Clearly, one of the areas that requires attention is criminal families, characterized by husband and wife partnerships. A starting point might be an investigation of capital accumulation by such criminal families and their investment patterns. Also, a searching look into female criminal roles and their changes over time as intermediates between the underworld and upperworld of the criminal justice systems in municipal America is sorely needed.

Organized crime has been a functional part of urban America providing goods and services for a variety of male and female patrons and clients and potential money and power for male and female criminals. Contrary to many accounts, organized crime was not the unique creation of any particular immigrant group such as the Italians, but rather flourished in a variety of ethnic and working-class communities. Criminal enterprises were one way of responding to poverty, and immigrant and native-born males and females realized this. In many cases illegal activities were a familial affair: there were real (not fictive) families of crooked bail bonders, pimps and madams, fences and thieves. Criminal enterprises were staffed by brothers, sisters, cousins, in-laws, mothers, and fathers. Male and female relatives channeled money back and forth from legal to illegal businesses and, when able, conveyed political protection.

Organized crime was frequently an adjunct of the economic, political, and social aspirations of communities such as New York's Lower East Side. Besides the goods and services provided to members of the community, illegal activities run and staffed by men and women pumped money into local real estate and legitimate businesses. Male and female syndicate criminals were major supporters and sometimes owners of such community enterprises as saloons, candy stores, pool parlors, restaurants, and gambling establishments. They also supplied work for the host of male and female intermediaries in the criminal justice system: lawyers, fixers, steerers, and bonders.

Blind Alleys and Dead Ends

American organized crime is a subtle and complex cultural phenomenon, a staple of the collective unconscious formed and re-formed through the fictive personalities of film and television stars, their creators and real-life imitators. Its fictional uniformities signal confusion in American attitudes about business, family life, sex, violence, individualism, and fraternity. And, as noted in the beginning of this chapter, just as the fictional gangster services the American psyche by his fortunate rise and fall, so the organized criminal tends to cater to certain ideological preconceptions held by mainstream social scientists. Central to the maintenance and development of these preconceptions is a stance toward American history which is a mixture of conspiracy theories coupled with a seeming disregard for historical methods and a heavy dose of male chauvinism. Implicit in a number of studies whose thrust is policy development is the idea that the alien conspiracy is an aberration on the body politic and social (Wilson 1970). There is a war at hand, so they argue, that must be understood to be successfully prosecuted (Lynch and Phillips 1971). The alien con-

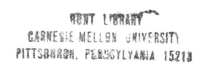

spiracy has infiltrated and undermined significant parts of the American economy and political system (*Law and the Social Order,* 1970). With echoes of Lincoln Steffens' moral homilies but with little of his deep fascination, the conspiracy theorists among the professional social scientists present organized crime within the context of a passion play.

Intriguing as this may be, it is well to note that this trend is not only unsophisticated but also quite retrograde. Social scientists have not always insisted upon a moral context instead of a historical and sociological one in the study of organized crime. Reflect for a moment on Robert Merton's (1968) work on political structure and the function of urban political bosses, as well as Daniel Bell's (1962) neglected study of the "Racket-Ridden Longshoremen." Both of these early works emphasized historical and sociological concerns in their schemas of the social system of organized crime. But today, while it is generally agreed that organized crime operates as a tripartite system consisting of the client who seeks the goods or services, the syndicate criminal who provides these goods and services, and the corrupt public official who is remunerated for his function of protecting the enterprise (Albini 1971: 63), little substantive historical analysis of this system has been generated.

This same basic point was made two decades ago by Eric McKitrick (1957) in his call for historical studies centered around the Merton model. But in only one sense has McKitrick's hope been answered, and that by a series of publications in urban history principally focusing on the structure of municipal politics and the functions of political machines during the Progressive Era (Miller 1968; Dorsett 1968; Crooks 1968; Lubove 1962). None of these have taken organized crime as their major preoccupation. They are invaluable guides detailing aspects of the social system of organized crime without coming to grips with criminal syndicates themselves. Beyond these historical works and several other exceptions it appears that McKitrick's advice and, therefore, Bell's and Merton's ideas have been less than fruitful. Certainly that is the conclusion offered by the historically minded sociologist William Chambliss (1976). Chambliss writes that the study of organized crime has been both biased and sterile overlooking the "real significance of the existence of [crime] syndicates." He also notes that social scientists have not consistently considered criminal syndicates "as intimately tied to, and in symbiosis with, the legal and political bureaucracies of the state." Social scientists, therefore, "have emphasized the criminality of only a portion of those involved."

The critical stance that Chambliss has in a sense rediscovered already had a major impact in a closely related field: the study of the Mafia phenomenon within the context of Italian/Sicilian history. Carried out by a combination of anthropologists sensitive to historical issues and radical historians (Blok 1974; Pizzorno 1966; J. Schneider 1969; P. Schneider 1972; Weingrod 1968; Boissevain 1974; Hess 1970), these studies view their task as locating the connections between the prevalence of private violence and the structure of economic and political life. For these scholars, following in the path of E. J. Hobsbawm's *Primitive Rebels* (1959), mafiosi are perceived as a variety of the political middlemen or power brokers, whose significance is predicated upon their capacity to acquire and maintain control over the paths linking the local infrastructure of the village to the superstructure of the larger society. They have integrated Merton's notions about political structure and the functions of power brokers, as well as ecological considerations characteristic of Bell's work, with developing analyses of patron-client networks. For them organized crime or Mafia is far from a simple parable of success or a simple conspiracy, alien or otherwise, or indeed an aspect of the ineluctable tendency toward bureaucratization. Rather, Mafia and syndicate criminals are among the consequences of competitive capitalism and state formation.

The point, then, is that American organized crime is the product of deep contradictions in American culture which are surely analogous to the contradictions responsible for the emergence and endurance of Mafia in Sicilian history. Contradictions, we must add, which cannot be pushed aside by ignoring history and interpreting criminology to be solely a policy science.

NOTES

1. This section has been based on Block (1977a).
2. New York *Times,* June 29, 1944; August 16, 1944; May 6, 1946; June 7, 1946; and June 10, 1946.
3. This discussion has been drawn from Block (1977b).

PART III

EPILOGUE

TOWARDS THE REALITY OF HISTORY

AS CONFLICT

Discussions about history are in many ways analogous to much of the contemporary writing on sex. Both phenomena appear to be protean and problematic in nature, susceptible to a host of interpretations and perenially interesting. They are also the subjects of a substantial literature which asks whether they are "art" or "science," or some novel combination of both. Increasingly, they are represented by an enormous series of anthologies and manuals, whose point is that history and sex are most difficult to understand, let alone practice. Clearly, "method" in both endeavors looms larger and larger. To plumb their mysteries, there is another segment of literature which is devoted to a detailed examination of the history and sex professionals. In addition, one can find both history and sex treated as transcendental forces, attributes of the gods. Closely related arguments hold that they are teleological in nature, their end being either a generalized eroticism or a perfect commonwealth. In fact, there is a rich and fascinating tradition which maintains that sexual repression is the engine of history or vice versa. Somewhat less metaphysical, history and sex are viewed instrumentally with the former's importance related to helping social scientists in need of perspective and the latter's being race maintenance. Obviously, they are among the fundamental data of human experience and existence. To equate the various approaches to history with the ways in which sex is understood is, we should add, in no way to denigrate history. Instead, it shows the degree of importance attached to the subject of history, for in the modern world sex is surely one of the most serious issues.

This epilogue, therefore, will first explore the significance of history by examining its relationship to the concept of time and the western world's perception of reality—transcendence and telos. Second, it deals with a crisis in western thought, which ultimately manifested itself through a devaluation of both historical transcendence and historical reasoning. The first aspect of this momentous change is traced through the work of philosophers Hans Meyerhoff and Karl Jaspers. We include an extended discussion of Karl Jaspers' work, which stands as a bridge attempting, in the twentieth century, to reunite scientific history with cosmological history under the imprimatur of existentialist philosophy. The second aspect of history's devaluation is seen through an analysis of ahistoricism in the social sciences. Finally, it is argued that this crisis shows clear signs of abating in the merging of techniques and methods in such disciplines as sociology and history. Specifically, it is claimed that "history from the bottom up" and conflict sociology share a similar ideological base, which is most recognizable in the recent work on crime and criminal justice.

Time as History

We begin with a few commonplaces: time is of the essence, and history is the story or study of time past. Trite as these statements may seem, they are nevertheless at the heart of the matter. They make no sense, for instance, outside a culture that is completely immersed in a notion of time as a constant becoming and in an idea of history which is being made intelligible. Time is motion from the beginning; it is what has been and what will be. Time as historical development is at the foundation of the western world's perception of reality. History is bound with what western civilization understands as the world. For some confirmation, consider the function of history so brilliantly discussed by Erich Auerbach in *Mimesis* (1963). In his analysis of the crucial distinction between antique modes of perceiving reality and those modes within which we continue to operate, the role of history is central. Auerbach's study begins with a comparison of the *Odyssey* and the *Old Testament*:

The two styles, in their opposition, represent basic types: on the one hand fully externalized description, uniform illumination, uninterrupted connection, free expression, all events in the foreground, displaying unmistakeable meanings, few elements of historical development and of psychological perspective; on the other hand, certain parts brought into high relief, others left obscure, abruptness, suggestive influence of the unexpressed, "background" quality, multiplicity of meanings and the need for interpretation, universal-historical claims, development of the concept of the historically becoming, and preoccupation with the problematic (p. 23).

According to Auerbach, the *Old Testament* is a presentation of "universal history." Time and history are coterminous; both begin with the supposedly knowable creation of the world, both will end with the "Last Days, the fulfilling of the Covenant, with which the world will come to an end" (p. 16). What is, therefore, radically different about the *Old Testament* in comparison with the *Odyssey* is its identification with history, its claim to *be* history—indeed the *only* history.

The realm and role of historical consciousness as the key to modern sensibilities is further exemplified by Auerbach in his explication of the work of Petronius. For Auerbach, Petronius reached the limit "to which realism attained in antiquity" (p. 31). The limit is clear from an investigation into the social boundaries of character representation. The boundaries are those of the comic—an extension of the realistic style into the serio-tragic was clearly impossible for antique realists because they could not "make clear the social forces underlying the facts and conditions which they present" (p. 31). In more precise terms, in the realistic literature of antiquity, the existence of society poses no historical problems. What problems it did confront were and could only be ethical. Antique writers were totally concerned with the vices and virtues of characters who existed in a time warp—eternally in the present. Petronius, great as he was, was incapable of describing the relationships between individual events and characters and the economic and political situations of the early Imperial period. If he could have, the reader would be forced into contending with another dimension beyond the individual ethical one— a general historical third dimension, as Auerbach suggested. That sort of presentation, however, would have been counter to the style within which Petronius operated, and, more importantly, would have called for a leap of imagination which he could not accomplish. Auerbach noted that Petronius simply could not conceive of the idea of historical forces.

The peculiar ahistorical manner of viewing individuals and events which was characteristic of antique literature in general, was also present in those magnificent works of history produced by such forefathers of the historical profession as Thucydides and Tacitus. They developed what Auerbach called an ethically oriented historiography notable for its "continuous account of foreground events" which were "statically aprioristic and ethical in content" (p. 34). Taken as a whole, therefore, the Greco-Roman literary tradition including the histories is distinctive for its inability to view its subjects as part of a process, as representatives of social forces, as compacted symbols for a world in motion—in time. In addition, because of the tradition's radical divorce from time as history, the antique works

are in an important sense uninterpretable. With everything in the foreground, with nothing shaded or half-hidden, with change over time out of
the question, there is no background upon which to ground varying interpretations. There are lessons to be learned, vices to be avoided, virtues to
be cultivated, but nothing that is truly problematic. It is only with the
representation of reality developed in the prophetic tradition that interpretation in a determined direction becomes a general method of compre-
hending reality. This is, of course, what occurs in the beginnings of the
Christian Era: "Paul and the Church Fathers reinterpreted the entire
Jewish tradition as a succession of figures prognosticating the appearance
of Christ, and assigned the Roman Empire its proper place in the divine
plan of salvation" (p. 16).

What is important here is not the particular vision of Christian theology, but that this theology was basically historical. Even though the
prophetic writers saw history as determined progress to something beyond
history, they nevertheless presented reality as the movement of the "deep
subsurface layers" of humanity. It is only after the manner or method of
viewing things is established, that the end of things becomes questionable.
At the beginning of the Christian Era, time was clearly two-dimensional:
temporal as history and eternal as prophecy. This dual dimensionality of
time provided a simple and familiar frame of reference for the western
world until the end of the Medieval period. But then came that series of
radical if not revolutionary changes in politics, religion, art, science, and
economics which ushered in the modern world and profoundly altered
the simple and familiar.

The Fragmentation of History

Among the most important effects of these immense changes was the
breakdown of the traditional concept of time as both history and eternity.
In this vein, philosopher Hans Meyerhoff (1968) noted that "there was a
sharp decline or virtual collapse of the dimension of eternity" (p. 89).
All the various notions which postulated an eternal world toward which
human history was ceaselessly advancing were either discarded or became
devoid of significance. Although the idea of eternity as the justification
and salvation of mankind was still retained and indeed promoted by reli-
ious spokesmen, it had "lost its force, function and significance when
placed within the context of the actual human and historical situation"
(p. 90). Meyerhoff argued that it was now a mere belief which had limited
correspondence to the changed and changing human condition. And as

belief in an eternity whose attributes included order and justness faded, the temporal dimension of time loomed larger and larger. Time as history became the medium for understanding humanity. Within this emerging consensus, history itself "became the only permanent, fixed substratum against which the varying manifestations of truths at different ages and in different cultures could be interpreted and evaluated" (p. 95). History would increasingly bear the burden of providing meaning for historical forces, the constant and relentless change that appeared more and more to characterize the world. By the loss of faith in time as eternity, history would now ironically double itself; it was the process of motion—the representation of reality—as well as the meaning of motion. It was in the nineteenth century that the dual role of history would reach its zenith.

In becoming both process and meaning, "history itself was raised to the status of a deity enthroned above and beyond the succession of temporal changes and the relative descriptions (or truths) elicited from the historical process" (p. 96). This meant that scholars would attempt to comprehend particular historical developments by reflecting on the fullness or totality of history. In this manner its attributes in the nineteenth century replicated the discarded dualities of historical theology. Temporal history was the shadow of the design buried in the meaning of history. One of the assumptions of nineteenth century historians, therefore, was that more and better histories collectively considered would ultimately reveal pattern in the flux—the why of it all. The plan of life, as it were, would be slowly realized through the laborious task of scientifically reconstructing the past of humankind. There was, of course, a certain nonsense inherent in this stance. Plumbing the past as the first step in the construction of meaning could be an endless task; the past was almost infinitely expandable. In addition, the more scientific history became, the more disputatious an enterprise it also became. Arguments centered around the choice of methods, the range of sources consulted, the verifiability of documents—in sum, the truth content of the first step. This meant that much historical work would be an exercise limited to the first step, the reconstruction of the past. Nevertheless, there was a certain serenity apparent in the enterprise. Secure in the belief that meaning was out there and that it would eventually be understood, professional historians could find personal satisfaction in viewing themselves as among the select artisans building an edifice without having to know its blueprint in advance. Reflection on the fullness of history would simply have to wait for another generation, the one which would inherit the totally reconstructed past.

Along with the extraordinary development, in terms of quantity, of what might be termed minimalist histories, the nineteenth century spawned historicist theories which claimed to have discovered the immutable historical law. The glory of the law was its identification with and, therefore, illumination of the inexorable method of change and hence the meaning of history. For our purposes it matters little whether the law and thus history was described in evolutionary, dialectical, or cyclical terms. What was significant was that the law was conceived to be eternally true and could thereby "guarantee a sense of order, continuity and permanence within the chaos of historical facts" (Meyerhoff 1968: 97). Along with timeless validity, all the historicist theories with the exception of the cyclical one incorporated a belief in progress as one of the attributes of the law of history. This idea of progress as one of the components allowed a "teleological reading of the theoretical law in accordance with human aspirations" (p. 97). The law revealed both the logic of motion as well as its end. As Meyerhoff put it, "it reconciled theory and practice" (p. 97). The world or reality was historical in the sense that its particular destiny would unfold over time in a particular way to a particular end: history was thus a law subject to its own logic that seemed to be outside the reach of man's idiosyncratic desires and immediate goals. It moved with a majesty of its own.

Unfortunately for the western world's peace of mind or perhaps as a consequence of its loss of peace, neither the serenity of the historical artisans patiently collecting data that would someday contribute to revelation nor the passionate certainty of the historical master builders of the nineteenth century could withstand the loss of belief in the idea of progress. Progress meant believing "that time is a cornucopia, that is, the most friendly, helpful instrument available to man in his perennial struggle for the good life or for the best of all possible worlds" (Meyerhoff 1968: 102). As they were originally formulated, the various historical laws had reconciled the increasing empirical descriptions of temporal change with eternal significance, a sort of secular version of historical theology. But a series of sharp and telling criticisms emerged which challenged all notions of a "unified theory of history" that disclosed a "unidirectional course" (p. 100). It is well to point out, however, that the criticisms did not seriously attack historicism as a method allowing for meaningful and valid descriptions on a limited scale. What was lost was the overarching sense of significance—the goal of history. Methodological historicism, as understood and practiced through most of this century, recognized numerous laws of limited application in contrast to the eternal law. Instead of an inexorable movement of history, it dealt with either several directions or no particular direction at all. Contemporary historical theorizing, until at least a few years ago, collected this diversity of positions and their lack of eternal meaning and tended to call it scientific pluralism.

In this century man has come to experience the second collapse of the dual dimensionality of time. Once again the end of things is not only problematic but almost unintelligible as a concept. The march of time appears senseless. Without a rational plan, without a design which explains temporal history, "time has ceased to be a friendly medium in which human beings could still feel at home despite the collapse of the dimension of eternity" (p. 104). What is most tragic about this situation is that the sense of reality which is historic at its foundation, is devoid of transcendence.

No century has had to face this tragedy of emptiness as resolutely as this one, for no century was ever faced with as much technological progress and destruction as ours. And as might be expected, this century has responded with several novel attempts at reconciling the traditional dual dimensions of time and history. The most interesting have been made by contributors to that exceptionally loose and diverse philosophical movement known as *existentialism.* Existentialist philosophy begins with the "temporality, or historicity, of man's existence" (Meyerhoff 1968: 138), and usually ends with some form of transcendence. Nowhere was this better exemplified than in the work of the German philosopher Karl Jaspers which demanded meaning in and from history as a bulwark against despair. There was, as we shall see, something humanely dramatic in Jaspers' philosophy of history as he tried to find the sublime in the worst of times.

Transcendence in the Twentieth Century

Jaspers worked on a history of the world which was both profound and idiosyncratic. To begin his work on world history, Jaspers stated that philosophy of history had been based on Christian historical theology. And, as we know, Christian philosophy of history saw the coming of the Savior as the axis of world history; the world is historically divided into two temporal divisions corresponding to before and after Christ. But, Jaspers noted that this faith was meaningful only for Christians. In contrast to Christian philosophy of history and similar attempts to develop a particularized version of world history as experienced by one people,

Jaspers proposed a historical axis "that will give rise to a common frame of historical self-comprehension for all peoples" (Jaspers 1953: 1). This axis of history was to be found in the period around 500 B.C., in the spiritual process that occurred between 800 and 200 B.C. He characterized this period as the time when man "becomes conscious of Being as a whole, of himself and his limitations." It was at this point that man awakened from the somnambulence of his prehistory. Man saw the void and experienced the terror of the world and therefore sought both liberation and salvation. This was the period of the Upanishads and Buddha in India, of Confucious and Lao-Tse in China, Zarathustra in Iran, the prophets in Palestine, and the Greece of Homer, Parmenides, Plato, Thucydides, and Archimedes (Jaspers 1953: 2).

It was during this long and remarkable period that the mythical age ended. Man emerged as an individual, philosophers appeared and reason and personality were revealed. As part of the transformation rationality struggled against myth, and religion became recognizably ethical. Jaspers saw the meaning of all this profound activity of the Axial period contained in our existential understanding of it. It was not enough to view the Axial period as a universal stage in the evolution of humanity. Instead, it had to be seen in Jaspers' terms as a "singular ramified historical process" (Jaspers 1953: 17). Its significance stemmed from its success as both the liberator and the creator of history as well as from its ability to be universally appreciated. The Axial period gained in importance as man immersed himself in its achievements; it gave to all something common, something shared, and in its commonness acted as a challenge to unbounded communication. It called for a worldwide "leap into expanding reality." These metaphors unfold the importance of this period for Jaspers. The contemporary salvation for man could only be found by being in the state of endless communication. According to Jaspers, there were no final, definitive answers; there was only tending and yearning—only existential being.

Because of the absence of any absolute, Jaspers' ultimate word was seemingly founded on ever-open communication rather than dogma. In consequence, Jaspers held man to be an end rather than a means encompassed by dogma. Historical research, then, was finding the "presence of our own roots, the sense of that past which, as great for us, belongs to our world, and on the other hand the search for even the remotest fact from which man still speaks to us" (Hennig: 581). He further stated that the present was in communication with the past in *Existenz* and was thus able to speak of possible futures. The past was no longer simply the causal condition of the present, but was a living part of present reality.

The Axial period then has immense significance, for both our present-day historical consciousness and the consciousness of our existential situation are determined by the way in which we perceive this period. It becomes "a question of the manner in which the unity of mankind becomes a concrete reality for us" (Jaspers 1953: 21).

Jaspers continued his schema of world history by postulating that man was now in a second pivotal age. This new age is characterized by modern science and technology and contains, he claimed, the first clearly new material and spiritual developments since the Axial. It is this new period which had its inception at the terminal stage of the Medieval period that is the immediate presupposition of contemporary spiritual life. Most significantly, this new pivotal age was the distinct creation of the western world. The question why the western world (Europe) created this new age was left unanswered. But that Europe entered this process of creation is unquestionable, and the conditions precluding it are enumerative. Jaspers elucidated some of these preconditions that are peculiarly western. There is in the West a "rationality that pursues its course without stay, holds itself open to the cogency of logically consistent thought and of empirical facts that must carry conviction to all men everywhere." The West is typified by an intellectual resoluteness that pursues questions to extremes, that places problems "before the either-or and so brings awareness of the underlying principles" (Jaspers 1953: 42). Clearly, both Max Weber and Søren Kierkegaard were world historical figures to Jaspers. As we can see, Jaspers' enumerative conditions were the workings of the Protestant ethic of Weber within the religious frame of Kierkegaard's transcendentalism. Extreme rationality placed before the either-or must unveil its underlying principles or retreat into a situation of despair. It is, therefore, the conjunction of the original, spiritual Axis with this new western creation that has produced what Jaspers called *Man in the Modern Age* (1957).

Modern man views this Technological age either with the despair born from the Axial period or with an overweening optimism born from the conjunction of the two epochs. Despair arises in the realization that contemporary existence has been metamorphosed by technology into a "technically perfect piece of machinery" and the planet into a "single great factory." Jaspers wrote that the first effects of this metamorphosis were disastrous: the individual experienced a profound dissatisfaction with himself, or even more disastrous, he entered into self-oblivion to become "a functional component of the machine." Jaspers continued noting that technology as a demon had been amply revealed. The demonology arises when the fashioning of life becomes the work of machines.

The mechanization of life means that "man himself becomes one of the raw materials to be purposefully worked over." Nothing of man, either his soul or his faith, is admissible to this new society that is not of utility to the machine. Thus, technology has within its power the destruction of the categorical imperative. Man's willing and his restraint in view of a universally valid law become irrelevant in a machine (Jaspers 1953: 98-123).

It is in this context that certain deadly phenomena have become manifest. For instance, Jaspers wrote that the masses, as opposed to the people, have become a decisive factor in the historical process. Masses are created when people become means. Also, the present situation of the world is overwhelmingly marked by the dissolution of traditional values. It is in this era's lack of faith, in fact, that nihilism has moved to the center becoming a dominant mode of thought. A spiritual vacuum has been created, according to Jaspers, which is causing man to lose himself either in nihilism or ideology. We live in an age of slogans and universal theories. He stated, "everything is the fault of capitalism, liberalism, Marxism, Christianity, or else those unable to defend themselves are picked on and serve as scapegoats: everything is the fault of the Jews, the Germans, etc." (Jaspers 1953: 134). This, then, is the present situation: we are rootless, and in our despair attach ourselves to absolute ideologies that are nothing but abdications from the truth. This abdication, Jaspers noted, is the great deceit for modern man as it spells the end of open communication.

To guide man past corruption, to give man an answer to despair, man must have faith, wrote Jaspers. It is in the certitude of this faith that man can learn that everything is not null and void, that the fear and trembling of life can be overcome. For Jaspers this faith is not a matter of volition, it does not consist of propositions, "but it is the Comprehensive, by which socialism, political freedom, and world order must be borne along their path, because it is from Faith alone that they receive their meaning" (Jaspers 1953: 214). There are three basic categories of faith: faith in man, faith in God, and faith in the possibilities of the world. Both faith in man and in the openness of the world are secured first by faith in God: "The Godhead is origin and goal, it is peace of mind" (Jaspers 1953: 219). In consequence of this faith, the forces that enable man to master his basic animal instincts are set in motion. History then, according to Jaspers, "is man's advance toward liberty through the cultivation of faith" (Jaspers 1953: 221). Though the question of the future of man's manifestation of faith is always open, Jaspers held it as probable that there would be another transformation wrought by the recurring power of the Biblical religion.

This is Jaspers' schema of history: it is open and boundless; it displays tendencies but not dogma; it tells man that he is moving but does not state where; it gives him a faith but no identity except with an unknowable transcendence. Jaspers turned, however, from the outline of history and its anticipation to the meaning of history. He asked why there is such a thing as history. His answer was because man is finite and unperfectible, and in his "metamorphosis through time" toward his awareness of the eternal, there is no other path than history. "Man's imperfection and his historicity are the same thing. History is at one and the same time happening and consciousness of happening, history and knowledge of history" (Jaspers 1953: 233-234). For an individual to be historical he must be unique, irreplaceable, single. And in the love of this individual, "the matrix of Being to which it is attached becomes simultaneously perceptible." Therefore, Jaspers reasoned, man's historicity which appears to be multiple must be seen as subject to the "imperative of the One" (Jaspers 1953: 247-249). For, he wrote, in all of man's dispersion, what is essential is that men are concerned with each other. This concern displays man's relation to others and it is seen as a movement, guided imperceptibly toward God. Conversely, this movement towards God, this feeling of relation, displays man's single origin and unity as created by God. Origin and goal are, therefore, the same: the unity of mankind is on display in history and history is unity in its task of display.

What can one say about Jaspers' philosophy of history beyond noting its desperate urge to believe that there is meaning in history and, therefore, in life, and that his philosophy ultimately collapses into an abstract, obscure, and benevolent religiosity? There is purpose, he claimed, but more importantly there is fellowship. And as the lesson of history is fellowship, its knowable goal must be fraternity. Compassion, kindness and respect for others, all others, are the hallmarks of the fully realized world which he so earnestly desires. For Jaspers this must be the end of things or else he is left with consuming despair over the victory of nihilism as exemplified by that zenith of demonic technology, the Nazi war machine (Jaspers 1947).

History and Social Science

For all its decency of purpose, its humaneness in claiming the world for the categorical imperative in the face of unrestrained will, however,

Jaspers' philosophy of history is finally irrelevant. To many contemporary historians, the efforts of Jaspers and other philosophers of history who consciously seek to reunite the dual dimensionality of time either within or without a religious and existentialist frame are absurd. They belong not to history and science but to literature and metaphysics. For many modern historians it appears to be more than enough to work at intelligent and scientific reconstruction of the past without bothering to engage in asking what it *all* means. As historian J. H. Hexter gleefully put it: "historians have been able to cut whatever filiation their discipline once had to substantive philosophies of history . . . which claimed that through the study of the whole past, history provided the key to the *whole* meaning of man, past, present, and future" (1971: 140). Along with the dumping of transcendentalism, historians, it is claimed, no longer have to concern themselves with demonstrating the immediate relevance of their work. History has been happily dethroned, Hexter commented, from its inflated position as the repository of final meaning for contemporary man and historians no longer must bear the burden of being either wizards or sages. In any case, he added, today "most people seem to look to the behavioral sciences for those varieties of secular salvation which history was once supposed to provide" (p. 141).

There is something ironic, however, in the humbling of history which Hexter celebrated. The position of devaluing the search for and the claims of universal history had the often unfortunate consequence of questioning the worth of any history. The developing pride in the new social sciences made them disdain not only meta-histories like Jaspers', but also the value of historical research per se. Typically, the latter point was based on the exalted idea that the social sciences were true sciences while history was basically some strange amalgam at best distantly related to scientific inquiry. Historical research itself was thus guilty of the same fundamental error as transcendental history: they both had more to do with intuition, need, desire, and finally art, than either had to do with science. If history was humbled when it surrendered transcendence, then it was humiliated when its techniques and methods were attacked. It was one thing for historians to celebrate their escape from meta-historical burdens, but quite another to find themselves and their work relegated to the slag heap of the humanities.

It is extremely important to note, however, that the social scientific fetish of scientism has in no way altered the sense of forces in motion and time as the core of reality. The perception of reality represented in the Bible still retains its hold, and is, as it should be, at the very foundation of all the sciences of man. This means that such modern disciplines as sociology, anthropology, economics, political science, and even biology are "historical sciences" insofar as they recognize and employ a "historical, genetic, or evolutionary method" (Meyerhoff 1968: 97). The point is that social phenomena are understood in all these disciplines as being historical regardless of what particular methods are used to explicate them or whether an individual researcher is interested in the past or the present.

This exemplifies both the irony and absurdity implicit in the denials of the validity of historical research. Surely it is true that transcendental histories like Jaspers have more in common with literature than science, and there is no argument with the evaluation that much historical research has been shabby and unscientific. But taken to its logical end, this attitude produces social scientific work that is consciously and methodologically ahistorical. This means that the devaluation of history has gone through several distinct steps beginning with the collapse of meta-historical efforts and ending with the denial of historicity. History, then, not only tells us nothing about our place in the cosmos, but precious little about anything in particular. The past is insignificant as a guide to the present or the future. In this sense, history has not even retained instrumental value. It is precisely here, however, that the *hubris* of social science has been most damaging. As we shall shortly consider, "ahistorical social science is as often narrow and superficial as sociologically primitive history, and it is certainly no less common" (Thernstrom 1969: 225).

No contemporary historian has examined the pitfalls and perils inherent in this type of social science research as intelligently as Stephan Thernstrom. His starting point as a young historian in the early 1960s was E. H. Carr's familiar dictum that "the more sociological history becomes, and the more historical sociology becomes, the better for both" (Carr 1961: 84). What concerned Thernstrom, however, was that Carr's point had been cited primarily by those interested in cataloging the sins of history. His purpose, then, was in redressing the balance through an analysis of the "uses of the past" by Yankee City researcher Lloyd Warner (Thernstrom 1969). As should be well known, the Yankee City project was a multivolume study conducted by a team of social science researchers led by Warner (1941, 1942, 1945, 1947, 1959) whose purpose was to study social stratification by as complete an examination of an American city— Newburyport, Massachusetts—as possible. What was immediately notable to Thernstrom about this massive assault upon Newburyport was that it was designed to avoid any histories of the city in order, it was claimed, to avoid falling "victim to the biases and preconceptions of the historian" (Thernstrom 1969: 228). But this made for an interesting dilemma. While avoiding histories and historians, the investigators could not avoid making historical assumptions about aspects of Newburyport. Upon what, Thernstrom asked, were these historical assumptions based? The rather stunning answer was that they were supposedly "scientifically derived from direct observation of the image of the past held by present members of the community" (p. 229). By not checking the historical record, the researchers were forced to accept contemporary opinion about the past as though it *were* the true past. And as Thernstrom pointed out, many of the historical assumptions were simply demonstrably false.

For instance, Thernstrom found that Warner's analysis of ethnic residential mobility was based on the premise that the relative social standing of the various neighborhoods of Newburyport had not changed at all between 1850 and 1933. But, Thernstrom noted, this significant assumption of residential stasis was based on faith rather than fact; the historical record was not consulted. In addition, Thernstrom showed that the Yankee City investigators proposed quantitative measures of the changing status of various groups over time without understanding that the composition of these groups was steadily changing. In the end, Thernstrom held that all of the substantive mistakes, and there were many, came from relying on the ahistorical "functionalist assumptions of the equilibrium school of social anthropology" (p. 239). It is a delusion, he stated, that one can understand a city such as Newburyport without an understanding of its real, not its mythic past.

What Thernstrom found inherent in the classic sociological work on Yankee City—structured mistakes resulting from a rigid ahistorical methodology—had also been noted by a number of scholars long interested in the development of the social sciences in general. In fact, Barrington Moore, Jr. (1965) contended earlier that a cavalier attitude toward history was perhaps the greatest error in modern social science. In drawing distinctions between the founders of social science in the nineteenth century and this century's interpreters, it was their involvement with history which appeared to Moore to provide the cutting edge of true significance. Moore held that what distinguished the earlier and much more profound thinkers was the notion that "all of them saw as their scientific problems those which the course of human history had put on the agenda as the significant ones of their epoch" (p. 113). The problems of contemporary social science in the late 1950s, Moore noted, stemmed from the radical decline in the historical perspective noticeable even earlier in Durkheim and Weber although neither totally succumbed to ahistoricism.

The crisis in the social sciences which Moore addressed was partially the result of the consequences of ahistoricism. Together with ahistorical thinking went a decline in the "capacity to analyze critically the existing social order" (p. 122). This meant that the great bulk of contemporary social science had become increasingly formal and abstract. The upshot of all these trends was that "modern sociology had less to say about society than it did fifty years ago" (p. 123). Moore's attack, much like Thernstrom's, was on the attributes of the structural-functionalist school which until recently dominated so much of the social scientific work. That the monolitic front of this approach has begun to crumble within the last decade, however, does not lessen the cogency of their arguments. And for our purposes, their claims are centrally germane as they have to do with both the meaning and uses of history in the contemporary world.

To continue Moore's arguments, he remarked that the ahistorical attitude was really made up of several positions vis-à-vis history. First and foremost was the simple disinclination to think historically. Second was the tendency when considering history to view it as "merely a storehouse of samples" (p. 131) to be used for ahistoricist and quasi-scientific purposes. The initial assumption behind this stance was that the facts of history are separate and discrete units. He blamed this assumption on the peculiar demands of statistical theory for single facts of equal importance. Even though it was not the case, he contended that the "significant facts of history are mere mechanical aggregates" (p. 132). In addition, the demand for uniformity leads away from consideration of the connections over time of various historical facts which, Moore believed, must be the central concern for contemporary social scientists as it once was for the founders. What seemed to most upset Moore as well as the other critics, then, was that by dropping historical questions or a historical approach in the name of science, social scientists dropped the critical stance. Unless problems are seen historically, social scientific work becomes mere descriptions of the status quo. And when that is the case, it all too often means implicit support for the way things are. History reveals connections and contradictions, the world of other possibilities from which the critical stance is sustained. Lose that, Moore warned, and one ends with abstractions which are technically proficient but concerned with trivial matters.

The strength of Moore's position was revealed in his closing statements on "strategy in social science":

Social scientists, we may conclude, condemn themselves to unnecessary frustrations by trying to erect an intellectual structure that will permit predictions in the manner of the natural sciences. Meanwhile, pre-occupied with its efforts to become 'scientific,' social science overlooks more important and pressing tasks. The main structural features of what society can be like in the next generation are already given by trends at work now. Humanity's freedom of maneuver lies within the framework created by its history. Social scientists and allied scholars could help to widen the area of choice by analyzing the historical trends that now limit it (p. 159).

Some Reconciliations

To this point we have considered several of the central themes dealing with the concept of time as exemplified in the meanings of history, including the profound changes in the value of history during the modern period. We have argued for history in the sense that without it life appears to be either absurd as the existentialists put it, or caught up in formally abstract and trivial matters. Especially important in this regard is the sterility inherent in formulating problems ahistorically as Thernstrom and Moore have demonstrated. But, it is one thing to discuss the banalities of ahistorical social science research and the decay of the metahistorical tradition, and quite another to leave the impression that modern scholarship remains in a quandary. If nothing else, Thernstrom and Moore are themselves examples of the care and diligence that some contemporary scholars were and are taking in investigating the relationships between historical and social scientific methods. Left unexplored is the recent and dramatic growth of work in social history and historical sociology, which display a mutuality of purpose and technique. There has been, during the last two decades, a number of significant studies which rather neatly mirror Carr's dictum.

As far as professional history is concerned, the best of this recent work usually can be found in the *Journal of Social History, Journal of Interdisciplinary History, Past and Present, Comparative Studies in Society and History,* and *History and Theory.* Probably the most fruitful examples of this expanding mutuality can be seen in the vigor by which historians have embraced statistical procedures first worked out in the related social sciences. Before celebrating this development, however, it is important to keep in mind another of J. H. Hexter's (1971) cautionary principles:

> The notion that in recent years all the Good Things in history come
> to it by way of quantification and the social sciences is not only
> false when retrojected into the past; it is wrong when projected into
> the future. It has not been nor is it ever likely to be true. It implies a
> conception of the resources available to the historical understanding
> far too narrow and pharisaical to do them justice. These resources
> are limited only by the full range of a historian's experiential knowl-
> edge, not by the exiguous bounds of his knowledge of statistical
> procedures and of the social sciences (p. 149).

Clearly then, we are not discussing all of the contemporary historical
profession nor arguing that all historical scholarship needs quantification.
Nevertheless, it is surely true that a great deal of what is currently best
and most exciting in professional history is the product of quantification
and the merging of historical and sociological perspectives.

The current fascination with statistical analysis among professional
historians can be traced, according to Jacob M. Price, to 1910, a point
which signaled the beginning of a long and desultory period of development within the historical profession, which created the proper ambiance
for historians "to seek greater precision through the fuller use of quantitative data and techniques" (1969: 3). Perhaps the most important among
the numerous reasons for the growing use of or interest in statistical
techniques was the division of history into such subdisciplines as economic
history and social history. In any case, the period which began in 1910
stretched to at least 1945 and marked in general only a very gradual transi-
tion in historians' interests in quantification. The culmination of this
period of slow growth was reached in 1945, Price held, with the publication of the *Historical Statistics of the United States* (U.S. Bureau of
Census, 1949), a project which involved social scientists, statisticians,
and historians. It was following this publication, Price added, that the
tendencies within the historical profession for statistical rigor and the
systematic investigation of statistical data became much more pronounced.

Outside of the startling mathematical developments in the field of
economic history led by American economic historians, the major ad-
vances in the application of quantification to historical analysis post-1945
were taken by French social historians and historical sociologists. Price
reported that Fernand Braudel's (1949) magnificent work on Mediterranean history in the sixteenth century, which incorporated statistical
data on population, prices, and commerce, marked a "symbolic turning
point" for the historical profession in general (p. 6). Braudel's *"succes*

d'estime," published in 1949, paved the way for French developments in historical demography and sociology whose influence on both American and continental scholars has been enormous.

A neat survey of historical work that exemplifies the merging of technique and purpose explicit in the work of Braudel and other French scholars such as Louis Henry, Emmanuel LeRoy Ladurie, and Pierre Goubert has been done by Edward Shorter in his guide *The Historian and the Computer* (1971). Shorter divided what he considered the best of the recent quantitative histories into two broad fields: political history and sociological history. Under political history he distinguished three subfields—legislative behavior, electoral behavior, and collective biography. Concerning legislative behavior, Shorter noted the work of Patrick and Trevor Higonnet on the French legislature of 1846-1848 (1967), and William O. Aydelotte's (1962-1963) study of voting patterns in the British House of Commons, also during the 1840s. Turning to the electorate, Shorter commented on Karl O'Lessker's (1968-1969) analysis of the German elections of 1930 and 1932, which indicated that supporters of Hitler were not the "politicized middle classes identified by other scholars, but a combination of traditional rightists and former nonvoters" (p. 15). The last category under political history was collective biography. Among the works discussed were Theodore K. Rabb's (1967) investigation of the striking expansion of English commerce at the turn of the seventeenth century through a detailed examination of commercial investors, as well as R. Burr Litchfield's (1969) study of the decline of Florentine patrician families.

Contemporary sociological history was divided by Shorter into studies of revolutions and mass movements, social structure, and finally demographic phenomena. Beginning with revolutions, Shorter related the methodological acuteness of Gilbert Shapiro's then uncompleted study of the French revolution, especially his analysis of the "*cahiers de doleances.*" Also noted was the prolific and exciting scholarship of Charles Tilly on collective violence and labor disturbances. Tilly, one of the most creative sociologist-historians, has been conducting a massive study designed to test the relationship between politics and mass movements (*The Rebellious Century,* 1975). Under social structure, the work of H. J. Dyos (1968) on the London suburb of Camberwell during the Victorian period as well as Lynn H. Lees' (1969) study of the Irish in nineteenth century London were cited as examples. The final work mentioned in this category was Sam Bass Warner's (1968) study of Philadelphia. Warner used computers in analyzing such sources as census returns and city directories for the years 1770-1780, 1830-1860, and 1920-1930 in order to plot the changes in the distribution of income, occupation, and ethnic groups in Philadelphia. Warner discovered a significant degree of both ethnic and occupational segregation and concluded that "an enduring tradition of 'privatism' is one of the forces most responsible for the ruin of the American city" (p. 25). The third aspect of sociological history is demography, the study of population. In this section the marvelous work of Louis Henry (1967) in the area of family reconstitution was recounted.

It seems apparent from Shorter's survey that much contemporary history is methodologically indistinguishable from other social scientific work. As historians have incorporated quantification into their analyses, they have been met by sociologists, demographers, economists, and political scientists employing a longitudinal approach. By the late 1960s, this merging of methods and approach reached the point where historian Richard T. Vann (1969) could ask whether demography for instance, must become historical. Quoting Louis Henry, Vann noted that " 'The lines of thought that classical demography followed often led to impasses because its methods were too rigorously focused on the present—on events of the moment' " (p. 75). Demography had to abandon its focus on the present if it expected to fully explore both nuptiality and fertility. Again quoting Henry, Vance wrote:

> If there are no permanent and rigid statistics in demography, there are certainly relations among phenomena. By studying these, we can hope to improve our knowledge and our ability to forecast. Only the observation of as long a chronological series as is possible will furnish all the relations observable up to the present. In demography, therefore, the important factor is not to possess the most recent information about the population of a certain country or city, but to be able to dispose of homogeneous retrospective statistics extending as far into the past as possible. If this is accepted, it is hardly a paradox to say that historical demography is all demography (p. 76).

Crime and the Plebes

It is well at this point to reconsider some of the notions raised earlier in the discussion of Barrington Moore's criticisms of ahistorical social science. Moore stressed two criteria for creative work in social science: the historical approach and its consequence, a critical stance. One might well wonder, therefore, if the recent explosion of historical work aided by the computer, featuring all the currently fashionable statistical manipulations, may not be drawing historians into technically proficient but essentially trivial exercises. In some cases this is undoubtedly true. However, in the main, the merging of social science methods with the historical approach has been both radical and liberating. In one sense it has to be, as can be seen by briefly returning to Richard T. Vann's (1969) discussion of history and demography:

> The establishment through statistical means of the existence of family limitation in the past is an extraordinary example of how the most intimate details in the private lives of quite obscure people, who produced no literary evidence at all, can nevertheless become the object of our knowledge. Even if they had done so, such was the force of repression that "direct" evidence would have been distorted, whereas the evidence of behavior, when quantitatively analyzed, is clear. Once again, the historian who looks directly for intentions finds his traditional historiographical tools failing; the methods of the quantitative social sciences turn out to be more suitable for historical explanation (p. 74).

The ability to understand the "private lives of quite obscure people" is the key to what is liberating in contemporary quantitative history. Statistical analysis is the means by which historical studies escape dwelling on elite and literate populations. It opens up for serious consideration the mass of past humanity whose lives are basically unapproachable with traditional historical methods. Quantification has finally fueled what has been called "history from the bottom up" (Lees and Lees 1976: xiv). At its most basic, history from the bottom up is the product of study animated by what Stephan Thernstrom and Richard Sennett call "an eagerness . . . to embrace the social experience of ordinary, unexceptional people" (1969: vii).

Among the many topics which have been either discovered or significantly reworked by empathetic historians and social scientists have been groups such as women, urban immigrants, adolescents, and criminals; institutions such as asylums, prisons, and the family; and lastly, processes such as social mobility, urbanization, family limitation, and public order. It is, of course, the recent work on crime, criminals, and social control which is of immediate concern. It must be kept in mind, however, that contemporary histories of crime and criminals have emerged from both the search for new sources and methods, and interest in nonelite populations. Consider, for example, *The Peoples of Philadelphia* (1973), a collection of essays edited by Allen F. Davis and Mark H. Haller covering the history of lower-class life in Philadelphia. Included in the twelve articles which deal with poverty, immigrants, residential mobility, and urban housing are several whose focus is crime, criminals and social control. Specifically, they analyze the relationship between nineteenth century urbanization and violence, the rise of gangs as a consequence of changes in the social functions, composition, and roles of fire companies, and overall crime patterns in the city during the mid-nineteenth century (Feldberg 1973; Laurie 1973; Johnson 1973).

Perhaps even more to the point, a recent edition of the *Journal of Social History* (summer 1975) was entirely composed of articles on crime and criminals. Among the contributions were J. M. Beattie's (1975) study of "The Criminality of Women in Eighteenth-Century England," Guido Ruggiero's (1975) "Sexual Criminality in the Early Renaissance," Wilbur R. Miller's (1975) comparative analysis of "Police Authority in London and New York, 1830-1870," and Barbara A. Hanawalt's (1975) fine work on "The Pattern of Crime Among the Fourteenth-Century English Nobility." Clearly, within the ranks of contemporary urban historians, social historians, historians of women, historical sociologists, and demographic historians, as well as most other groups of social scientists whose work is marked by an interest in the history of lower-class life, the study of crime and related subjects is more and more the fashion.

To truly appreciate the upsurge of interest in the history of crime and affiliated topics, a survey of dissertations in history over the course of the twentieth century as well as a perusal of several of the leading historical journals is revealing. Consider histories of the police. In 1936 Walter Prescott Webb's article on the Texas Rangers appeared in the *Southwestern Historical Quarterly* (Webb 1936). Eleven years later the *New England Quarterly* published an article on the Boston police strike (Lyons 1947). However, from 1961 through 1973 there were at least six studies in major historical journals including two dissertations on the police completed at the University of Chicago and Cornell University (Jeffries 1961; Baenziger 1969; Friend 1971; Johnson 1972; Watts 1973; Greenberg 1973). Turning to dissertations and articles on the history of crime and aspects of urbanization the point is much clearer. With only one minor exception (Wilcox 1941), all the articles and dissertations in this area appeared in the first half of the 1970s. This includes nine dissertations from such institutions as the University of Rochester, the University of Minnesota, Notre Dame University, Rice University, The University of Chicago, UCLA, and the University of Maryland (Bonkrude 1970; Feldberg 1970; Schneider 1971; Boyer 1972; Helper 1972; Johnson 1972; Monkkonen 1973, Block 1975; Rhines 1975). And finally, if one constructed a more inclusive list composed of histories of crime and criminal justice institutions in America, their distribution would appear as follows:

	1890s	1920s	1930s	1940s	1950s	1960s	1970s
Number of articles and dissertations	2	1	6	4	7	7	18

Over 43 percent of the studies were undertaken during the first six years of the current decade, and obviously well over 50 percent during the last sixteen years. And as can be seen from the titles of just two of the most recent dissertations, the range of issues covered in this contemporary historical work on crime and criminal justice is substantial: Charlotte C. Rhines (1975) "A City and its Social Problems: Poverty, Health and Crime in Baltimore, 1865 – 1875"; Estella B. Freedman (1976) "Their Sister's Keepers: The Origins of Female Corrections in America."

Without meaning to overstate the case, it does seem that the perils of ahistoricism are recognized and increasingly surmounted by a varied collection of social scientists. At the same time, it appears that the historical establishment now is producing and supporting work whose techniques and methods derive from the allied social sciences. At the very least, then, the instrumental value of history, which seemed to be threatened only a short time ago, has been vigorously resurrected. But the recent efforts in history and the social sciences which we have been cataloging signal even more important developments. Histories of crime and criminal justice, for example, are part of an effort within segments of the historical profession to escape older, more conservative models of the American past. Interest in exploring aspects of lower-class life which include the host of social pathologies and problems is based on the premise that our present has been structured out of past conflicts whose features are typically oppression and repression. History from the bottom up, or *plebeian history* as E. P. Thompson calls his work (1975: 255), stems from a renascent Marxism or perhaps more accurately an eclectic radicalism indebted to Marxist principles. This means, of course, that meta-historical attitudes have also slipped back into the fray. Slipped back is appropriate because they are usually implicit in the radical style and are surely far removed from the ones articulated by mid-century existentialists.

What has happened within professional history has been paralleled by develoments within sociology. The rise of plebeian history is matched by the rise of the conflict school in sociology. The differences between the conflict approach and its major academic enemy, functionalism, have been neatly summarized by William J. Chambliss (1973), who writes that "the conflict perspective sees social inequality as being a chief source of social conflict" (p. 4). Functionalists, on the other hand, tend to either disregard the fact of social conflict or when noting it, view it as merely an attribute of man. They are, he holds, almost incapable of seeing conflict as the consequence of structured social inequality. As part of their myopia, functionalists view the state and law as institutions representative of the whole society acting primarily to further the common good. In contrast, conflict theorists see law and the state as oppressive instruments used by the "ruling classes for their own benefit" (p. 4). Conflict theory might be described as sociology from the bottom up. Significantly, it is historicist at its core.

History, it appears, is ultimately inescapable as it is the foundation of the western world's perception of reality. Its power as both the scientific reconstruction of the past as well as the meaning of it all recur whenever researchers regardless of whether they are sociologists, demographers, or professional historians shake themselves loose from the tyranny of ideology, opting instead for the critical stance. Historical studies of crime and criminal justice are significant not simply because they have instrumental value and clear up mistakes, but because they can also provide a base for what is now called *The New Criminology* (Taylor, Walton, and Young 1974).

PART IV

APPENDICES

REFERENCE AND RESEARCH GUIDE:

A Commentary on Historical Sources

This section offers a commentary and listing of a variety of works pertinent to the topics covered in this book. It has been intended to help the researcher, student, and general reader locate various kinds of source materials for further study, and to supplement many of the sources already cited. In addition, and where appropriate, annotations are included, as well as some additional descriptions and commentary on many of the major areas covered in the text. Essentially, four main areas of inquiry are approached: (1) the nature and method of history; (2) folklore and history; (3) the American "Wild West"; and (4) organized crime. Since the study of folklore is a field far beyond the traditional areas of criminology, we offer a more extended discussion of its content. As in the text of this volume, most sources are indicated only briefly by author and date of publication; the complete citations appear in APPENDIX B: References.

The Nature and Method of History

The study of history has been one of humankind's more enduring scholarly activities, and the volume of works prepared on its subject matter is awesome. Consequently, our intention here in this preliminary section is to suggest only a sampling of materials dealing with the nature and method of history.

For those with only a minimal background in historical study, Lester D. Stephens' (1974) *Probing the Past* represents an excellent introduction. It examines the nature, scope, and uses of history, and discusses the relationship of history to the other social sciences. Once past the introductory stage, one of the most moving and profound works to turn to is Marc

Bloch's *The Historian's Craft* (1953). Written in a simple style, the book is an intelligent guide through the difficult terrain of professional history. Another study in much the same vein is E. H. Carr's challenging *What is History* (1961). As is already clear, one of Carr's central points calls for more sophisticated, interdisciplinary work especially between history and sociology.

If one seriously considers Carr's suggestion, there are a number of studies which must be consulted. For instance, *Explanation in Social Science* (Brown 1963) and the reader *Sociology and History: Theory and Research* (Cahnman and Boskoff 1964) raise provocative questions about the logic and manner of interdisciplinary work. Also concerned with the relationship of history to the social sciences is *History as Art and as Science* (Hughes 1964). One chapter in particular is relevant as it raises the significant issue of the relationship between history and psychoanalysis. Hughes writes:

> For the historian as for the psychoanalyst, an interpretation ranks as satisfactory not by passing some formal scientific test but by conveying an inner conviction. For both, plural explanations are second nature. . . . Indeed, for both of them the word "cause" is admissible only if defined with extreme flexibility; most of the time they prefer to express their interpretations in terms more clearly suggesting the possibility of alternative ways of looking at the matter. Both deal in complex configurations, searching for a thread of inner logic that will tie together an apparent chaos of random words and actions (p. 47).

Another work which explores the merging of history and psychoanalysis is the reader edited by Bruce Mazlich (1963), *Psychoanalysis and History*.

To return to history and sociology, other valuable studies include *History as Social Science* (Landes and Tilly 1971) and Shorter's (1971) *The Historian and the Computer*. To ponder both the meaning of history and history's relationship to other social science disciplines, one must also consider the arguments raised by J. H. Hexter in *Doing History* (1971). In a witty, elegant and provocative manner Hexter makes clear what professional history is:

> What I love to watch the skillful pro do is make those easy-looking but difficult right moves that, whatever the situation may be, distinguish the winners from the losers. Lawrence Stone rendering visible the deterioration of the social value of aristocratic status in early seventeenth-century England by tracing the fall in the market value of titles of honor. Roland Mousnier detecting the hostility of regional

France to the royal center in noble incitement and support of peasant revolts against the king's tax collectors. Edmund Morgan tracing the topography of old and current local feuds in the alignment of opposition to and support of the mother country in the Stamp Act crisis. . . . Sir John Neale, by the masterly mobilization of a few scraps of evidence, reversing a venerable judgement on the extent to which the initial settlement of the English Church in 1559 was the work of the virgin queen (pp. 6-7).

Clearly, what excites Hexter is the sophisticated and economical use of historical methods. And on the methods of historical study, there are many helpful volumes. Initially, *The Modern Researcher* (Barzun and Graff 1962; 1970) describes the basic methods used by historians, while a more detailed discussion of research issues appears in Gustavson (1955) and Garraghan (1946). For informative and interesting commentaries on historians' search for evidence, Robin W. Winks' (1968) edited volume *The Historian as Detective* is especially recommended, as well as the Lipset and Hofstadter (1968) volume *Sociology and History: Methods*.

The question of method(s) in historical writing and research is exceptionally broad, involving oftentimes rather sweeping philosophical questions. There is no way around it: once the methods are questioned or examined so the purpose of history is raised. In almost all of the books already noted, the authors deal with both issues. The implicit connections between purpose and method are made explicit in G. J. Renier's (1965) intriguing *History: Its Purpose and Method*. Renier's study is dominated by a notion of history which is both pragmatic and instrumental. Another work which confirms the relationship between methods and philosophy is W. H. Walsh's (1960) *Philosophy of History: An Introduction*. In this same vein one should consider Sydney Hook's (1963) collection of essays *Philosophy and History*. Among the essays are Morton White's "The Logic of Historical Narration," Leo Gershoy's "Some Problems of a Working Historian," Carl G. Hempel's "Reasons and Covering Laws in Historical Explanation," and Bruce Mazlich's "On Rational Explanation in History."

Finally, no guide to history would be complete without mentioning those works which deal with the history of historical writing. One place to start is with *A History of Historical Writing* (Barnes 1962). Additionally, there are two superb collections of the changing styles and concerns of historians edited by Hans Meyerhoff (1959), and Fritz Stern (1956).

Folklore and Oral Tradition

Professional folklorists, like their counterparts in other fields, have produced the usual outpouring of books, articles and reference works. The purpose of the following section is to provide the historical criminologist interested in folklore as a source of evidence with a useful but concise introduction to major perspectives, theories, methods, and materials on folklore generally, and the folklore of deviance specifically. As such, the section is necessarily selective, but the annotated sources frequently include extensive bibliographic material to guide the scholar further into the folklore literature. In addition, many include extensive illustrations of folklore materials.

Like other disciplines focused on human social life, folklore is characterized by conflict over and ambiguity of definitions. The following selections are certainly not exhaustive but offer a range of perspectives on important folklore themes and provide materials for the historical criminologist to develop an awareness of crucial issues and a working knowledge of folklore products and processes and folklorists' problems and practices. The references, with some overlap, are divided into seven sections. These include: (1) folklore texts and overviews; (2) methodological discussions; (3) references, bibliographies, and indexes; (4) journals; (5) theoretical approaches and issues; (6) folklore genres, and (7) folklore of crime and deviance.

TEXTS AND OVERVIEWS

Before moving into the intensive study of a particular folklore item, general knowledge of the discipline can be gained from the following texts and collected essays by leading American folklorists.

A useful introduction to the field is Jan Brunvand's, *The Study of American Folklore: An Introduction* (1968). This text is organized around folklore genres in current circulation in American oral tradition and material culture. The materials of folklore study are subdivided into verbal, partly verbal and nonverbal forms, with each subsection consisting of the most important genre. Each genre chapter contains a definition, examples of the genre, suggested lines of analysis, subtypes of the genre, and bibliographic references. An introductory section explores the crucial issues, what is folklore? what is folklore study? and who are "the folk"? Brunvand's most recent contribution, *Folklore: A Study and Research Guide* (1976), also includes a beginning discussion of folklore materials and folklore study with a brief but useful glossary of key terms and concepts. The book is a research guide for the beginner and has an extensive survey of folklore reference guides and substantive contributions. This excellent research guide consists of seven subareas: (1) bibliographies and references; (2) journals and series; (3) histories, surveys and texts; (4) theories; (5) genres; (6) studies of text, texture, and context of folklore; and (7) studies of the folk.

A wide-ranging and useful compilation is Tristram Potter Coffin's, *Our Living Traditions: An Introduction to American Folklore* (1968). A large number of contributors, some of them leading folklorists, provide more detailed discussions of folklore definitions, the field of folklore, folklore methods, and various genres.

One of the more prolific contemporary folklorists, Richard Dorson, also produced a text and overview of the field, appropriately entitled: *American Folklore* (1959a). Dorson approaches folklore in the context of American history and offers interpretive discussions of the lore of different groups and eras central to the country's development. In addition to a dated but useful bibliography, Dorson provides a table of motifs—transhistorical and transcultural recurrent themes—used in the text. An essential introductory work for the historian is Dorson's *American Folklore and the Historian* (1971). This theoretical and methodological collection consists of reprints of Dorson's contributions to the interface between folklore and history and covers such topics as the historical grounding of American folklore, folklore in literature, "fakelore," and the utility of folklore study for historical research in general and local history in particular.

Dorson has also published three compilations on general folklore subjects and issues. The first of these, *Folklore: Selected Essays* (1972c), offers articles on folklore as a field of study, theory, method, genre discussions and two essays on the trustworthiness of folklore as an historical source and the utility of folklore evidence for the history of nonelites. Another work edited by Dorson is *Folklore and Folklife: An Introduction* (1972d). This collection opens with a comprehensive overview of current approaches to folklore study and is a brief but essential discussion for the uninitiated. The theoretical introduction is followed by essays on various genres and a section on the methods of folklore study. Dorson's most recent contribution is *Folklore and Fakelore; Essays Toward a Discipline of Folk Studies* (1976b), a multifaceted collection of his previously published essays. The prospects of academic folkloristics, general theoretical issues, discussions of the oral process, examples of recent field work, and media folk heroes are the general subject headings. The essays "Folklore in the Modern World" and "Oral Literature, Oral History, and the Folklorist," are important contributions to the definition of folklore and its relationship to related areas of study.

A former student of Dorson's, Alan Dundes, also surveys the field in two anthologies. The first of these, *The Study of Folklore* (1965), opens with a concise discussion of the definition of folklore and the field of folkloristics, and includes material by recognized leaders of the discipline on the definition of folklore, modes of transmission, origin and diffusion of folklore items, folklore forms, functions and meanings of folklore, and selected folklore studies. The second work is a collection of Dundes' essays entitled: *Analytic Essays in Folklore* (1975a). These essays include his contributions to folklore theory and method and numerous studies of diverse genres from "structural" and psychoanalytic perspectives. Some of the more provocative discussions of the function and meaning of folklore, folklore genres and specific folklore items are included in this book, which also provides an ample bibliography.

Another useful overview is the *Standard Dictionary of Folklore, Mythology and Legend* (1972) edited by Maria Leach and Jerome Fried. This is a revised edition of a work that covers numerous folklore topics in an uneven but sometimes useful manner.

METHODOLOGICAL DISCUSSIONS

Although it is unlikely that criminologists will collect their own folklore, the evaluation of available folklore materials will be facilitated by some knowledge of folklorist's methods of collecting, archiving, and analyzing. These selections provide a basic introduction to folklore methods and each references additional sources on the subject. Several of the works cited above in "Texts and Overviews" also have useful methodological articles. In addition to general folklore methods, key contributions to the relationship of folklore and oral tradition to historical study are listed.

The most comprehensive discussion of folklore collection methods is Kenneth S. Goldstein (1964). The guide is similar to other social science field work guides and has chapters on the definition of the problem, prefield preparations, establishing and maintaining rapport, observation and interviewing techniques, and supplementary methods. A useful bibliography of writings relevant to folklore methodology is included. The interested reader can refer to Richard Dorson, *Folklore and Folklife: An Introduction* (1972d), for several methodological essays with more up-to-date references.

An old but recently reissued treatise on folklore and historical method is George Gomme, *Folklore As An Historical Science* (1968) first published in 1908. A more recent contribution is historian Jan Vansina's *Oral*

Tradition: A Study in Historical Methodology (1965), translated by H. M. Wright. There is no complete overlap between oral tradition and folklore but Vansina's discussion serves as an essential reference. He covers the definition of oral tradition, its relationship to written history, modes of transmission, sources and types of distortion of oral testimony, methods of collecting, evaluating and interpreting oral testimony, and the characteristics of oral traditional genres.

REFERENCES, BIBLIOGRAPHIES, AND INDEXES

This section lists some of the general academic sources—bibliographies and abstracts; and references more unique to folklore study—archive directories and thematic indexes.

Bibliographic listings and abstracts of folklore writings appear in several publications. From 1955 to 1962 the *Journal of American Folklore* included a supplement consisting of international works, and *Southern Folklore Quarterly* provided references from 1937 to 1973. The former reference was replaced by *Abstracts of Folklore Studies* which was published until 1975. Since that time, the *Publications of the Modern Language Association* has included a comprehensive folklore bibliography. A nonfolklore bibliography with a few references dealing with the relationship of folklore and oral tradition to historical study is Manfred Waserman, compiler, *Bibliography on Oral History* (1975).

Much folklore material is not published but is included in archives at various universities. A list of these archives and their addresses is Peter Aceves and Magnus Einarsson-Mullarky, *Folklore Archives of the World* (1968).

A major task for many folklorists is the identification and cataloging of recurrent themes in folk literature. These "motifs" or "types" can be found in Stith Thompson's *Motif-Index of Folk Literature,* six volumes, second edition (1955-58), and his *The Types of the Folktale (1961).*

JOURNALS

Folklore materials can be found in several national and regional journals and, occasionally, in nonfolklore publications. Among the most important folklore journals are the *Journal of American Folklore* and the *Journal of the Folklore Institute.* A more complete listing of regional and specialty journals can be found in Jan Brunvand, *Folklore: A Study and Research Guide* (1976), pages 40 to 43. Also of interest is the *Journal of Popular Cul-*

ture, which often publishes folklore material in addition to its regular treatment of topics of interest to folklorists from the popular culture perspective.

THEORETICAL APPROACHES

Folklore as a separate discipline has developed an eclecticism that draws
on fields as diverse as psychoanalysis, history and literature—cutting across
the usual boundary between social sciences and the humanities. This diversity has facilitated a more flexible definition of the field but with considerable conflict and confusion. The following sources provide an overview
of major theoretical approaches and an introduction to current issues
central to theories of folklore as a communicative process.

Three previously mentioned works include important theoretical discussions and are fully referenced in the section on "Texts and Overviews."
These are Richard Dorson's *Folklore and Folklife: An Introduction*
(1972d), his *American Folklore And The Historian* (1971), and Alan
Dundes' *Analytic Essays In Folklore* (1975a). The latter includes essays
from the structural perspective in folklore, a point of view more fully
examined in Pierre Maranda and Eli Kongas' edited publication: *Structural
Analysis Of Oral Tradition* (1971). The contributors, anthropologists,
linguists, and folklorists, apply the perspective to myth, ritual, folk drama,
folktale, riddle and folksong in attempt to reveal the processes of human
communication about the nature of man and his universe.

The more general anthropological approach to folklore is portrayed in
a special issue on "Culture and Folklore" edited by Jerome Mintz (1965)
and published in the *Journal of the Folklore Institute.* Several useful
critiques of past definitions of folklore and important new approaches to
the field and its theoretical underpinnings appear in *Toward New Perspectives In Folklore.* This collection of essays appeared in the *Journal of
American Folklore* 81 (1971) and as a special publication of the American
Folklore Society edited by Americo Paredes and Richard Bauman (1972).
The articles by Roger Abrahams, "Personal Power and Social Restraint in
the Definition of Folklore"; Richard Bauman, "Differential Identity and
the Social Base of Folklore", Dan Ben-Amos, "Toward a Definition of
Folklore in Context"; and Alan Dundes, "Folk Ideas as Units of Worldview" all raise important theoretical questions about folklore.

Definitions and theories of folklore often hinge on the materials included and the definitions of the "folk" and the "lore" involved. Important issues concerning the definition of the "folk" are included in *The
Urban Experience and Folk Tradition,* another special publication of the
American Folklore Society and edited by Americo Paredes and Ellen

Stekert (1971). The issue of the relationship of oral tradition to written modes of communication is currently important. Discussion and references can be found in Richard Dorson, "Folklore in the Modern World," pages 33 to 73 in his *Folklore and Fakelore* (1976a), and illustrative material supporting an argument for folklore in print can be found in Alan Dundes and Carl Patger, editors, *Urban Folklore from the Paperwork Empire* (1975).

FOLKLORE GENRES

Much folklore scholarship, especially the work of more literary oriented folklorists, centers on folklore genres. Genres are the subtypes or forms of folklore such as ballad, legend, or folksong, and knowledge of each is useful for accessing and analyzing folklore materials. In this section, an overview of genre study references is followed by a selective discussion of genres most relevant to the concerns of historical criminologists.

Useful overviews of genres are found in Jan Brunvand's two texts, *The Study Of American Folklore: An Introduction* and *Folklore: A Study and Research Guide,* cited above. Several important theoretical essays can be found in Alan Dundes' *Analytic Essays In Folklore,* also mentioned above.

Brunvand's (1976) recent overview of folklore materials classifies material into four main categories—folksay; folk literature; folk beliefs, customs, games; and folklife or material culture—each of which includes traditional genres. For purposes of this essay, folk literature is most important. This is not to say that other genres within the remaining categories are irrelevant, but that those genres included in folk literature most likely contain information on crime or deviance. Of the other categories, folksay covers the study of expressions, proverbs, riddles and rhymes; folk beliefs, customs, and games focus on festivals, superstitions, gestures, dances; and folklife concentrates on arts, crafts, architecture, clothing styles. These genres should not be ignored entirely for purposes of a specific study. For example, a student of banditry would gain useful insights about public perceptions of outlawry during one of the many festivals held in communities with a bandit tradition.

Folk literature consists of several interrelated genres, each of which also has numerous subtypes. The most important are folktale; legend; myth; folksong; ballad; folk poetry—especially the "toasts" of urban blacks; and jokes. These genres interrelate and change in historical importance, often creating difficulty in the classification of any particular item. The following references comprise a beginning list for the interested scholar and an introduction into issues of folklore classification and interpretation. Supplementing these initial references is a brief attempt to provide a working definition of each genre and to suggest its crucial features and its significance for historical criminologists.

For the legend genre, the collection of essays edited by Wayland Hand and published as *American Folk Legend* (1971) is especially useful. A beginning overview of writings on myth is Richard Dorson's (1976c) "Mythology and Folklore: A Review Essay," in his *Folklore and Fakelore*. Several special issues of journals have featured myth discussion. Among them see Thomas A. Sebeok (1955), Henry A. Murray (1959a), and Melville Jacobs (1966). A study that illustrates the more contemporary approach to myth is Henry Nash Smith, *Virgin Land: The American West As Symbol and Myth* (1950).

For the folksong see D. K. Wilgus's *Anglo-American Folksong Scholarship Since 1898* (1959). Scholars interested in the ballad should refer to MacEdward Leach and Tristram P. Coffin's anthology: *The Critics and the Ballad* (1961). Malcom G. Laws' revised edition of *Native American Balladry* (1964) includes references to numerous ballads and explanatory chapters on the ballads, their meaning and content, the relationship of American to British balladry, the ballad as a depiction of national "spirit," and an exploration of the ballad's relationship to historical fact.

A less well-known genre, the "toast," deserves attention. Defined as the oral epic poetry of the urban black, this genre is a particularly intriguing form of folklore. Useful collections and discussions are: Bruce Jackson, *Get Your Ass in the Water and Swim Like Me* (1974); Roger D. Abrahams, *Deep Down in the Jungle: Negro Narrative Folklore from the Streets of Philadelphia* (1970); and William Labov et al., "Toasts," in Alan Dundes' anthology: *Mother Wit From The Laughing Barrel: Readings in the Interpretation of Afro-American Folklore* (1973).

Myth, legend, and *folktale* are all traditional narratives or stories which show great variety in content but follow certain basic forms or outlines. According to Brunvand (1968: 101), "Folktales are traditional prose narratives that are strictly fictional and told primarily for entertainment, although they may illustrate a truth or point a moral." As such, they are of limited value except as indicators of moral beliefs. Some acquaintance with folktales is advisable simply to clarify the differences between them and those genres believed to be true—myth and legend.

The *legend* is especially important for criminologists due to its belief component. A useful definition is provided by Georges (1971: 5), "A legend is a story or narrative, set in the recent historical past, that is believed to be true by those by whom and to whom it is communicated." Though the elements of this definition are widely accepted, Georges goes on to demonstrate its indeterminacy. Degh (1971b) also recognizes this indeterminacy and points out that genres are continually mixing and merging, producing transitional forms and *seemingly* new forms that, in fact, maintain a consistent form, function, or meaning. These changes are a strength of folklore and reveal adjustment of the communicative process to a changed social environment. The legend genre is increasingly important since it is considered more of a communal product and its fragmentary form minimizes constraints on the communication of ideas.

Just as each specific legend has numerous variants, the *genre* of legend displays widespread variation in its characteristics between societies and across time (Dorson 1971b). Even so, its core function remains intact, as each genre is considered as a specific manifestation of a collective mental attitude. As Degh says:

> Folk legend varies, but only within the narrow limits of its frame. Like all the other basic forms of narration, the legend corresponds to a basic mental attitude composed of conscious and unconscious functions. This attitude itself is not subject to modifications, but social and historical changes may influence the nature of the legend more than they do any other genre of folklore (1971b: 59-60).

This feature of legend creation and maintenance as a response to new problems posed for the society or group is also discussed by Dundes (1971) and is amply reflected in differences in legendary accounts of banditry.

Of course, other genres aid in collective adjustment to social problems, but legend has the crucial aspect of being believed. Because of this belief by folklore performers and their audiences, legend provides a more versatile source of evidence. First, legends are composed of and shaped according to prevailing folk beliefs (Mullen 1971) and serve as indicators of those beliefs. Second, when contrasted with nonlegendary accounts or the legends of other groups, they portray the role of collective strain and interest in defining reality. Finally, since legends do have a factual core, they can provide minimal but useful information on historical events and persons. Regardless of that, when contrasted with other accounts, the factual basis of legend is often questioned, and, indeed, as one commentator declares: "one man's legend is another man's myth" (Georges 1971: 13).

The preceding statement best expresses the prevailing layman's usage of *myth* as a widely held misconception or false belief. Folklorists, however, tend to treat the term without pejorative overtones, and prefer a definition like Brunvand's depicting myths as "the sacred, traditional narratives of a culture, charters for belief, and validation of ritual" (1976: 139).

The genre labeled *myth* is difficult to define with any hope of consensus. Formerly myth was associated *only* with traditional societies and cultures and was limited to sacred stories told about the remote past and centering on the actions of gods and other supernatural beings. Following this definition, folklore collectors do *not* find traditional myths in modern societies (Dorson 1959b), but it is currently recognized that all societies have myths in some sense. The genre of myth exists in a different form, a much less elaborate and precise one, often akin to a symbol or image that functions to support an ideology or lifestyle. Friedman contends that

> the mythology of complex cultures is cryptotypical, that such mythologies are covert systems of assumptions, values, beliefs, personal wishes socialized and social wishes internalized, which reveal themselves only in the images and metaphors in which they get expressed (1971: 43).

Myth need no longer be limited to sacred narrative, and is often applied to widespread visions that activate societies like "Manifest Destiny" or "free enterprise" (Dorson 1971c). But this conception of myth, appropriate for secular, scientific culture must be used with discrimination lest it be broadened to include *all* imaginative products of mankind (Murray 1959b), but that selectivity must not arbitrarily limit the *types* of objects referred to (Bidney 1955).

A favorite activity of scholars is to show myth to be false or unverifiable when juxtaposed with historical fact, but the salient cultural fact is that:

> In matters of myth, the so-called truth does not satisfy. We make an overriding truth of what satisfies us by preserving our illusions; it need only pretend to be historically verifiable. In any case, it is not the facts of the legend that are profoundly meaningful to us, but rather the ethos (Friedman 1971: 44).

The meaning and function of myth does not lie in its relationship to fact but in its importance as an emotional catalyst for social action and as a basis for group harmony and unity—in short, the "charters for belief" of a society or group.

The revised conception of myth as a genre seems to preclude it as an identifiable item. Myths are included as elements or background assumptions of other folklore genre items. For example, the legend of Jesse James or the ballad of Robin Hood, contain clusters of meaning which, extracted and abstracted from the concrete account, might be called "the myth of the bandit." The distinction is, in part, a matter of levels of abstraction. Legends and ballads are concrete narratives based on abstract beliefs, some of which may be, separately or in combination, a representation of collective ideals—a vision or myth that sustains and directs social action.

There is more agreement among folklorists about *folksong*. Folksongs in Brunvand's terms simply "consist of words and music that circulate orally in traditional variants among members of a particular group" (1968: 130). They are often performed simultaneously in the popular realm of electronic media, especially since the folksong revival of the 1960s, and may not even have a popular *origin* as long as they are *maintained* in oral tradition. Of special interest is the prison worksong (to be discussed in more detail below), a musical device of southern black convicts to regulate prison work, pass the time, and release tension. As Jackson notes, it is "a long tradition in the south of the black man being permitted to sing things he is not permitted to say" (1972: 30). Consequently, these worksongs reveal insights into the "pains of imprisonment" and cover a range of topics including guards, escape, freedom, and other aspects of prison life.

Folksongs offer a wide range of topics but the *ballad,* "a narrative folksong which dramatizes a memorable event" (Laws 1964: 2), often emphasizes crime and deviance topics. Laws' overview of American balladry includes much material on murder, suicide, outlawry, and other forms of violence. Though it is less and less viable as a folklore genre, the ballad is a particularly useful subtype of folksong since it purports to be a true account of some event. The core of truth may be embellished for artistic or entertainment purposes, but the historical basis of many ballads, especially those about crime and murder, has been confirmed. Like the legend, the ballad offers insights into folk beliefs, images, and stereotypes about crime.

Most folklore genres cut across social groupings and have existed for centuries. But new and transitional genre forms arise on occasion and may be more circumscribed in audience. One such genre is the "*toast*." Toasts are "narrative poems from black American oral tradition" (Jackson 1974:

vii) and are largely limited to blacks and told in typically male-only con-texts. Toasts have been found among blacks in widely dispersed geographi-cal settings (Wepman, Newman, and Binderman 1974) and are usually performed in a theatrical manner (Abrahams 1970). The toast has been characterized as "epic poetry," sometimes believed to be true, which depicts "the sporting life" of urban blacks. Toasts usually involve topics like gambling, fighting, and pimping and provide an "insider's" conception of the nature, causes and consequences of deviance. The predominant role models of the "badman" and the "trickster" portray the world view of male, black, street life as unpredictable, insecure, threatening, and gamelike. This world view reflects the social position of blacks and in one discussion the authors conclude:

> This outlook, found throughout the toasts and the black experience they reflect, is a function of poverty and social impotence. The Life promotes a highly visible reference group, successful role models whose "colorful, swaggering style of cool bravado" has irresistible appeal for many disaffected black youths. . . . Toasts, then, like all folk poetry are enlightening as well as entertaining. They vividly depict the spirit of a black subculture—the Life—in our cities (Wep-man, Newman, and Binderman 1974: 223-224).

Jackson also emphasizes the connection between life as a black man in urban America and the interpretation of the genre. He claims that toasts contain no under-the-surface meaning but rely on prior knowledge shared by teller and audience. In this way, "the kind of complex meaning evoked from a folk poem is meaning *about* the way the poem relates to the tellers or the culture—little within the thing itself" (1974: ix). They are com-munal products. Private meaning is avoided.

Toasts are often collected in prison, and consequently, crime-related topics are heavily represented, since the function of the genre is, in part, the release of the fears and anxieties of the group. In this same way, the toast outside the prison serves as a counterpoint to the dominant, white-controlled society, and, consequently, it reveals the values, beliefs, and role models of the black subculture. This is not to underplay the enter-tainment value of the toast. Whether in prison or on the street, toast performances are enjoyed, considered humorous, and in some communi-ties the label toasts are exchanged for "jokes."

The final genre of folk literature relevant to this essay is the joke. Humor in all forms often reveals the images, beliefs, stereotypes and norms of a social group in the process of entertaining.

THE FOLKLORE OF CRIME AND DEVIANCE

Acquaintance with the folklore of banditry is common, and bandit themes are an important area of study. However, other types of deviance are also portrayed in folklore, indicating a broader utility of folklore as historical evidence. The folklore of crime and the folklore of deviant groups have not been a primary concern of folklorists but have been found by Richard Dorson (1971a) to be major themes in his initial collections of urban folklore. The salience of crime as a folklore topic is partly a function of the genre selected and the social group studied. The genre of ballads and toasts contains a high proportion of crime-related material. The folklore of subordinate groups tends to reflect their "deviant status," either directly as in the case of prison inmates or indirectly as in the case of counterculture youth and blacks.

Putting differences of genre and social group aside, folklore on crime and deviance provides insights into all the modes of utility discussed above in relation to bandits. The following discussion differentiates the folklore *of* deviant groups from the folklore *about* deviance and deviant groups. A complete analysis would contrast these perspectives. The present effort is intended to be suggestive and introduce the interested scholar to some current lines of folklore inquiry.

Among the range of deviant subcultures whose folklore has been published are those of prison inmates, heroin addicts, youth culture drug users, street hustlers, and gay men.

Bruce Jackson (1972) collected and published worksongs from inmates in the Texas prison system and drew insights from them on what he called "making it in hell." The genre is unique to black prisoners in the South and does not extend outside the prison walls. Jackson collected the songs through extensive field work in the prison system and included references to other publications and recordings. Although the songs arose when prison conditions were more harsh, they still function to protect the inmate physically, interpersonally, and psychologically. The *functions* of the worksongs include: (1) setting a work rhythm that protects slower workers from guards' reprisals; (2) passing time; (3) gaining some control over the work; and (4) relieving the tension of imprisonment. This latter function is revealed in the persistence of certain themes:

> The constants of the songs and of the life are the most obvious: the guards, escape, sentence length, geographical places remembered or longed for or heard of, sickness, death, guns, and the work itself. The songs concentrate on the devices and forms of control, and the manifestation of impotence (1972: xvi).

These themes persist despite an overall emphasis on women and freedom and indicate that "the singer is concerned with his relationship to certain institutions of the state, certain legal situations, certain interpersonal relationships" (1972: 38), and in expressing those relationships in song, he reveals some of what imprisonment is all about.

The folklore of heroin addicts draws heavily from the "toasts" of urban blacks. Agar (1971) and Fiddle (1972) studied institutionalized addicts and their folklore. Agar interpreted the toasts as a focus for the cultural themes of the urban addict subculture, the images, values, goals, and attitudes held by addicts. However, his informants stressed the entertainment value of folklore performance and would lend no other significance to it. In addition to description of addict skills, lifestyle and the effects of heroin, the toasts present conflicting images of addict life as either a positive counterpoint to a hypocritical system or as a physically and socially harmful venture.

Dorson offers an initial look at the popular culture (1976a) and folklore (1973b) of the youthful drug-using counterculture. Though the traditional nature of such folklore is in dispute, many genres are represented, and aspects of the drug culture lifestyle such as the paranoia about arrest; stories of bad drug experiences; perceptions of the legal establishment as hypocritical; attitudes toward and against the police and the "establishment"; and the rudiments of a folk hero tradition are depicted.

The hustling world of black men in Los Angeles offered a setting for folklore collection by Reynolds (1974). He found a group of black men who intertwined legal activity with gambling, prostitution, and pornography, and who entertained themselves in long drinking sessions spiced up with performances of "toasts." These included widespread traditional toasts of the urban black community and local ones depicting the hustling career of the performers.

Dresser (1974) did fieldwork in a gay bar and found a vital joking tradition that included material on images of gays, relationships with heterosexuals, and depictions of sexual practices. She concluded that gay folklore serves three important functions: (1) it signals membership in the subculture; (2) it produces solidarity among gays; and (3) it provides a tension release from the stresses of a deviant lifestyle.

Undoubtedly, other deviant groups also have informal folklore traditions that remain to be studied and may provide new data for historical criminologists. Of course, folklore of deviant groups also includes *their* own deviance. The following material approaches the deviant from the allegedly nondeviant's perspective.

The bandit or outlaw looms large in the folklore about crime. Laws (1964) lists several ballads about bandits; and the combination of oral and literary tradition for Billy the Kid (Steckmesser 1965); of oral legend and journalistic discussion for Jesse and Frank James (Settle 1966); and of local legend and folksong for the little-known Beanie Short (Wilgus and Montell 1971) served to establish the outlaw theme. Steckmesser (1966) attributes the persistence of bandit folklore to the folk belief in the Robin Hood stereotype of rob-from-the-rich-to-give-to-the-poor, but not all bandits are glorified in that manner. Interestingly, it does not require a "Robin Hood" character to establish the outlaw as a folk hero. In their study of a rebel guerrilla, Wilgus and Montell found ample folk memory of victimization after one hundred and six years in a pattern of bandit activity that did not stress a Robin Hood theme, although some of their informants portrayed the bandit as a clever prankster. Despite local tales that depict murderous activity, "Many who tell of him seem almost proud that he injured or killed their ancestors, a fact that distinguishes them from other persons who cannot tell similar tales" (Wilgus and Montell 1971: 136). The bandit as a focus for folklore reveals the diversity and continuity of outlaw traditions as an indicator of definitions of deviance. Although the folk hero label seems to attach to the outlaw regardless of whether the theme is one of rebellion, revenge, or self-motivated armed robbery, a diversity of definitions still applies, some applaud, some lament, and some curse. The high visibility of banditry, and its function as a personification of the beliefs and grievances of a subordinate group, give that phenomenon special significance to the criminologist interested in the nature, sources, and consequences of public perceptions.

Contrary to the Robin Hood theme of bandit lore, the "badman" of urban, black toasts celebrates "meanness" (Abrahams 1970). The badman theme pervades the black street community, especially in the South (Brearley 1973), and is the primary role model in many toasts. The toasts portray an attitude of despair and hopelessness as a backdrop to the heroism and final dignity of the hero who plays the game right (Labov et al. 1973). The world view of the toasts, whether they are badman or trickster tales, has been depicted as a "function of poverty and social impotence" of the black community (Wepman, Newman, and Binderman 1974: 223). The heroes of toasts typically violate the norms of the dominant white society and exemplify:

> total rejection of white middle-class society. The heroes are all "bad," they claim the virtues of courage, physical strength, clarity

and coolness of mind, and knowledge of the rules of the game and ways of the world. They explicitly reject respect for the law; romantic love; pity and gratitude; chivalry or special consideration for women (Labov et al. 1973: 335-336).

The values, world view and role models of street youth and adults comprise the underlying themes of the story told about the fast and often violent action of the subculture. These toasts are performed before an audience for entertainment, but place the performer and audience in social context. The badman displays vicious though heroic opposition to the hegemony of the system and cannot be coerced because "he doesn't mind dying." But the lack of self-control of the badman is complemented by the cool and controlled trickster, who eschews danger and aims for an ostentatious life, often as a pimp. Jackson (1974) suggests that the exaggerated role models of the toasts are viewed with ambivalence since they simultaneously depict the lure of success and the dangers of street life. Toasts focus on a character who uses either verbal or physical skill or both to survive. The interrelationship of these is presented in Jackson's description of the three most frequently heard toasts:

> "Stackolee" is about an irrational badman who engages in gratuitous violence and joyless sexuality, a man who fires his gun a lot but is almost totally nonverbal. He is the archetypal bully blindly striking out. . . . His sheer strength and big pistol bring him fame, but there are for him no solutions. . . .

> "Signifying Monkey" is about a jungle trickster who by clever word-play—signifying—manages to send his archfoe, Lion, off to be stomped and mangled by the stately Elephant. The Monkey uses wile and cleverness to accomplish what he cannot accomplish with brawn. . . . He usually "wins" but his gains are not unmixed, for although he gets someone else to trample his enemy he still must stay off the ground if he wants to stay alive.

> "Titanic" is about a laborer named Shine, who combines the ability of the physical hero with the verbal skill of the trickster or pimp hero. Shine cracks jokes as he swims away from the sinking ship and drowning whites; he ends up safely on dry land in orgies of sex and booze. Shine and the various Pimp heroes succeed through both verbal and physical skill, and their successes are the greatest (Jackson 1974: 13-14).

The toast represents the lasting problems of human relations of black street life in an exaggerated way. The pimps, prostitutes, hustlers, badmen, and tricksters of the toasts confront the problems commonly experienced by the audience. But they meet life's difficulties with style, and, if failure is their due, it is a spectacular "fall." The persistence of the toast as a genre is threatened by other communicative modes, but as it continues to entertain audiences on the streets or in the prisons, it serves as a unique datum on the deviant lifestyles and attitudes of one part of the urban community.

The highly personalized, though socially based, violence of the bandit and the badman are complemented by the folklore of more explicitly collective forms of violence. Roger Abrahams (1971) extended the analysis of the urban, black world view of the toast to the riots of the 1960s in black slum communities. He argued that the pattern of heroics exemplified by the toasts was reflected in the violence and aggression of the riots as well as in the day-to-day lives of street youth. In his view, the riots were an expression of yearning within the circumscribed world view created in reaction to the frustration of subordinance.

Montell (1970) used oral history interviews to establish the history of a small post-Civil War settlement of emancipated blacks. This account more openly depicts the violence of racial prejudice. The oral traditional narratives of the former settlers and their descendants included much embroidery but presented a core of legends of folk heroes and villians, and established the history of the community as wracked with violence and killing from a feud spawned by whites' hatred and harrassment of black settlers. Although folk attitudes influenced the accounts, the geographical persistence, interracial congruity, and agreement with written records convinced the author that the oral tradition offered a personal history of the folk: "the joy, humor, pathos and indestructable spirit of the local group" (Montell 1970: xviii).

Violence related to the early American labor movement is also celebrated or denounced in oral tradition. The struggle of mine workers in the United States occasionally led to violent sabotage or confrontation and to popular traditions about the Rocky Mountain Dynamite Man— Harry Orchard—who allegedly killed forty-two men with his zealous union-supporting activity (Holbrook 1941); and the Molly Maguires, who allegedly sabotaged and killed in Pennsylvania mining strikes. Dorson (1973b) discussed the folklore about the Molly Maguires, including ballads and legends, and highlighted the conflicting portrayal of them as either sadistic, cold-blooded murderers or as fighters for economic justice. He recounted a shift in folk definitions from the early emphasis on mining life as an arduous but honorable pursuit to the later focus on the cleavage between miners and owners and the violent activities of the Molly Maguires as the folk heroes of the exploited workingmen.

These folk accounts of violence between blacks and whites and between labor and capital often diverge from the hard facts of written documents or add the history of groups neglected by the chronicles of history, and they offer invaluable evidence for the historian attempting to study the history of collective violence in the United States.

As Lynn (1969) noted, violence has been a recurring theme in American literature and folklore. But in ballad and legend, the murder story lacking intimations of social conflict was the favorite. Laws' (1964) compilation of ballads native to the United States included numerous murder stories. Many of these were also collected by Burt (1958) who included only ballads for which the murder could be verified by other records. These ballads represent diverse motives and murder types but the collection is limited to the ballad texts alone with no attempt to determine the social context of ballad origin and acceptance. Holbrook's (1941) collection of narrative accounts of sensational murder cases was also limited but indicated the potential for a more inclusive analysis.

Laws provides a comparative analysis of British and American ballads and points out that the treatment of murder differs greatly. American ballads portray murder as shocking, whereas British ballads accept it as commonplace; the latter display none of the American repugnance for the bloody details of murder and do not express the typically American sentimental and emotional tone. Laws argues that American ballads also show other consistencies, attributable to the shortness of ballad tradition and the consistency in moral standards for viewing murder. The British tradition exhibits the values and morals of centuries and is therefore less consistent. Laws goes on to attribute the British-American differences to the national "spirit." The contrast of white and black ballad portrayals of murder is intriguing. Laws notes that the black balladeer is a "dramatist first, moralist second," and emphasizes the character rather than the event. He characterized black ballads as "highly personal expressions of characteristic racial attitudes" (1964: 84) and explains some of the features of black attitudes as an outgrowth of racial discrimination. "The social distinctions drawn among white men between criminal and non-criminal have not been equally emphasized among Negroes, who so often have been victims of the white man's laws," Laws (1964: 86-87) claims. Ballads are similar to toasts in their "badman" emphasis and perspective and include a frequent note of sympathy for the killer.

The white murder ballad focuses on the event and portrays characters in stereotyped roles, emphasizing murder as a moral outrage. Certain stereotyped murder situations are repeated. One subtype, depicting the killing of a girl by her lover, is found in fifty accounts (Field 1951). Anne Cohen (1973) made an intensive study of one of the more popular "murdered girl" ballads and found both newspaper and ballad accounts following certain stereotyped formulae of character, motive, situation, and action. Across time, the details of the murder were continually replaced by stock themes. Cohen analyzes some of the recurrent themes and speculates that the murdered girl stereotype reflected popular ideas about society flowing from dominant values. The tension between rural and urban interests in the late 1800s was especially prevalent in the imagery of the innocent country girl lured to her doom in the evil city. The analysis of the content, context, and comparative differences between groups in accounting for murder appears to be a profitable direction for students of deviance interested in the social basis of perceptions. The flexibility of the folklore account allows the definitional process to operate and reveals the force of values, ideas and attitudes in the dehistorization process, but still has value to the historian.

The folklore of crime and deviance is certainly a neglected area since scholars prefer the more controlled data sources of survey techniques. However, the folk communication process has unique features that make it a potentially valuable source of data on deviant behavior and perceptions and attitudes toward it. Hopefully, folklorists and historical criminologists will find shared interest and move toward a more complete understanding of the "problem of crime" in a balanced historical perspective.

The American "Wild West"

At the close of Chapter 3 we offered a quote from Walter Noble Burns (1925: 68-69), who maintained that the history of Billy the Kid is clouded by legend, and that history has neglected him. We also suggested that historians lost the "Wild West" as an area of serious research by default, and that, in general, much of the material in this field of inquiry is ahistorical. This is not to say, however, that there is nothing of value to be obtained from the existing literature on the West. On the contrary, while much of our understanding of outlaws, bandits, and gunfighters is either based on legend or is historically false, there is also a large body of literature that is of significant value to the serious researcher. The materials cited below represent a preliminary listing of works that ought to be noted in research endeavors on crime in the American West.

THE SETTLERS' WEST

Any examination of crime on the western frontier must necessarily begin with a conscious understanding of the growth of the West and the emerging social and cultural conditions which led to the era of outlaws and gunslingers. One might begin with Daniel J. Boorstin's (1965) *The Americans: The National Experience,* which examines the patterns of national self-discovery in the years between the Revolutionary War and the Civil War. In addition, Martin F. Schmitt and Dee Brown's (1974) *The Settlers' West* offers a capsule account of western expansion across the Great Plains and Rocky Mountains, the Texas-Oklahoma scrub country, the Southwest deserts, and the California gold fields.

While these two references offer a broad picture of western expansion, of even greater importance are the in-depth analyses of specific areas. Materials on the history of California, including the gold rush days and the vigilante era appear in Bean (1968), Chidsey (1968), Groh (1966), and Lewis (1966), each of which offer an extensive bibliography on local history. Stretching across to the Kansas territory and the Kansas-Missouri border wars, Alice Nichols' (1954) *Bleeding Kansas* provides a complete analysis of the border conflict combined with a forty-two-page commentary on appropriate references. A significant figure in the Kansas-Missouri wars, the Civil War, and the emergence of outlawry was William Clarke Quantrill, the guerrilla chief with whom Jesse and Frank James were once associated. An excellent and correct history of Quantrill and his times appears in Castel (1962), yet to be avoided is the more popular *Quantrill and the Border Wars* (Connelley 1956), which appears as a highly prejudiced account in which the author makes many historical errors and reflects a strong contempt for his subject.

The general texture of the West cannot be fully understood without some examination of the railroad and its impact on social and economic change. A comprehensive overview of the subject is Stewart H. Holbrook's (1962) *The Story of American Railroads* and Richard O'Connor's (1971) *Iron Wheels and Broken Men.* Robert G. Athearn's (1971) *Union Pacific Country* and John F. Stover's (1975) *History of the Illinois Central Railroad* examine specific railroad empires, the latter being one of eight volumes published in the Macmillan *Railroads of America Series.* Other useful works on the railroad include Howard (1962) and Hubbard (1945).

THE OUTLAWS AND GUNSLINGERS

Anyone seriously interested in the study of the western outlaw should obtain a copy of Ramon F. Adams' (1969) *Six Guns and Saddle Leather.*

This excellent work is an annotated bibliography of some 2,500 books and pamphlets on western outlaws and gunmen. In addition, Adams' (1964) *Burs Under the Saddle* offers an extended commentary on more than 400 volumes, which have aided the cause in the historical distortion of the American West. A brief review of these volumes might lead one to believe that there is little of value in the outlaw literature, but some excellent histories are available. For example, one can fully rely on Wayne Gard's (1936) *Sam Bass,* Joseph G. Rosa's (1964) *They Called Him Wild Bill,* Ramon F. Adams' (1960) *A Fitting Death for Billy the Kid,* William A. Settle's (1966) *Jesse James Was His Name,* Bailey C. Hanes' (1968) *Bill Doolin, Outlaw O. T.,* Frank Waters' (1960) *The Story of Mrs. Virgil Earp: The Earp Brothers of Tombstone,* Matt Warner and Murray E. King's (1940) *The Last of the Bandit Raiders,* William A. Keleher's *The Fabulous Frontier* (1945) and his *Violence in Lincoln County* (1937), J. Evetts Haley's (1948) *Jeff Milton, A Good Man With a Gun,* and Walter Prescott Webb's (1935) *The Texas Rangers.* In terms of the myth and reality of the outlaw and gunslinger, two excellent pieces are Joseph G. Rosa's (1969) *The Gunfighter: Man or Myth?* and Kent L. Steckmesser's (1965) *The Western Hero in History and Legend.*

These are certainly not the only reliable works on Western Americana, and what follows is an examination of some of the more or less dependable materials in specific areas of inquiry that might be examined for comparative purposes.

THE LEGEND MAKERS

Initially, there is a cluster of more than a thousand volumes, which, while interesting in their presentation of the West, are of no value as historical sources. Their only utility is for those who wish to study how the erroneous and ahistorical information emerged and was repeated. And second, there are the "histories," "biographies," and "memoirs" that border more on fiction than on fact. All of these works cannot be presented here, but some comment is offered on the more visible ones encountered in our research.

The first to be addressed is the *dime novel.* The original dime novels have become scarce items, having been inexpensively printed with little concern for historic preservation. For those interested in the flavor of the early dime novels, several have been reprinted in E. F. Bleiler's (1974) *Eight Dime Novels,* including Edward L. Wheeler's (1877) *Deadwood Dick, The Prince of the Road,* Prentiss Ingraham's (1881) *Adventures of Buffalo Bill From Boyhood to Manhood,* and the John W. Morrison publication *Frank James on the Trail* (Anonymous 1882). It might be added here that the dime novel treatment of crime was not limited to western outlawry. The houses of Beadle and Adams, Street & Smith, and others included fictional detective series, as well as such "true-life" examinations as *La Mafia; The New Orleans Italian Fiends' Oath; The "Dock Rats" of New York; Trapping the Moonshiners;* and *The League of the Counterfeiters.* For a study of the dime novel, one might wish to examine Johannsen (1950) and Mott (1947). In addition, Frank L. Schick's (1958) *The Paperbound Book in America* offers a history of paperbacks and includes an extremely useful bibliography on the subject.

Legend-making, as we have already seen, was not limited to the dime novelist. There were also those who produced full-length volumes written in the sensational dime novel style which relied little on historical fact. All of James William Buel's (1880; 1881a; 1881b) works fall into this category. One of Buel's larger works, carrying the title *Heroes of the Plains; or, Lives and Wonderful Adventures of Wild Bill, Buffalo Bill . . . and Other Celebrated Indian Fighters . . . Including a True and Thrilling History of Custer's "Last Fight" . . . also a Sketch of the Life of Sitting Bull and his Account of the Custer Massacre as Related to the Author in Person* (1881b), is most typical of the legend-making genre. The author repeats the false story of Wild Bill Hickok that first appeared in *Harper's Magazine;* he claims to have come into possession of Hickok's diary, given him by Hickok's widow, although her son-in-law denies that Wild Bill ever kept a diary; he places the Rock Creek, Nebraska affair in Kansas and claims that during the "fight," Hickok sustained a fractured skull, three gashes in his chest, cuts on his forearm, hip, and right leg, his cheek slashed open, plus numerous bullet wounds. In addition, he makes the statement, "This combat, of one man fairly whipping ten acknowledged desperadoes, has no parallel, I make bold to say, in any authentic history . . ." which appeared fifty years later, word for word, in Wilbert E. Eisele's (1931: 52) *The Real Wild Bill Hickok.* It might be added here that Buel's volume *Heroes of the Plans* was widely disseminated, for it was republished in 1882, 1883, 1884, 1886, and 1891.

As noted earlier in Chapter 3, one of the most prolific sources of misinformation has been the "old-timer" who wrote his "memoirs," and several examples were cited in our discussion of Billy the Kid. To these we might add Stone (1905), Abbott (1939), Cook (1923), Guyer (1938), and Gardner (1944). And there are dozens of others. Yet by contrast, there are also many useful works in this category, including French (1965a, b), Phillips (1925), Bonney (1971), and Raymond (1940).

HISTORIES AND BIOGRAPHIES

The biographers and historians of the frontier West have produced an interesting assortment of literature—some of it reliable, the overwhelming majority resembling historical fiction. On the more positive side, reliable works on outlaws and lawmen of greater and lesser renown, and on specific events in western history, can be located with some effort. In addition to those items already mentioned, accurate discussions of Jesse and Frank James and the Younger brothers can be found in Cantrell (1973), Croy (1949), and Huntington (1895). The Reno brothers, the first organized group of train robbers, are examined in Shields (1939) and Drago (1964). In addition to Adams (1960), Billy the Kid is well documented in Hoyt (1929), while Wild Bill Hickok's Rock Creek Station affair has been correctly treated in Bloyd (n.d.). Rube Burrow, an outlaw who specialized in train robberies from Texas to Alabama during the 1880s, is well described in Agee (1890); Bill Wilson, the Missouri outlaw, is thoroughly examined by Arthur (1938); for a discussion of the Dalton brothers, see Elliot (1892); and on the California outlaws in general, Joseph Henry Jackson's (1949) *Bad Company* reflects some excellent and scholarly research.

Belle Starr, more popularly referred to as "the bandit queen," can be found in Rascoe (1941), and useful materials on Calamity Jane are located in McClintock (1939) and Mumey (1950).

Much has been written about Robert Leroy Parker, more commonly known as "Butch Cassidy." His outlaw career extended from the 1880s through the turn of the twentiety century, and it is generally believed that he was killed in Bolivia after he, along with the Sundance Kid (Harry Longbaugh) and his lover Etta Place, journeyed to South America and robbed banks and payroll wagons while working in the tin mines. Lula Parker Beteson's (1975) *Butch Cassidy, My Brother* presents a complete history of the life of Butch Cassidy, and puts to rest the fable about his alleged death in South America.

Turning to an alternative side of lawlessness in the West, "hanging judge" Issac C. Parker has been thoroughly discussed in Croy (1952) and Harman (1898); materials on the Texas Rangers appear in Kilgore (1973) and Stephens (1970); and on the peace officers and gunfighters such as John Selman, Bat Masterson, Bill Tilghman, and John Wesley Hardin, see, Debo (1953), Hardin (1896), Jennings (1899), Cunningham (1934), Metz (1966), Thompson (1943), and Tilghman (1949). And finally, Pat Jahns' (1957) biography of Doc Holliday can be deemed reliable, and discussions of the lawmen and gunmen of Dodge City, Kansas appear in Wright (1913).

Looking to the less reliable sources, only the more popular and most persistent works will be noted here. Initially, although it has been cited in several places in this volume, Walter Noble Burns' (1925) *Saga of Billy the Kid,* in print now for more than half a century, is so romantic a piece of folklore that it should be avoided as a historical reference. Similarly, his *The Robin Hood of El Dorado* (1932) perpetuates the fiction about Joaquín Murieta. Similarly, the complete works of Carl W. Breihan (1953; 1957; 1959; 1961a, b; 1963) should be thoroughly avoided. Breihan deals with the better known outlaws and gunmen, repeatedly using the fictional device of imaginary thoughts. Furthermore, he repeatedly misspells the names of well-known figures, and general errors of fact are rampant, beginning in his prefaces and enduring through each final chapter.

It might be noted here that most of the works listed above have been cited in their first editions. Although many of the early editions have become rare items, they are available in numerous reprint editions. Furthermore, most of the significant older works have been republished by the University of Oklahoma Press in their "Western Frontier Library" series.

THE WESTERN MOVIE

The impact of the Western movie and that of the TV Western was discussed only briefly, but there are several volumes dealing with their structure and history. For further reading in these areas, see, Jon Tuska's (1976) *The Filming of the West,* and George N. Fenin and William K. Everson's (1973) *The Western.*

Organized Crime

Organized crime is an area of research and concern for both academicians from several social science disciplines and more-or-less popular writers, primarily reporters. Taken together they have produced a wide-ranging literature dealing in all manner of ways with some aspect or other of organized crime. The secondary sources not only cover a multiplicity of areas, but are also of exceptionally uneven quality. What follows is a discussion of selected works arranged in four fairly distinct but nevertheless loose categories: biographies and memoirs; organized crime, corruption, and urban studies; illicit criminal activities; and new approaches.

BIOGRAPHIES

Probably no other category in the organized crime literature is as academically suspect as this one, comprised primarily of pseudo-studies clearly designed to romanticize and sensationalize. Nothing is more obvious in this regard than the memoirs of J. Richard "Dixie" Davis (1939), which appeared serially in *Collier's* magazine. Aside from his somewhat inadvertent propagation of the mythology of the purge, Davis's story recounts his own adventures as Dutch Schultz's attorney and so-called "mouthpiece for the mob." It is, all in all, a rather dismal piece. Some three decades later, gangster Vincent Teresa (1973) in his *My Life in the Mafia* would provide an account of the alleged New England Mafia every bit as tiresome as Davis's story of New York mobsters. In both cases, as in so many other criminal memoirs, the historical reliability of the stories is highly questionable.

America's most famous organized criminal is undoubtedly Al Capone, whose career has been chronicled in at least two biographies and several films. The first biography of Capone was published in the early 1930s (Pasley 1966), and proved to be sensitive and thoughtful. A more complete account of Capone has been provided by John Kobler (1971), who not only updated the Capone story but carried it through his death in 1947. Kobler ends his account of Capone's life with a brief coda on Capone's son that should cause reflection on family mobility and organized crime. One other study of organized crime dealing almost completely with Capone deserves to be mentioned here. It is Kenneth Allsop's (1961) *The Bootleggers,* which adequately examines Capone's career. More interesting, however, Allsop reflects on the fascination of Capone's persona. When Al Capone came to Chicago, he was employed by John Torrio, another ex-New York gangster who is reported to have been the organizing genius of Chicago bootlegging. It was the Torrio gang and enterprises which Capone, in a sense, inherited in the mid-1920s when Torrio left Chicago. The standard account of Torrio's life can be found in McPhaul (1970).

Others among America's most infamous modern criminals to have their lives told are Meyer Lansky and his one-time partner Benjamin "Bugsy" Siegel. Hank Messick (1971) is Lansky's biographer, and he attempts to portray him as this century's master manipulator of organized crime. Lansky's career began in the 1920s and is still going on according to newspaper accounts. He is credited with providing the leadership behind the post World War II gambling empires in Las Vegas and the Caribbean.

The story of "Buggsy" Siegel is a simple account of his rise and gruesome fall as Lansky's advance man in the West. Other prominent syndicate criminals to have published biographies include "Dutch Schultz" (Sann 1971), Carlo Gambino (Meskil 1973), and Lucky Luciano (Gosch and Hammer 1974).

The best that can be said about the works mentioned above and their unnamed and best forgotten companions is that they do provide some chronology of events in America's underworlds, and sometimes, mostly inadvertently, highlight transformations in criminal organizations. Most importantly, they detail but rarely document the working relationships among criminals, criminal justice officers, politicians, and businessmen. What they almost never do is approach their topic with analytical sophistication. They really believe, for instance, that simple greed and moral imbecility are sufficient to explain criminality. And as would be expected, there is little consideration beyond the sentimental of such phenomena as the problems of immigrants or second-generation Americans in an urban, secular environment.

ORGANIZED CRIME, CORRUPTION, AND URBAN STUDIES

Turning from those works which are specifically written as life histories of infamous criminals, we encounter next a long and interesting series dealing with the social system of organized crime, the relationships binding together upper- and under-world figures. The most famous popular study cast in the above mold is *Murder, Inc.* (Turkus and Feder 1951). This account of the origins of the so-called *National Crime Syndicate,* composed of sketches of Louis Buchalter, Abe Reles, and other gangsters of the 1920s and 1930s, provides a vast amount of detail about corruption and collusion within New York's political system. The basis for *Murder, Inc.* was an investigation into so-called contract murder. The most startling claim was that murder was one of the businesses conducted by the *National Crime Syndicate.* Other works similar to *Murder, Inc.,* but considerably less ambitious and, indeed, useful, are Mockridge and Prall's (1954) *The Big Fix* and Ed Reid's (1953) *The Shame of New York.* The first is a fairly faithful but pedestrian report of police corruption in Brooklyn uncovered by an investigation into the Harry Gross gambling racket. Reid's book, on the other hand, attempts to establish the criminal leadership of Thomas Luchese as America's leading "Mafia Don" through the 1940s. The story of Luchese is replete with numerous factual errors unskillfully woven together with solid data gathered by the New York Crime Commission.

While the above accounts must be cautiously approached, there are a number of substantial and first-rate accounts of organized crime and corruption. One of the best is Andy Logan's (1972) *Against the Evidence: The Becker-Rosenthal Affair.* Logan, a reporter for the *New Yorker,* wrote a passionate and moving account of the 1912 murder of gambler Herman Rosenthal and the subsequent trial and execution of Police Lieutenant Charles Becker for supposedly engineering the crime. Logan convincingly demonstrates that Becker was framed by Manhattan District Attorney Charles Whitman, who used this sordid triumph to further his political climb. In recounting the story, Logan reveals an enormous amount of detail concerning the relationships between gamblers and politicians in Progressive Era New York. Another marvellous study which discusses in part the social system of organized crime is Herbert Mitgang's biography (1963) of Judge Samuel Seabury. Aptly titled *The Man Who Rode the Tiger,* it contains some extraordinary chapters dealing with corruption during the tenure of James Walker as Mayor of New York. During the early 1930s, Seabury led three technically separate investigations of New York's criminal justice and political system. Both the quality and quantity of corruption uncovered by Seabury were monumental (New York State Supreme Court 1932).

Continuing in this same field, there are a number of other studies which are useful, insightful, and rewarding. Dealing primarily with the structure of urban politics and corruption, they include Lincoln Steffens' (1948) famous series of essays published as *The Shame of the Cities;* John Gardiner's (1970) analysis of organized crime and corruption in Reading, Pennsylvania; Seymour Mandelbaum's (1965) *Boss Tweed's New York,* an attempt to understand corruption by utilizing contemporary communication theory; Walton Bean's (1952) classic analysis of graft and corruption in early San Francisco; Lyle Dorsett's (1968) study of the notorious Pendergast machine in Missouri; and V. O. Key's (1934) doctoral dissertation on corruption in Chicago. Among the few important theoretical analyses of corruption is Robert K. Merton's (1968) *Social Theory and Social Structure,* which contains a challenging discussion of the function of political machines. A major historical essay on this same theme is Samuel Hays (1964) "Politics of Reform in Municipal Government in the Progressive Era." Hays argues that political corruption was a "central element" in the reform movement which characterized the first decade or so of this century. The corruption arose because the structure of urban politics was unresponsive to members of a new urban upper class. Corruption, Hays continues, was the method by which this new upper class circumvented the democratic and decentralized city politics of that day, until that time when they could legitimately refashion municipal government.

Also helpful in unravelling the nature of urban politics is the Banfield and Wilson (1963) study *City Politics*. All students of organized crime and corruption should be familiar with John Landesco's (1968) pioneering analysis *Organized Crime in Chicago,* which originally appeared in 1929 and still remains the finest book on Chicago crime to this time. Landesco's work should be supplemented, however, with a careful reading of two superb articles by Mark H. Haller. The first is "Urban Crime and Criminal Justice: The Chicago Case" (1970), and the other is "Organized Crime in Urban Society: Chicago in the Twentieth Century" (1971-1972). Harold Lasswell and Jeremiah McKenna (1972) have written an important account of the impact of organized crime on a particular Brooklyn neighborhood, Bedford-Stuyvesant. Their study documents the damage wrought by certain illegal activities to inner-city areas. And finally, William Foote Whyte's (1955) classic *Street Corner Society* is also concerned with organized crime and urban life.

ILLICIT CRIMINAL ACTIVITIES

In looking at the historical and sociological literature dealing with organized crime there are some important and significant works whose intent is the analysis of specific criminal enterprises. Among the types of enterprises discussed are such activities as labor racketeering, gambling, bootlegging, and narcotics. Under the topic of labor racketeering, which is all too often a term used to discredit trade unions, the most comprehensive work is *The Imperfect Union* (Hutchinson 1970). It is a somewhat uneven historical account of racketeering in such diverse trades and industries as garment manufacturing, construction, and transportation. In this same regard, one should consider Daniel Bell's (1962) "Racket-Ridden Longshoremen." David J. Saposs (1958) and Simon Rottenberg (1960) have both written solid theoretical essays on trade union corruption. A very substantial but often neglected study of labor racketeering was published in the *Columbia Law Review* in the summer of 1937. Written by a member of Special Prosecutor Thomas E. Dewey's staff, the article "Legal Implications of Labor Racketeering," describes a number of employer and racketeer conspiracies which were the foundations of labor racketeering. This brings us to an important point: with the exception of the above essay, most of the social scientific interpretations distort the true nature of graft and corruption in the American labor movement. Rather than being a function of the drive for unioniza-tion, the development of racketeering in unions illustrates the extent to which timely decisions by the owners of industry can usurp a labor move-ment by institutionalizing corruption and thereby negating the potential effectiveness of labor organizations (Block and Chambliss 1977). One of the very few scholars to approach union racketeering from this perspec-tive is Rhodri Jeffreys-Jones (1974), whose long essay should be con-sidered a major contribution toward shifting the interpretive balance.

Unlike the bulk of studies on labor racketeering which suffer from an antilabor bias, most of the scientific material on narcotics is simply silent concerning organized crime. There are, in fact, only two studies dealing with narcotics and organized crime which can be recommended. They are Block (1977d) and Alfred W. McCoy (1973) *The Politics of Heroin in Southeast Asia.* Both are historical, with McCoy offering a panoramic description of the international narcotics trade and Block discussing the structure of cocaine syndicates in early twentieth century New York.

Another area to receive individual attention is gambling. In fact, gam-bling, which has often been described as organized crime's chief source of revenue, has perhaps the most extensive literature. Examples would include the American Bar Association's Commission on Organized Crime (1952) report of a "Model Anti-gambling Act," Russell Baker (1950) "Equitable Remedy to Combat Gambling in Illinois," and Charles B. Hagan (1951) "Wire Communications Utilities and Bookmaking," as well as numerous other articles in law reviews whose thrust has been legalistic. Their basic concern has been methods to control organized gambling through new legislation including consideration of legalizing certain aspects of organized gambling. Recently, however, Mark H. Haller (1976) has written a thoughtful, historical essay for the Commission on the Review of National Policy Toward Gambling. Haller discusses "the impact of bootleggers upon the structure and control of gambling in American cities" and in so doing provides one of the few historically sophisticated accounts of organized gambling during this century.

Concerning bootlegging, most of the literature is anecdotal at best. It is primarily covered in the unreliable biographies of America's more notorious racketeers mentioned previously. There is, however, a substan-tial literature both historical and sociological dealing with prohibition which should be closely examined, the most outstanding being Norman H. Clark's (1976) *Deliver Us from Evil.*

Other criminal activities which have been written about include prosti-tution and fencing. The material on prostitution, indeed on women in organized crime, has been discussed or cited in Chapter 4. The most important exception, however, is the superb study *Vice in Chicago* (Reckless 1933). There is no literature on fencing, but there is a fine study of a professional fence written by Carl B. Klockars (1974), who combines historical and sociological materials on fencing with outstanding field work.

NEW APPROACHES

The newest and best work on organized crime is in many ways an answer to those who claim that there is Italian/Sicilian dominance in organized crime. Much of the work to be discussed is not simply critical of the popular biographies etc. of Cosa Nostra criminals, but is more concerned with the academic sociologists who claim to have found a rigid underworld government (Cressey 1967a, 1967b, 1969; and Furstenberg 1969).

The two strongest critiques have been done by Joseph L. Albini (1971) and Dwight C. Smith, Jr., (1975 and 1976). Albini's work is a direct refutation of the Cosa Nostra criminologists. After an exhaustive reading of the historical literature, Albini points out the gross historical naiveté of most contemporary reports. Albini then goes on to present a counter-image of organized crime. He sees it as composed of innumerable shifting patron-client networks and coalitions.

The Mafia Mystique (Smith 1975) is a more powerful study. In explaining his purpose, Smith writes:

> My intent is to illustrate how the moral entrepreneurship of earlier generations was able to capitalize on our willingness to emphasize differences between some criminals and the rest of us, and thereby to establish for present consumption a series of expectations about what organized crime is and how we should deal with it. Those expectations do indeed add up to a mystique. Beneath the labels and symbols of "Mafia" today is an artificial concept expressed in inadequate and highly questionable assumptions and beliefs (p. 23).

Smith proceeds to "demythologize" this image by placing it within, in part, a survey of American cultural history. Smith is concerned with showing the interplay between cultural stereotypes manufactured by the press, novelists, and film makers, and their manipulation by policy-planners. This is made most explicit in the wonderfully titled chapter "Educating or Brainwashing? The Co-opted Stereotype," which deals with image management during the 1960s:

The campaign against criminal conspiracy as the heart of organized crime continued, however, with a persistence matching the "Mafia" campaign waged by the Federal Narcotics Bureau in the fifties. The focus shifted from Washington to Albany, as New York State sponsored a series of conferences on combating organized crime, held from 1965 to 1967. The conferences received little public attention and achieved only limited goals for the state. But specific results were less significant than the fact that the meetings sustained a network of law-enforcement personnel who had been principal supporters of Valachi's testimony (p. 220).

The impact of the New York meetings and the network was only apparent when President Lyndon Johnson established the President's Commission on Law Enforcement and Administration of Justice in 1966. As Smith maintained, the "network was available to give substantial conceptual support to the task force that the commission formed to study organized crime." And it was the conclusions reached by the commission which shaped so much contemporary opinion.

Other scholars who have broken down the efforts of the policy-makers include Francis A. J. Ianni with Elizabeth Reuss-Ianni (1972), William H. Moore (1974), and Humbert S. Nelli (1976). The Iannis are anthropologists who conducted a field study of a functioning "crime family" for over two years. It is their view that Italian-American crime families are really a "number of lineages linked together into a composite clan." They go on noting that the "universality of this clan organization and the strength of its shared behavior system" makes it appear that Italian-American criminal syndicates are similar. And furthermore, they conclude "that it is this similarity which has inclined observers to maintain that the different crime families constitute some sort of highly organized national or even international crime conspiracy" (p. 192).

Moore and Nelli are historians, and their approach is radically different from the Iannis. Nevertheless, their conclusions are important parts of the current demythologizing process. Moore's interest is in the Kefauver investigation into organized crime in the early 1950s. Moore ably demonstrates not only the origins of that crucial investigation, but the manner in which false conclusions were drawn by the committee, especially in the area of organized crime's structure. Nelli presents the first historically reliable study of "Italians and Syndicate Crime in the United States." He relies and reports on a wealth of *primary* sources available to scholars of organized crime. Unlike the biographers discussed before, Nelli brings a subtle and sensitive understanding of the problems of immigrants and second-generation Americans in an urban, secular environment to bear upon the development of organized criminal activities. With Nelli's study, we have come full circle in our discussion. He exemplifies how a judicious search for reliable material can produce a first-rate history of even the most sensational American syndicate criminals.

APPENDIX B

REFERENCES

The following list includes all items cited throughout the text and the *Reference and Research Guide.* It should be noted that excessively long subtitles were a common practice in books published decades ago. In this reference list, *main titles* are indicated, with subtitles reported only in instances where it may be pertinent to the discussion in the text, or where it is not of excessive length. Burton Rascoe's (1941) biography of Belle Starr, for example, was originally published under the full title of *Belle Starr, "The Bandit Queen." The True Story of the Romantic and Exciting Career of the Daring and Glamorous Lady Famed in Legend and Story Throughout the West. . . . The True Facts About the Dastardly Deeds and the Come-uppence of such Dick Turpins, Robin Hoods, and the Youngers, the Jameses, the Daltons, the Starrs and the Jenningses. The Real Story with Court Records and Contemporary Newspaper Accounts and Testimony of the Old Nesters, Here and There in the Southwest. . . .* but in this reference list it will be noted only by its main title, *Belle Starr, "The Bandit Queen."*

ABBOTT, E. C. (1939) *We Pointed them North: Recollections of a Cowpuncher.* New York: Farrar & Rinehart.

ABRAHAMS, R. D. (1966) "Some Varieties of Heroes in America." Journal of the Folklore Institute 3.

——— (1969) "On Meaning and Gaming." Journal of American Folklore 28.

——— (1970) *Deep Down in the Jungle: Negro Narrative Folklore from the Streets of Philadelphia.* Chicago: Aldine.

——— (1971) "The Negro Stereotype: Negro Folklore and the Riots," in Americo Paredes and Ellen Stekert (eds.) *The Urban Experience and Folk Tradition.* Austin: University of Texas Press.

——— (1972) "Personal Power and Social Restraint in the Definition of Folklore," in Americo Paredes and Richard Bauman (eds.) *Toward New Perspectives in Folklore.* Austin: University of Texas Press.

ACHEVES, P. and M. EINARSSON-MULLARKY (1968) *Folklore Archives of the World.* Bloomington, Ind.: Folklore Forum, Bibliographic and Special Series, 1.

ADAMS, R. F. (1948) *The Old Time Cowhand.* New York: Macmillan.

——— (1960) *A Fitting Death for Billy the Kid.* Norman: University of Oklahoma Press.

——— (1964) *Burs Under the Saddle.* Norman: University of Oklahoma Press.

ADAMS, R. F. (1969) *Six Guns and Saddle Leather*. Norman: University of Oklahoma Press.

AGAR, M. H. (1971) "Folklore of the Heroin Addict: Two Examples." Journal of American Folklore 84.

AGEE, G. W. (1890) *Rube Burrow, King of Outlaws, and His Band of Train Robbers*. Chicago: Henneberry.

ALAGOA, E. J. (1968) "The Use of Oral Literary Data for History: Examples from Niger Delta Proverbs. Journal of American Folklore 81: 235-242.

ALBINI, J. L. (1971) *The American Mafia: Genesis of a Legend*. New York: Appleton-Century-Crofts.

ALLSOP, K. (1961) *The Bootleggers: The Story of Chicago's Prohibition Era*. New Rochelle, N.Y.: Arlington House.

AMEN, J. H. (1942) *Report of Kings County Investigation, 1938-1942*.

AMERICAN BAR ASSOCIATION. Commission on Organized Crime. (1952) *Model Anti-gambling Act*.

ANONYMOUS (1881) *The Cowboy's Career, or the Dare Devil Deeds of "Billy the Kid," the Noted New Mexico Desperado*. Chicago: Belford, Clark.

ANONYMOUS (1882) *Frank James on the Trail*. New York: John W. Morrison.

ARTHUR, G. C. (1938) *Bushwhacker; A True Story of Bill Wilson, Missouri's Greatest Desperado; A Story of Blood*. Rolla, Mo.: Rolla Printing Company.

ASBURY, H. (1927) *The Gangs of New York: An Informal History of the Underworld*. New York: Alfred A. Knopf.

――― (1933) *The Barbary Coast: An Informal History of the San Francisco Underworld*. New York: Alfred A. Knopf.

――― (1940) *The Chicago Underworld*. New York: Alfred A. Knopf.

ATHEARN, R. G. (1971) *Union Pacific Country*. Chicago: Rand McNally.

AUERBACH, E. (1953) *Mimesis: The Representation of Reality in Western Literature*. Princeton, N.J.: Princeton University Press.

AYDELOTTE, W. O. (1962-63) "Voting Patterns in the British House of Commons in the 1840's." Comparative Studies in Society and History 5.

BADGER, J. E. (1881a) *Joaquin, the Terrible. The True History of the Three Bitter Blows that Changed an Honest Man to a Merciless Demon*. New York: Beadle & Adams.

――― (1881b) *Joaquin, The Saddle King. A Romance of Murieta's First Fight*. New York: Beadle & Adams.

BAENZIGER, A. P. (1969) "The Texas State Police During Reconstruction." Southwestern Historical Quarterly 72.

BAKER, P. (1965) *The Wild Bunch of Robbers Roost*. Los Angeles: Westernlore.

BAKER, R. (1950) "Equitable Remedy to Combat Gambling in Illinois." Chicago-Kent Law Review 28.

BANFIELD, E. C. and J. Q. WILSON (1963) *City Politics*. New York: Vintage.

BARNES, H. E. (1962) *A History of Historical Writing*. New York: Dover.

BARZINI, L. (1971) *From Caesar to the Mafia: Sketches of Italian Life*. New York: Library Press.

BARZUN, J. and H. F. GRAFF (1962) *The Modern Researcher*. New York: Harcourt Brace & World.

――― (1970) *The Modern Researcher*. New York: Harcourt Brace & World.

BASCOM, W. (1965a) "Folklore and Anthropology," in Alan Dundes (ed.) *The Study of Folklore*. Englewood Cliffs, N.J.: Prentice-Hall.

––– (1965b) "Four Functions of Folklore," in Alan Dundes (ed.) The Study of Folklore. Englewood Cliffs, N.J.: Prentice-Hall.

BAUMAN, R. (1969) "Towards a Behavioral Theory of Folklore: A Reply to Roger Welsch." Journal of American Folklore 82.

––– (1972a) "Differential Identity and the Social Base of Folklore," in Americo Paredes and Richard Bauman (eds.) *Toward New Perspectives in Folklore*. Austin: University of Texas Press.

––– (1972b) "Introduction," in Americo Paredes and Richard Bauman (eds.) *Toward New Perspectives in Folklore*. Austin: University of Texas Press.

BEAN, W. (1952) *Boss Ruef's San Francisco: The Story of the Union Labor Party, Big Business, and the Graft Prosecution*. Berkeley and Los Angeles: University of California Press.

––– (1968) *California: An Interpretive History*. New York: McGraw-Hill.

BEATTIE, J. M. (1975) "The Criminality of Women in Eighteenth Century England." Journal of Social History 8.

BECHDOLT, F. (1922) *When the West Was Young*. New York: Century.

BECKER, S. (1959) *Comic Art in America*. New York: Simon & Schuster.

BELL, D. (1962) *The End of Ideology: On the Exhaustion of Political Ideas in the Fifties*. New York: Free Press.

BEN-AMOS, D. (1972) "Toward a Definition of Folklore in Context," in Americo Paredes and Richard Bauman (eds.) *Toward New Perspectives in Folklore*. Austin: University of Texas Press.

––– (1973) "A History of Folklore Studies–Why Do We Need It?" Journal of the Folklore Institute 10.

BENJAMIN, H. and R.E.L. MASTERS (1964) *Prostitution & Morality: A Definitive Report on the Prostitute in Contemporary Society and an Analysis of the Causes and Effects of the Suppression of Prostitution*. New York: Julian.

BENSON, L. (1967) "An Approach to the Scientific Study of Past Public Opinion." Public Opinion Quarterly 31.

BENTON, J. J. (1943) *Cow by the Tail*. Boston: Houghton Mifflin.

BETESON, L. P. (1975) *Butch Cassidy, My Brother*. Provo, Utah: Brigham Young University Press.

BIDNEY, D. (1955) "Myth, Symbolism, and Truth." Journal of American Folklore 68.

BLEILER, E. F. [ed.] (1974) *Eight Dime Novels*. New York: Dover.

BLOCH, M. (1953) *The Historian's Craft*. New York: Vintage.

BLOCK, A. A. (1975) "Lepke, Kid Twist and the Combination: Organized Crime in New York City, 1930-1944," Ph.D. dissertation, UCLA.

––– (1977a) "History and the Study of Organized Crime." Urban Life (forthcoming).

––– (1977b) "The Search for Women in Organized Crime." Paper presented at the 28th Annual Meeting of the American Society of Criminology, Tucson, Arizona, November 4-7, 1976.

––– (1977c) "Aw . . . Your Mother's in the Mafia: Women Criminals in Progressive New York." Contempory Crises.

––– (1977d) "The Snowman Cometh: Coke in Progressive New York." Paper presented at the Missouri Valley History Conference, Omaha, Nebraska.

BLOCK, A. A. and W. J. CHAMBLISS (1977) "The Role of Employers in the Development of Labor Racketeering." Paper presented at European Group for the Study of Deviance, Barcelona, Spain.

BLOCK, E. B. (1959) *Great Train Robberies of the West*. New York: Avon.

BLOK, A. (1972) "The Peasant and the Brigand: Social Banditry Reconsidered." Comparative Studies in Society and History 14.

——— (1974) *The Mafia of a Sicilian Village, 1860-1960: A Study of the Violent Peasant Entrepreneur*. New York: Harper & Row.

BLOYD, L. (n.d.) *Jefferson County History*. Fairbury, Nebraska: Holloway.

BOISSEVAIN, J. (1974) *Friends of Friends: Networks, Manipulators and Coalitions*. New York: St. Martin's.

BONKRUDE, H. L. (1970) "Crime and Its Threat in Minneapolis and St. Anthony to 1880." Ph.D. dissertation, University of Minnesota.

BONNEY, E. (1850) *Banditti of the Prairies*. Chicago: E. Bonney.

BOORSTIN, D. J. (1965) *The Americans: The National Experience*. New York: Random House.

BOYER, L. R. (1972) "The Golden City and Nassau Street Riots: New York City, 1970." Ph.D. dissertation, Notre Dame University.

BRAUDEL, F. (1949) *La Mediterrane et le Monde Mediterraneen a l'Epoque de Philippe II*. Paris: Librairie Armand Colin. English edition (1972) *The Mediterranean and the Mediterranean World in the Age of Philip II*. New York: Harper & Row.

BREARLEY, H. C. (1973) "Ba-ad Nigger," in Alan Dundes (ed.) *Mother Wit From the Laughing Barrel: Readings in the Interpretation of Afro-American Folklore*. Englewood Cliffs, N.J.: Prentice-Hall.

BREIHAN, C. W. (1953) *The Complete and Authentic Life of Jesse James*. New York: Frederick Fell.

——— (1957) *Badmen of Frontier Days*. New York: Robert M. McBride.

——— (1959) *Quantrill and His Civil War Guerrillas*. Denver: Sage Books.

——— (1961a) *Great Gunfighters of the West*. London: John Long.

——— (1961b) *The Day Jesse James Was Killed*. New York: Frederick Fell.

——— (1963) *Great Lawmen of the West*. London: John Long.

Brewer's Dictionary of Phrase and Fable (n.d.). New York: Harper & Brothers.

BROWN, R. (1963) *Explanation in Social Science*. London: Routledge & Keegan Paul.

BROWNE, R. B. (1972) "Popular Culture: Notes Toward a Definition," in Ray Browne and Ronald Ambrosetti (eds.) *Popular Culture and Curricula*. Bowling Green, Ohio: Bowling Green University Popular Press.

BRUNVAND, J. (1968) *The Study of American Folklore*. New York: W. W. Norton.

——— (1970) "On Abraham's Besom." Journal of American Folklore 83.

——— (1971) "New Directions in the Study of Folklore." Folklore 82.

——— (1972) "Popular Culture in the Folklore Course," in Ray Browne and Ronald Ambrosetti (eds.) *Popular Culture and Curricula*. Bowling Green, Ohio: Bowling Green University Popular Press.

——— (1976) *Folklore: A Study and Research Guide*. New York: St. Martin's.

BUCHAN, D. (1968) "History and Harlaw." Journal of the Folklore Institute 5.

BUEL, J. W. (1880) *Life and Marvelous Adventures of Wild Bill, the Scout*. Chicago: Belford, Clarke.

——— (1881a) *Heroes of the Plains*. St. Louis: Historical Publishing Company.

——— (1881b) *The Border Outlaws*. St. Louis: Historical Publishing Company.

BUNTLINE, N. (1886) *Buffalo Bill and his Adventures in the West*. New York: J. S. Ogilvie.

BURNS, W. N. (1925) *The Saga of Billy the Kid*. Garden City, N.Y.: Garden City.

––– (1932) *The Robin Hood of El Dorado; the Saga of Joaquín Murrieta, the Famous Outlaw of California's Age of Gold*. New York: Coward-McCann.

BURT, O. W. (1958) *American Murder Ballads and Their Stories*. New York: Oxford University Press.

BYNUM, D. (1973) "Oral Evidence and the Historian: Problems and Methods," in Richard Dorson (ed.) *Folklore and Traditional History*. The Hague: Mouton.

CAHNMAN, W. J. and A. BOSKOFF [eds.] (1964) *Sociology and History: Theory and Research*. New York: Free Press.

California Police Gazette (1859) "The Life of Joaquin Murieta, the Brigand Chief of California. . . ." 1 (September 3–November 5).

CALLAHAN, J. P. (1926-1928) "Kansas in the American Novel and Short Story." Kansas State Historical Society Collections, Vol. 17.

CALLISON, J. J. (1914) *Bill Jones of Paradise Valley, Oklahoma*. Chicago: M. A. Donohue.

CANTRELL, D. (1973) *Younger's Fatal Blunder: Northfield, Minnesota*. San Antonio: Naylor.

CARR, E. H. (1961) *What is History?* New York: Alfred A. Knopf.

CASTEL, A. (1962) *William Clarke Quantrill: His Life and Times*. New York: Frederick Fell.

CASTLEMAN, H. N. (1944) *The Texas Rangers*. Girard, Kansas: Haldeman-Julius.

CHALFANT, W. A. (1928) *Outposts of Civilization*. Boston: Christopher.

CHAMBLISS, W. [ed.] (1973) *Sociological Readings in the Conflict Perspective*. Reading, Mass.: Addison-Wesley.

––– and M. Mankoff (1976) *Whose Law, What Order? A Conflict Approach to Criminology*. New York: John Wiley.

CHANDLER, D. L. (1975) *Brothers in Blood: The Rise of Criminal Brotherhoods*. New York: E. P. Dutton.

CHESNEY, K. (1970) *The Victorian Underworld*. New York: Schocken.

CHIDSEY, D. B. (1968) *The California Gold Rush*. New York: Crown.

CLARK, N. H. (1976) *Deliver Us From Evil: An Interpretation of American Prohibition*. New York: W. W. Norton.

CLINARD, M. B. and R. QUINNEY (1967) *Criminal Behavior Systems: A Typology*. New York: Holt, Rinehart & Winston.

COFFIN, T. P. (1968) *Our Living Traditions: An Introduction to American Folklore*. New York: Basic Books.

COHEN, A. B. (1973) *Poor Pearl, Poor Girl!: The Murdered Girl Stereotype in Ballad and Newspaper*. Austin: University of Texas Press.

COHEN, D. (1972) "The Origin of the 'Jackson Whites': History and Legend Among the Ramapo Mountain People." Journal of American Folklore 85.

Congressional Globe, Tuesday, December 5, 1848.

CONNELLEY, W. E. (1956) *Quantrill and the Border Wars*. New York: Pageant.

COOK, J. H. (1923) *Fifty years on the Old Frontier, as Cowboy, Hunter, Guide, Scout, and Ranchman*. New Haven, Conn.: Yale University Press.

CORLE, E. (1949) *The Royal Highway*. Indianapolis: Bobbs-Merrill.

COSSLEY-BATT, J.L.E. (1928) *The Last of the California Rangers*. New York: Funk & Wagnalls.

COSTELLO, A. E. (1884) *Our Police Protectors*. New York: Author's edition.

COURSEY, O. W. (1924) *Wild Bill*. Mitchell, S.D.: Educator Supply.

COWDRICK, J. C. (1884) *Silver-Mask, the Man of Mystery*. New York: Beadle & Adams.

CRESSEY, D. R. (1967a) "The Structure and Functions of Criminal Syndicates," in Task Force Report: Organized Crime. President's Commission on Law Enforcement and Administration of Justice. Washington, D.C.: U.S. Government Printing Office.

——— (1967b) "Methodological Problems in the Study of Organized Crime as a Social Problem." The Annals 374.

——— (1969) *Theft of the Nation: The Structure of Organized Crime in America*. New York: Harper & Row.

CROOKS, J. B. (1968) *Politics and Progress: The Rise of Urban Progressivism in Baltimore, 1895-1911*. Baton Rouge: Louisiana State University Press.

CROY, H. (1949) *Jesse James Was My Neighbor*. New York: Dwell, Sloan & Pearce.

——— (1952) *He Hanged them High. An Authentic Account of the Fanatical Judge who Hanged Eighty-Eight Men*. Boston: Little, Brown.

CUNNINGHAM, E. (1934) *Triggermometry, A Gallery of Gunfighters*. San Antonio: Press of the Pioneers.

CUNNINGHAM, J. C. (1938) *The Truth About Murrietta; Ancedotes and Facts Related by Those Who Knew Him and Disbelieve His Capture*. Los Angeles: Wetzel.

DA ALLEPPO, G. M., and G. H. CALVARUSO (1910) *Le Fonte Arabiche Nel Dialetto Sicilano*. Roma: Etmanno Loescher.

DACUS, J. A. (1882) *Illustrated Lives and Adventures of Frank and Jesse James and the Younger Brothers, The Noted Western Outlaws*. St. Louis: N. D. Thompson.

DANE, G. E. (1941) *Ghost Town*. New York: Tudor.

DAVIS, A. F., and M. H. HALLER [eds.] (1973) *The Peoples of Philadelphia: A History of Ethnic Groups and Lower-Class Life, 1790-1940*. Philadelphia: Temple University Press.

DAVIS, D. B. (1957) *Homicide in American Fiction, 1798-1860: A Study in Social Values*. Ithaca, N.Y.: Cornell University Press.

——— (1969) *The Slave Power Conspiracy and the Paranoid Style*. Baton Rouge: Louisiana State University Press.

DAVIS, J. R. (1939) "Things I Couldn't Tell Till Now." Collier's 104.

DAVIS, K. S. (1976) Kansas: A Bicentennial History. New York: W. W. Norton.

DEBO, A. [ed.] (1953) *The Cowman's Southwest. . . . The Reminiscences of Olive Nelson*. Glendale, Calif.: Arthur H. Clark.

DEGH, L. (1971a) "Prepared Comments," in Americo Paredes and Ellen Stekert (eds.) *The Urban Experience and Folk Tradition*. Austin: University of Texas Press.

——— (1971b) "The 'Belief Legend' in Modern Society: Form, Function, and Relationship to Other Genres," in Wayland Hand (ed.) *American Folk Legend*. Berkeley and Los Angeles: University of California Press.

DORSETT, L. W. (1968) *The Pendergast Machine*. New York: Oxford University Press.

DORSON, R. (1959a) *American Folklore*. Chicago: University of Chicago Press.

––– (1959b) "Theories of Myth and the Folklorist." Daedalus 88.

––– (1971) *American Folklore and the Historian*. Chicago: University of Chicago Press.

––– (1971a) "Is There a Folk in the City?" in Americo Paredes and Ellen Stekert (eds.) *The Urban Experience and Folk Tradition*. Austin: University of Texas Press.

––– (1971b) "How Shall We Rewrite Charles M. Skinner Today?" in Wayland Hand (ed.) *American Folk Legend*. Berkeley and Los Angeles: University of California Press.

––– (1971c) "Oral Tradition and Written History: The Case for the United States," in Richard Dorson (ed.) *American Folklore And The Historian*. Chicago: University of Chicago Press.

––– (1971d) "Fakelore," in Richard Dorson (ed.) *American Folklore And The Historian*. Chicago: University of Chicago Press.

––– (1971e) "Defining the American Folk Legend," in Richard Dorson (ed.) *American Folklore And The Historian*. Chicago: University of Chicago Press.

––– (1971f) "Local History and Folklore," in Richard Dorson (ed.) *American Folklore And The Historian*. Chicago: University of Chicago Press.

––– (1972a) "Introduction: Concepts of Folklore and Folklife Studies," in Richard Dorson (ed.) *Folklore and Folklife*. Chicago: University of Chicago Press.

––– (1972b) "History of the Elite and History of the Folk," in Richard Dorson (ed.) *Folklore: Selected Essays*. Bloomington: Indiana University Press.

–– (1972c) *Folklore: Selected Essays*. Bloomington: Indiana University Press.

––– [ed.] (1972d) *Folklore and Folklife: An Introduction*. Chicago: University of Chicago Press.

––– (1973a) "Sources for the Traditional History of the Scottish Highlands and Western Islands," in Richard Dorson (ed.) *Folklore and Traditional History*. The Hague: Mouton.

––– (1973b) *America in Legends*. New York: Random House.

––– (1976a) "Folklore in the Modern World," in Richard Dorson (ed.) *Folklore and Fakelore*. Cambridge: Harvard University Press.

––– (1976b) *Folklore and Fakelore: Essays Toward a Discipline of Folk Studies*. Cambridge: Harvard University Press.

––– (1976c) "Mythology and Folklore: A Review Essay," in Richard Dorson (ed.) *Folklore and Fakelore*. Cambridge: Harvard University Press.

DOUGHTY, F. W. (1890) *Old King Brady and Bill the Kid*. New York: Frank Tousey.

DOVE, W. F. (1936) "Artificial Production of the Fabulous Unicorn." The Scientific Monthly 42.

DRAGO, H. S. (1964) *Outlaws on Horseback*. New York: Dodd, Mead.

DRESSER, N. (1974) " 'The Boys in the Band Is Not Another Musical': Male Homosexuals and Their Folklore." Western Folklore 33.

DUNDES, A. [ed.] (1965) *The Study of Folklore*. Englewood Cliffs, N.J.: Prentice-Hall.

––– (1971) "On the Psychology of Legend," in Wayland Hand (ed.) *American Folk Legend*. Berkeley and Los Angeles: University of California Press.

––– (1972) "Folk Ideas as Units of Worldview," in Americo Paredes and Richard Bauman (eds.) *Toward New Perspectives in Folklore*. Austin: University of Texas Press.

——— (1975) "The American Concept of Folklore," in Alan Dundes (ed.) *Analytic Essays in Folklore*. The Hague: Mouton.

——— [ed.] (1975a) *Analytic Essays in Folklore*. The Hague: Mouton.

——— and C. PATGER (1975) *Urban Folklore from the Paperwork Empire*. Austin: American Folklore Society.

DUPREE, L. (1967) "The Retreat of the British Army from Kabul to Jalalabad in 1842: History and Folklore." Journal of the Folklore Institute 4.

DURANT, W. and A. DURANT (1968) *The Lessons of History*. New York: Simon & Schuster.

DYOS, H. J. [ed.] (1968) *The Study of Urban History*. London: Edward Arnold.

EDWARDS, W. B. (1953) *The Story of Colt's Revolver*. Harrisburg, Penn.: Stockpole.

EISLE, W. E. (1931) *The Real Wild Bill Hickok*. Denver: William H. Andre.

ELLIOT, D. S. (1892) *Last Raid of the Daltons*. Coffeyville, Kansas: Coffeyville Journal Print.

EVERY, E. V. (1930) *Sins of New York as "Exposed" by the Police Gazette*. New York: Frederick A. Stokes.

FABEL, E. (1881) *Billy the Kid, the New Mexican Outlaw; or, the Bold Bandit of the West*. Denver: Denver Publishing Co.

FELDBERG, M. J. (1970) "The Philadelphia Riots of 1844: A Social History." Ph.D. dissertation, University of Rochester.

——— (1973) "Urbanization as a Cause of Violence: Philadelphia as a Test Case," in A. Davis and M. Haller (eds.) *The Peoples of Philadelphia: A History of Ethnic Groups and Lower-Class Life 1790-1940*. Philadelphia: Temple University Press.

FELDMAN, E. (1967) "Prostitution, The Alien Woman and the Progressive Imagination, 1910-1915." American Quarterly 11.

FENIN, G. N. and W. K. EVERSON (1973) *The Western: From Silents to the Seventies*. New York: Penguin.

FIDDLE, S. (1972) *Toasts: Images of a Victim Society*. Exodus House.

FIELD, A. (1951) "Why Is the 'Murdered Girl' So Popular?" Midwest Folklore 1.

FIELDER, M. (1965) *Wild Bill and Deadwood*. New York: Bonanza.

FINNEGAN, R. (1970) "A Note on Oral Tradition and Historical Evidence." History and Theory 9.

FISCHER, D. H. (1970) *Historians' Fallacies: Toward a Logic of Historical Thought*. New York: Harper & Row.

FLORIN, L. (1962) *Ghost Town Album*. Seattle: Superior.

FORD, T. L. (1926) *Dawn and the Dons. The Romance of Monterey*. San Francisco: A. M. Robertson.

FREEDMAN, E. B. (1976) "Their Sister's Keepers: The Origins of Female Corrections in America." Ph.D. dissertation, Columbia University.

FRENCH, W. (1965a) *Some Recollections of a Western Ranchman: New Mexico, 1883-1899*. New York: Argosy-Antiquarian.

——— (1965b) *Further Recollections of a Western Ranchman*. New York: Argosy-Antiquarian.

FRIDGE, I. (1927) *History of the Chisum War; or, Life of Ike Fridge*. Electra, Texas: J. D. Smith.

FRIEDMAN, A. B. (1971) "The Usable Myth: The Legends of Modern Mythmakers," in Wayland Hand (ed.) *American Folk Legend*. Berkeley and Los Angeles: University of California Press.

FRIEND, L. (1971) "W.P. Webb's Texas Rangers." Southwestern Historical Quarterly 74.

FURSTENBERG, M. H. (1969) "Violence and Organized Crime," in *Crimes of Violence*. Staff Report Submitted to the National Commission on the Causes and Prevention of Violence, Vol. 13, Appendix 18. Washington, D.C.: U.S. Government Printing Office.

GARD, W. (1936) *Sam Bass*. Boston: Houghton Mifflin.

GARDINER, J. A. (1970) *The Politics of Corruption: Organized Crime in an American City*. New York: Russell Sage.

GARDNER, R. H. (1944) *The Old Wild West: Adventures of Arizona Bill*. San Antonio: Naylor.

GARRAGHAN, G. J. (1946) *A Guide to Historical Method*. New York: Fordham University Press.

GARWOOD, D. (1948) *Crossroads of America: The Story of Kansas City*. New York: W. W. Norton.

GATES, P. W. (1966) *Fifty Million Acres: Conflicts Over Kansas Land Policy, 1854-1890*. New York: Atherton.

GENTILE, N. (1963) *Vita di Capomafia*. Roma: Editori Ruiniti.

GEORGES, R. (1971) "The General Concept of Legend: Some Assumptions to be Examined and Reassessed," in Wayland Hand (ed.) *American Folk Legend*. Berkeley and Los Angeles: University of California Press.

GLASSCOCK, C. B. (1934) *A Golden Highway: Scenes of History's Greatest Gold Rush Yesterday and Today*. Indianapolis: Bobbs-Merrill.

GOLDSTEIN, K. (1964) *A Guide for Field Workers In Folklore*. Hatboro, Penn.: Folklore Associates.

GOLLOMB, J. (1927) *Master Highwaymen*. New York: Macaulay.

GOMME, G. (1968) *Folklore As An Historical Science*. Detroit: Singing Tree Press.

GORDON, C. H. (1974) *Riddles in History*. New York: Crown.

GOREN, A. A. (1970) *New York Jews and the Quest for Community: The Kehillah Experiment, 1908-1922*. New York: Columbia University Press.

GOSCH, M. and R. HAMMER (1974) *Last Testament of Lucky Luciano*. Boston: Little, Brown.

GOTTSCHALK, L. (1969) *Understanding History*. New York: Alfred A. Knopf.

GOULART, R. (1972) *Cheap Thrills: An Informal History of Pulp Magazines*. New Rochelle, N.Y.: Arlington House.

GOULD, R. (1966) "Indian and White Versions of the Burnt Ranch Massacre: A Study in Comparative Ethnohistory." Journal of the Folklore Institute 3.

GREENBERG, D. S. (1973) "Persons of Evil Name and Fame: Crime and Law Enforcement in the Colony of New York, 1691-1776." Ph.D. dissertation, Cornell University.

GROH, G. W. (1966) *Gold Fever*. New York: William Morrow.

GURR, T. R., P. N. GRABOSKY, and R. C. HULA (1977) *The Politics of Crime and Conflict: A Comparative History of Four Cities*. Beverly Hills: Sage Publications.

GUSTAVSON, C. (1955) *A Preface to History*. New York: McGraw-Hill.

GUYER, J. S. (1938) *Pioneer Life in West Texas*. Brownwood, Texas: n.p.

HAGAN, C. B. (1951) "Wire Communications Utilities and Bookmaking." Minnesota Law Review 35.

HALEY, J. E. (1948) *Jeff Milton, A Good Man With A Gun*. Norman: University of Oklahoma Press.

HALL, T. (1920) *California Trails, Intimate Guide to the Old Missions*. New York: Macmillan.

HALLER, M. H. (1970) "Urban Crime and Criminal Justice: The Chicago Case." The Journal of American History 58.

––– (1971-1972-W) "Organized Crime in Urban Society: Chicago in the Twentieth Century." Journal of Social History 5.

––– (1976) "Bootleggers and American Gambling, 1920-1950." Commission on the Review of National Policy Toward Gambling. Gambling in America, Appendix I. Washington, D.C.: U.S. Government Printing Office.

HAMILTON, T. M. (1932) *The Young Pioneer*. Washington, D.C.: Library Press.

HANAWALT, B. A. (1975) "Fur-Collar Crime: The Pattern of Crime Among the Fourteenth-Century English Nobility." Journal of Social History 8.

HAND, W. [ed.] (1971) *American Folk Legend*. Berkeley and Los Angeles: University of California Press.

HANES, B. C. (1968) *Bill Doolin, Outlaw O. T.* Norman: University of Oklahoma Press.

HANSEN, G. W. (1927) "The Rock Creek Ranch Events and the Trail of Wild Bill." Nebraska History Magazine 10.

HARDIN, J. W. (1896) *The Life of John Wesley Hardin*. Seguin, Texas: Smith & Moore.

HARLOW, A. F. (1931) *Old Bowery Days: The Chronicles of a Famous Street*. New York: D. Appleton.

––– (1934) *Old Waybills*. New York: D. Appleton.

HARMAN, S. W. (1898) *Hell on the Border: He Hanged Eighty-Eight Men*. Fort Smith, Ark.: Phoenix.

HASKELL, M. R. and L. YABLONSKY (1969) *Crime and Delinquency*. Chicago: Rand McNally.

HAWGOOD, J. A. (1969) *America's Western Frontiers: The Exploration and Settlement of the Trans-Mississippi West*. New York: Alfred A. Knopf.

HAYS, S. P. (1964) "The Politics of Reform in Municipal Government in the Progressive Era." Pacific Northwest Quarterly.

HELPER, M. (1972) "Color, Crime and the City." Ph.D. dissertation, Rice University.

HENNIG, J. (1957) "Jaspers' Attitude Toward History," in P. A. Schilpp (ed.) *The Philosophy of Karl Jaspers*. New York: Tudor.

HENRY, L. (1967) *Manuel de demographie historique*. Genevea and Paris: Librairie Droz.

HENRY, S. O. (1930) *Conquering Our Great American Plains*. New York: E. P. Dutton.

HERBERS, J. (1969) "Special Introduction" to H. D. Graham and T. R. Gurr (eds.) *Violence in America: Historical and Comparative Perspectives*. New York: Bantam.

HESS, H. (1970) *Mafia: Zentrale Herrschaft und Lokale Gegenmacht*. Tübingen: J.C.B. Mohr.

HEXTER, J. H. (1971) *Doing History*. Bloomington: Indiana University Press.

HIGONNET, P. and T. HIGONNET (1967) "Class, Corruption and Politics in the French Chamber of Deputies, 1846-1848." French Historical Studies 5.

HILL, J. L. (n.d.) *The End of the Cattle Trail*. Long Beach, Calif.: George W. Moyle.

HITTELL, T. H. (1898) *History of California*. N. J. Stone.

HOBSBAWM, E. J. (1959) *Primitive Rebels: Studies in Archaic Forms of Social Movement in the 19th and 20th Centuries*. Manchester, England: Manchester University Press.

HOBSBAWM, E. J. (1969) *Bandits*. Harmondsworth, England: Penguin.

—— (1972) "Social Bandits: Reply." Comparative Studies in Society and History 14.

HOCKETT, H. C. (1955) *The Critical Method in Historical Research and Writing*. New York: Macmillan.

HOLBROOK, S. H. (1941) *Murder Out Yonder: An Informal Study of Certain Classic Crimes in Back-Country America*. New York: Macmillan.

——— (1962) *The Story of American Railroads*. New York: Bonanza.

HOLLON, W. E. (1974) *Frontier Violence: Another Look*. New York: Oxford University Press.

HOOK, S. [ed.] (1963) *Philosophy and History*. New York: New York University Press.

HOPWOOD, R. F. (1971) " 'The Importance of Being Earnest;' Reflections on the Popular Culture Symposium Held at Queen's University, Kingston, Ontario." Journal of Popular Culture 4.

HOWARD, R. W. (1962) *The Great Iron Trail*. New York: Bonanza.

HOWES, C. C. (1952) *This Place Called Kansas*. Norman: University of Oklahoma Press.

HOYT, H. F. (1929) *A Frontier Doctor*. Boston: Houghton Mifflin.

HUBBARD, F. H. (1945) *Railroad Avenue: Great Stories and Legends of American Railroading*. New York: McGraw-Hill.

HUGHES, H. S. (1964) *History as Art and as Science: Twin Vistas on the Past*. New York: Harper & Row.

HUGHES, W. J. (1964) *Rebellious Ranger: Rip Ford and the Old Southwest*. Norman: University of Oklahoma Press.

HUNEKER, J. (1921) *Unicorns*. New York: Charles Scribner's.

HUNTINGTON, G. (1895) *Robber and Hero, The Story of the Raid on the First National Bank of Northfield, Minnesota, by the James-Younger Band of Robbers in 1876*. Northfield, Minn.: Christian Way.

HUTCHINSON, J. (1970) *The Imperfect Union: A History of Corruption in American Trade Unions*. New York: E. P. Dutton.

IANNI, F. A. with E. REUSS-IANNI (1972) *A Family Business: Kinship and Social Control in Organized Crime*. New York: New American Library.

INCIARDI, J. A. (1974) "Vocational Crime," in Daniel Glaser (ed.) *Handbook of Criminology*. Chicago: Rand McNally.

——— (1975) *Careers in Crime*. Chicago: Rand McNally.

INGRAHAM, P. (1881) *Adventures of Buffalo Bill from Boyhood to Manhood*. New York: Beadle & Adams.

——— (1882) *Wild Bill, the Pistol Dead Shot; or Dagger Dan's Double*. New York: Beadle & Adams.

——— (1884) *Wild Bill, the Pistol Prince, From Early Boyhood to His Tragic Death*. New York: Beadle & Adams.

——— (1889) *Wild Bill, The Pistol Prince*. New York: J. Ives.

JACKSON, B. (1972) *Wake Up Dead Man: Afro-American Worksongs from Texas Prisons*. Cambridge, Mass.: Harvard University Press.

——— (1974) *Get Your Ass in the Water and Swim Like Me: Narrative Poetry from Black Oral Tradition*. Cambridge, Mass.: Harvard University Press.

JACKSON, J. H. (1949) *Bad Company*. New York: Harcourt, Brace & World.

JACOBS, M. [ed.] (1966) "The Anthropologist Looks at Myth." Journal of American Folklore 79.

JAHNS, P. (1957) *The Frontier World of Doc Holliday, Faro Dealer from Dallas to Deadwood*. New York: Hastings House.

JAMES, J. (1889) *Jesse James, My Father: The First and Only True Story of His Adventures Ever Written*. Independence, Mo.: Sentinel.

JASPERS, K. (1947) *The Question of German Guilt*. New York: Dial.

——— (1953) *The Origin and Goal of History*. London: Routledge & Kegan Paul.

——— (1957) *Man in the Modern Age*. New York: Doubleday.

JEFFREYS-JONES, R. (1974) "Violence in American History: Plug Uglies in the Progressive Era." Perspectives in American History, Vol. 8. Cambridge: Charles Warren Center for Studies in America History.

JEFFRIES, C. C. (1961) "The Character of the Terry's Texas Rangers." Southwestern Historical Quarterly 64.

JENARDO, D. (1881) *The True Life of Billy the Kid*. New York: Frank Tousey.

JENNINGS, D. (1967) *We Only Kill Each Other: The Life and Bad Times of Bugsy Siegel*. Greenwich, Conn.: Fawcett.

JENNINGS, N. A. (1899) *A Texas Ranger*. New York: Charles Scribner's.

JOHANNSEN, A. (1950) *The House of Beadle and Adams and its Dime and Nickel Novels*. Norman: University of Oklahoma Press.

JOHNSON, D. R. (1972) "The Search for an Urban Discipline: Police Reform as a Response to Crime in American Cities, 1800-1875." Ph.D. dissertation, University of Chicago.

——— (1973) "Crime Patterns in Philadelphia, 1840-70," in A. Davis and M. Haller (eds.) *The Peoples of Philadelphia: A History of Ethnic Groups and Lower-Class Life, 1790-1940*. Philadelphia: Temple University Press.

JONES, D. (1973) "Clenched Teeth and Curses: Revenge and the Dime Novel Outlaw Hero." Journal of Popular Culture 7.

JOSSERAND, M. H. and J. STEVENSON (1972) *Pistols, Revolvers, and Ammunition*. New York: Crown.

JOYNT, C. B. and N. RESCHER (1965) "The Problem of Uniqueness in History," in G. H. Nadel (ed.) *History and Theory*. New York: Harper & Row.

KELEHER, W. A. (1937) *Violence in Lincoln County, 1869-1881*. Albuquerque: University of New Mexico Press.

——— (1945) *The Fabulous Frontier; Twelve New Mexico Items*. Sante Fe: Rydall.

KELLER, W. (1956) *The Bible as History: A Confirmation of the Book of Books*. New York: William Morrow.

KELLY, C. (1958) *The Outlaw Trail*. New York: Bonanza.

KEY, V. O. (1934) "The Techniques of Political Graft in the U.S." Ph.D. dissertation, University of Chicago.

KILGORE, D. E. (1973) *A Ranger Legacy: 150 Years of Service in Texas*. Austin: Madrona Press.

KING, H. F. (1956) "The Banishment of Prudery: A Study of the Issue of Prostitution in the Progressive Era." Ph.D. dissertation, Columbia University.

KLEIN, B. (1973) "The Testimony of the Button," in Richard Dorson (ed.) *Folklore and Traditional History*. The Hague: Mouton.

KLETTE, E. (1928) *The Crimson Trail of Joaquin Murieta*. Los Angeles: Wetzel.

KLOCKARS, C. B. (1974) *The Professional Fence*. New York: Free Press.

KNEELAND, G. J. (1913) *Commercialized Prostitution in New York City*. New York: Century.

KOBLER, J. (1971) *Capone: The Life and World of Al Capone*. New York: Putnam.

LABOV, W. et al. (1973) "Toasts," in Alan Dundes (ed.) *Mother Wit From the Laughing Barrel: Readings in the Interpretation of Afro-American Folklore*. Englewood Cliffs, N.J.: Prentice-Hall.

LAKE, S. N. (1931) *Wyatt Earp, Frontier Marshall*. Boston: Houghton Mifflin.

LANDESCO, J. (1968) *Organized Crime in Chicago*. Part III of the Illinois Crime Survey, 1929. Chicago: University of Chicago Press.

LANDES, D. and C. TILLY (1971) *History as Social Science*. Englewood Cliffs, N.J.: Prentice-Hall.

LARKIN, M. [ed.] (1931) *Singing Cowboy, A Book of Western Songs*. New York: Alfred A. Knopf.

LASSWELL, H. D. and B. McKENNA (1972) *The Impact of Organized Crime on an Inner City Community*. New York: Policy Sciences Center.

LAURIE, B. (1973) "Fire Companies and Gangs in Southwark: The 1840's," in A. Davis and M. Haller (eds.) *The Peoples of Philadelphia: A History of Ethnic Groups and Lower Class Life, 1790-1940*. Philadelphia: Temple University Press.

LAWS, M. G. (1964) *Native American Balladry*. Philadelphia: American Folklore Society.

LAWSON, W. B. (1902) *Jesse James's Diamond Deal, or Robbing the Red Hands*. New York: Street & Smith.

LEACH, M. and T. P. COFFIN [eds.] (1961) *The Critics and the Ballad*. Carbondale, Ill.: Southern Illinois University Press.

LEACH, M. and J. FRIED [eds.] (1972) *Standard Dictionary of Folklore, Mythology, and Legend*. New York: Funk & Wagnalls.

LEES, A. and L. Lees [eds.] (1976) *The Urbanization of European Society in the Nineteenth Century*. Lexington, Mass.: D.C. Heath.

LEES, L. H. (1969) "Patterns of Lower-Class Life: Irish Slum Communities in Nineteenth-Century London," in S. Thernstrom and R. Sennet (eds.) *Nineteenth-Century Cities: Essays in the New Urban History*. New Haven, Conn.: Yale University Press.

"Legal Implications of Labor Racketeering" (1937) Columbia Law Review 37.

LEWIS, O. (1966) *Sutter's Fort: Gateway to the Gold Fields*. Englewood Cliffs, N.J.: Prentice-Hall.

LEY, W. (1959) *Exotic Zoology*. New York: Viking.

LIPSET, S. M. and R. HOFSTADTER [eds.] (1968) *Sociology and History: Methods*. New York: Basic Books.

LITCHFIELD, R. B. (1969) "Demographic Characteristics of Florentine Patrician Families, Sixteenth to Nineteenth Centuries." Journal of Economic History 29.

LOGAN, A. (1972) *Against the Evidence: The Becker—Rosenthal Affair*. New York: Avon.

LOMAX, J. A. (1947) *Adventures of a Ballad Hunter*. New York: Macmillan.

LOOMIS, N. M. (1968) *Wells Fargo*. New York: Bramhall.

LORD, J. (1926) *Frontier Dust*. Hartford, Conn.: Edwin Valentine Mitchell.

LOVE, N. (1907) *The Life and Adventures of Nat Love, Better Known in the Cattle Country as "Deadwood Dick."* Los Angeles: Wayside Press.

LOVE, R. (1926) *The Rise and Fall of Jesse James*. New York: Putnam.

LUBOVE, R. (1963) *The Progressives and the Slums: Tenement House Reform in New York City, 1890-1917*. Pittsburgh: University of Pittsburgh Press.

LYONS, R. (1947) "The Boston Police Strike of 1919." New England Quarterly 2.
LYNCH, W. S. and J. W. PHILLIPS (1971) "Organized Crime, Violence and Corruption." Journal of Public Law 20.
LYNN, K. (1969) "Violence in American Literature and Folk Lore," in Hugh Graham and Ted Gurr (eds.) *Violence in America.* New York: Signet.

McADOO, W. (1906) *Guarding a Great City.* New York: Harper.
McCLINTOCK, J. S. (1939) *Pioneer Days in the Black Hills.* Deadwood, S.D.: John S. McClintock.
McCLURE, S. S. (1909) "The Tammanyzing of a Civilization." McClure's Magazine 34.
McCOY, A. N. (1973) *The Politics of Heroin in Southeast Asia.* New York: Harper & Row.
McKITRICK, E. L. (1957) "The Study of Corruption." Political Science Quarterly 72.
McLAUGHLIN, D. (1975) *Wild and Wooly: An Encyclopedia of the Old West.* Garden City, N.Y.: Doubleday.
McPHAUL, J. (1970) *Johnny Torrio: First of the Gang Lords.* New Rochelle, N.Y.: Arlington House.
MAAS, P. (1968) *The Valachi Papers.* New York: Bantam.
MANDELBAUM, S. (1965) *Boss Tweed's New York.* New York: John Wiley.
MARANDA, P. and E. KONGAS [eds.] (1971) *Structural Analysis of Oral Tradition.* Philadelphia: University of Pennsylvania Press.
MAZLICH, B. [ed.] (1963) *Psychoanalysis and History.* Englewood Cliffs, N.J.: Prentice-Hall.
MEIGHAN, C. (1960) "More on Folk Traditions." Journal of American Folklore 73.
MERCATANTE, A. S. (1974) *Zoo of the Gods: Animals in Myth, Legend and Fable.* New York: Harper & Row.
MERTON, R. K. (1968) *Social Theory and Social Structure.* New York: Free Press.
MESKIL, P. (1973) *Don Carlo: Boss of Bosses.* New York: Popular Library.
MESSICK, H. (1971) *Lansky.* New York: Putnam.
METZ, L. C. (1966) *John Selman, Texas Gunfighter.* New York: Hastings House.
MEYERHOFF, H. [ed.] (1959) *The Philosophy of History in Our Time.* Garden City, N.Y.: Doubleday.
——— (1968) *Time in Literature.* Berkeley and Los Angeles: University of California Press.
MILLER, W. R. (1975) "Police Authority in London and New York 1830-1870." Journal of Social History 8.
MILLER, Z. L. (1968) *Boss Cox's Cincinnati: Urban Politics in the Progressive Era.* New York: Oxford University Press.
Minneapolis Star (1975) "Army calls massacre label unfair." (December 29).
MINTZ, J. [ed.] (1965) "Culture and Folklore." Journal of the Folklore Institute 2.
MITGANG, H. (1963) *The Man Who Rode the Tiger: The Life of Judge Samuel Seabury and the Story of the Greatest Investigation of City Corruption in this Century.* New York: Viking.
MOCKRIDGE, N. and R. H. PRALL (1954) *The Big Fix.* New York: Henry Holt.
MONAGHAN, J. (1951) *The Great Rascal: The Exploits of the Amazing Ned Buntline.* Boston: Little, Brown.
MONKKENON, E. H. (1973) "Crime and Poverty in a Nineteenth Century City: The

Dangerous Class of Columbus Ohio, 1860-1885." Ph.D. dissertation, University of Minnesota.

MONTELL, W. L. (1970) *The Saga of Coe Ridge.* Knoxville: University of Tennessee Press.

MOODY, R. (1963) *The Old Trails West.* New York: Thomas Y. Crowell.

MOORE, B. (1965) *Political Power and Social Theory.* New York: Harper & Row.

MOORE, J. M. (1935) *The West.* Wichita Falls, Texas: Wichita Printing Co.

MOORE, W. H. (1974) *The Kefauver Committee and the Politics of Crime, 1950-1952.* Columbia: University of Missouri Press.

MOTT, F. L. (1947) *Golden Multitudes.* New York: Macmillan.

MULLEN, P. B. (1971) "The Relationship of Legend and Folk Belief." Journal of American Folklore 84.

MUMEY, N. (1950) *Calamity Jane, 1852-1903.* Denver: Range Press.

MURRAY, H. A. [ed.] (1959a) "Myth and Mythmaking." Daedalus 88.

――― (1959b) "Introduction to the Issue 'Myth and Mythmaking'." Daedalus 88.

NELLI, H. S. (1976) *The Business of Crime: Italians and Syndicate Crime in the United States.* New York: Oxford University Press.

NEVINS, A. (1962) *The Gateway to History.* Garden City, N.Y.: Doubleday.

New York State Senate Committee to Investigate the Police Department of the City of New York (1895). Report and Proceedings. Albany: J. B. Lyon.

New York State Supreme Court, Appellate Division–First Judicial Department (1932). Final Report of Samuel Seabury, Referee. (Reprinted by Arno Press, 1974.)

NICHOLS, A. (1954) *Bleeding Kansas.* New York: Oxford University Press.

O'CONNOR, R. (1973) *Iron Wheels and Broken Men: The Railroad Barons and the Plunder of the West.* New York: Putnam.

OLDER, F. (1940) *Love Stories of Old California.* New York: Coward-McCann.

O'LESSKER, K. (1968-1969) "Who Voted for Hitler? A New Look at the Class Basis and Nazism." American Journal of Sociology 74.

"Organized Crime: Developing Devices for Debilitating Desperadoes," (1970) Law and Social Order.

PALAVESTRA, V. (1966) "Tradition, History and National Feeling." Journal of the Folklore Institute 3.

PAREDES, A. (1958) *With a Pistol in his Hand.* Austin: University of Texas Press.

――― and E. STEKERT [eds.] (1971) *The Urban Experience and Folk Tradition.* Austin: American Folklore Society, University of Texas Press.

PAREDES, A. and R. BAUMAN [eds.] (1972) *Toward New Perspectives In Folklore.* Austin: American Folklore Society, University of Texas Press.

PARKER, J. M. (n.d.) *An Aged Wanderer. A Life Sketch of J. M. Parker, A Cowboy on the Western Plains in the Early Days.* San Angelo, Texas: Elkhorn Wagon Yard.

PASLEY, F. D. (1966) *Al Capone: The Biography of a Self-Made Man.* London: Faber & Faber.

PENDERGAST, D. and C. MEIGHAN (1959) "Folk Traditions as Historical Fact: A Paiute Example." Journal of American Folklore 72.

PHILLIPS, P. C. [ed.] (1925) *Forty Years on the Frontier as Seen in the Journals and Reminiscences of Granville Stuart, Gold-Miner, Trader, Merchant, Rancher, and Politician.* Cleveland: Arthur H. Clark.

PITRE, G. (1884) *Le Tradizioni cavel leresche popolari in Sicilia.* Parigi: F. Vieweg.

––– (1894) "La Mafia," in L. Capirana *L'isola del Sole.* Catania: N. Giannotta.

––– (1898) "La Sicilia, nei Canti popolari e nella novellistica contemporanea." Conferenze letta il 12 maggio nella sola del Liceo Musicale di Bologna a beneficio dle Comitato Bolognese della Societa Dante Alighieri.

––– (1902) *Curiosita de use popolari.* Catania: N. Giannotta.

PIVAR, D. J. (1973) *Purity Crusade: Sexual Morality and Social Control, 1868-1900.* Westport, Conn.: Greenwood Press.

PIZZORNO, A. (1966) "Amoral Familism and Historical Marginality." International Review of Community Development 15/16.

PRICE, J. M. (1969) "Recent Quantitative Work in History: A Survey of the Main Trends." History and Theory, Beiheft 9.

PRITCHARD, J. B. [ed.] (1955) *Ancient Near Eastern Texts.* Princeton, N.J.: Princeton University Press.

RABB, T. K. (1967) *Enterprises and Empire: Merchant and Gentry Investment in the Expansion of England, 1575-1630.* Cambridge, Mass.: Harvard University Press.

RADBRUCH, G. (1950) *Elegantiae juris criminalis.* Basel: Verlag Für Recht und Gesellschaft.

RASCOE, B. (1941) *Belle Starr, "The Bandit Queen."* New York: Random House.

RAYMOND, D. (1940) *Captain Lee Hall of Texas.* Norman: University of Oklahoma Press.

RECKLESS, W. (1933) *Vice in Chicago.* Chicago: University of Chicago Press.

REID, E. (1953) *The Shame of New York.* New York: Random House.

––– (1969) *The Grim Reapers: The Anatomy of Organized Crime in America.* Chicago: Henry Regnery.

RENIER, G. J. (1965) *History: Its Purpose and Method.* New York: Harper & Row.

REYNOLDS, A. M. (1974) "Urban Negro Toasts: A Hustler's View From L.A." Western Folklore 33.

RHINES, C. C. (1975) "A City and its Social Problems: Poverty, Health, and Crime in Baltimore, 1865-1875." Ph.D. dissertation, University of Maryland.

RICHARDSON, J. F. (1970) *The New York Police: Colonial Times to 1901.* New York: Oxford University Press.

RIDGE, J. R. (1854) *The Life and Adventures of Joaquín Murieta, the Celebrated California Bandit.* San Francisco: W. B. Cook.

ROBINSON, D. (1973) "The Impact of Al-Hajj 'Umar on the Historical Traditions of the Fulbe," in Richard Dorson (ed.) *Folklore and Traditional History.* The Hague: Mouton.

ROSA, J. G. (1964) *They Called Him Wild Bill: The Life and Adventures of James Butler Hickok.* Norman: University of Oklahoma Press.

––– (1967) *Alias Jack McCall. A Pardon or Death?* Kansas City, Mo.: Kansas City Posse of the Westerners.

––– (1969) *The Gunfighter: Man or Myth?* Norman: University of Oklahoma Press.

ROTTENBERG, S. (1960) "A Theory of Corruption in Trade Unions." National Institute of Social and Behavioral Sciences, Series Studies in Social and Economic Sciences, Symposia Studies Series No. 3. (Washington, D.C.)

RUGGIERO, G. (1975) "Sexual Criminality in the Early Renaissance: Venice 1338-1358." Journal of Social History 8.

RUSCHE, G. and O. KIRCHHEIMER (1939) *Punishment and Social Structure.* New York: Columbia University Press.

SABIN, E. L. (1929) *Wild Men of the Wild West.* New York: Thomas Y. Crowell.

SANN, P. (1971) *Kill the Dutchman: The Story of Dutch Schultz.* New Rochelle, N.Y.: Arlington House.

SANTAYANA, G. (1905) *The Life of Reason.* London: Constable.

SAPOSS, D. J. (1958) "Labor Racketeering: Evolutions and Solutions." Social Research 25.

SAVAGE, R. H. (1892) *The Little Lady of Lagunitas; A Franco-Californian Romance.* New York: American News and J. J. Little.

SCHICK, F. L. (1958) *The Paperbound Book in America.* New York: R. R. Bowker.

SCHMITT, M. F. and D. BROWN (1974) *The Settlers' West.* New York: Ballantine.

SCHNEIDER, J. C. (1969) "Family Patrimonies and Economic Behavior in Western Sicily." Anthropological Quarterly 42.

SCHNEIDER, J. C. (1971) "Mob Violence and Public Order in the American City, 1830-1885." Ph.D. dissertation, University of Minnesota.

SCHNIEDER, P. (1972) "Coalition Formation and Colonialism in Sicily." European Journal of Sociology 13.

SEBEOK, T. A. [ed.] (1955) "Myth: A Symposium." Journal of American Folklore 68.

SELIGMAN, E.R.A. (1912) *The Social Evil: With Special Reference to Conditions Existing in the City of New York.* New York: Putnam.

SELLIN, T. (1976) *Slavery and the Penal System.* New York: Elsevier.

——— (1963) "Organized Crime as a Business." The Annals 347.

SENSING, T. (1968) "Sensing the News," Athens, Ga.: Bannerherald, February 5.

SETTLE, W. A. (1966) *Jesse James was his Name.* Columbia: University of Missouri Press.

SHEPARD, O. (1930) *The Lore of the Unicorn.* London: Allen & Unwin.

SHIELDS, R. W. (1939) *Seymour, Indiana, and the Famous Story of the Reno Gang, Who Terrorized America with the First Train Robberies in World History.* Indianapolis: H. Lieber.

SHINN, C. H. (1948) *Mining Camps: A Study in American Frontier Government.* New York: Alfred A. Knopf.

SHIRLEY, G. (1957) *Law West of Fort Smith.* New York: Henry Holt.

——— (1965) *Henry Starr: Last of the Real Badman.* New York: David McKay.

SHORTER, E. (1971) *The Historian and the Computer: A Practical Guide.* New York: W. W. Norton.

SIMEONE, W. (1958) "Robin Hood and Some Other Outlaws." Journal of American Folklore 71.

SMITH, D. C. (1975) *The Mafia Mystique.* New York: Basic Books.

——— (1976) "Mafia: The Prototypical Alien Conspiracy." The Annals 423.

SMITH, H. N. (1950) *Virgin Land: The American West As Symbol And Myth.* Cambridge, Mass.: Harvard University Press.

SOITO, P. (1949) *A Hundred Years of Pleasanton.* San Francisco: Philips & Van Orden.

STECKMESSER, K. (1965) *The Western Hero in History and Legend.* Norman: University of Oklahoma Press.

——— (1966) "Robin Hood and the American Outlaw: A Note on History and Folklore." Journal of American Folklore 79.

STEFFENS, L. (1948) *The Shame of the Cities.* New York: Peter Smith.

STENRING, K. (1970) *The Book of Formation.* New York: Ktav.

STEPHENS, L. D. (1974) *Probing the Past: A Guide to the Study and Teaching of History.* Boston: Allyn & Bacon.

STEPHENS, R. W. (1970) *Walter Durbin, Texas Ranger and Sheriff.* Clarendon, Texas: Clarendon Press.

STERN, F. [ed.] (1956) *The Varieties of History: From Voltaire to the Present.* Cleveland: Meridian.

STEWART, M. A. (1882) *Rosita: A California Tale.* San Jose: Mercury Steam Print.

STONE, W. H. (1905) *Twenty-Four Years A Cowboy and Ranchman in Southern Texas and Old Mexico.* Author's edition.

STOVER, J. F. (1975) *History of the Illinois Central Railroad.* New York: Macmillan.

STREET & SMITH (1902) *Catalogue of Street & Smith's Novels.* New York: Street & Smith.

SUTHERLAND, E. H. and D. R. CRESSEY (1974) *Criminology.* Philadelphia: J. P. Lippincott.

SUTTON, C. (1873) *The New York Tombs: Its Secrets and Mysteries.* New York: United States Publishing Co.

TALESE, G. (1971) *Honor Thy Father.* New York: World.

TAYLOR, I., P. WALTON, and J. YOUNG (1973) *The New Criminology: For A Social Theory of Deviance.* New York: Harper & Row.

TERESA, V. (1973) *My Life in the Mafia.* Greenwich, Conn.: Fawcett.

THERNSTROM, S. (1969) *Poverty and Progress: Social Mobility in a Nineteenth Century City.* New York: Atheneum.

――― and R. SENNETT [eds.] (1969) *Nineteenth-Century Cities: Essays in the New Urban History.* New Haven, Conn.: Yale University Press.

THOMES, W. H. (1872) *The Whaleman's Adventures in the Sandwich Islands and California.* New York: Lee, Shepard & Dillingham.

THOMPSON, E. P. (1975) "The Crime of Anonymity," in *Albion's Fatal Tree: Crime and Society in Eighteenth-Century England.* New York: Pantheon.

THOMPSON, G. G. (1943) *Bat Masterson.* Topeka: Kansas State Printing Plant.

THOMPSON, S. (1955-1958) *The Motif-Index of Folk Literature.* 6 vols. Copenhagen: Rosenkilde & Bagger.

――― (1961) *The Types of the Folktale.* Helsinki: Folklore Fellows Communications 184.

TILGHMAN, Z. A. (1949) *Marshall of the Last Frontier.* Glendale, Calif.: Arthur H. Clark.

TILLY, C., L. TILLY, and R. TILLY (1975) *The Rebellious Century, 1830-1930.* Cambridge, Mass.: Harvard University Press.

TOBIAS, J. J. (1967) *Urban Crime in Victorian England.* New York: Schocken.

TRIPLETT, F. (1882) *The Life, Times, and Treacherous Death of Jesse James.* Chicago: J. H. Chambers.

TURKUS, B. B. and S. FEDER (1951) *Murder, Inc.: The Story of the Syndicate.* New York: Farrar, Straus & Young.

TURNER, G. K. (1909) "The Daughters of the Poor." McClure's Magazine 34.

TURNER, G. (1972) *George Turner's Book of Gun Fighters.* Amarillo: Baxter Lane.

TUSKA, J. (1976) *The Filming of the West.* Garden City, N.Y.: Doubleday.

U.S. Bureau of Census (1949) *Historical Statistics of the U.S. 1789-1945.* Washington, D.C.: U.S. Government Printing Office.

VAN DOREN, C. [ed.] (1974) *Webster's American Biographies.* Springfield, Mass.: G & C Merriam.

VANN, R. T. (1969) "History and Demography." History and Theory, Beiheft 9.

VANSINA, J. (1965) Oral Tradition. Translated by H. M. Wright. Chicago: Aldine.

——— (1971) "Once Upon a Time: Oral Traditions as History in Africa." Daedalus 100.

VARNA, A. (1957) World Underworld. London: Museum Press.

VOLD, G. B. (1967) "The Organization of Criminals for Profit and Power," in M. B. Clinard and R. Quinney Criminal Behavior Systems: A Typology. New York: Holt, Rinehart & Winston.

WALSH, W. H. (1960) Philosophy of History: An Introduction. New York: Harper & Row.

WARD, W. (n.d.) Jesse James' Ruse, or The Mystery of the Two Highwaymen. Cleveland: Arthur Westbrook.

WARNER, M. and M. E. KING (1940) The Last of the Bandit Raiders. Caldwell, Idaho: Caxton.

WARNER, S. (1968) The Private City: Philadelphia in Three Periods of its Growth. Philadelphia: University of Pennsylvania Press.

WARNER, W. L. and J. O. LOW (1947) The Social System of the Modern Factory. New Haven, Conn.: Yale University Press.

WARNER, W. L. (1959) The Living and the Dead: A Study of the Symbolic Life of Americans. New Haven, Conn.: Yale University Press.

——— and P. LUNT (1941) The Social Life of a Modern Community. New Haven, Conn.: Yale University Press.

——— (1942) The Status System of a Modern Community. New Haven, Conn.: Yale University Press.

WARNER, W. L. and L. SROLE (1945) The Social Systems of American Ethnic Groups. New Haven, Conn.: Yale University Press.

WARSHOW, R. (1970) The Immediate Experience: Movies, Comics, Theater and Other Aspects of Popular Culture. New York: Atheneum.

WASERMAN, M. (1975) Bibliography On Oral History. New York: Oral History Association.

WATERMAN, W. C. (1932) Prostitution and its Repression in New York City. New York: Columbia University Press.

WATERS, F. (1960) The Story of Mrs. Virgil Earp: The Earp Brothers of Tombstone. New York: Clarkson N. Potter.

WATTS, E. J. (1973) "The Police in Atlanta, 1890-1905." Journal of Southern History 39.

WEBB, W. P. (1935) The Texas Rangers: A Century of Frontier Defense. Boston: Houghton Mifflin.

——— (1936) "The Texas Rangers: A Century of Frontier Defense." Southwestern Historical Quarterly 39.

WEINGROD, A. (1968) "Patrons, Patronage, and Political Parties." Comparative Studies in Society and History 10.

WELSCH, R. (1968) "A Note on Definitions." Journal of American Folklore 81.

WEPMAN, D., R. B. NEWMAN, and M. B. BINDERMAN (1974) "Toast: The Black Urban Folk Poetry." Journal of American Folklore 87.

WHEELER, E. L. (1877) Deadwood Dick, The Prince of the Road. New York: Beadle & Adams.

WHYTE, W. F. (1955) Street Corner Society. Chicago: University of Chicago Press.

WILCOX, S. (1941) "The Laredo City Election and Riot of April, 1886." Southwestern Historical Quarterly 45.

WILGUS, D. K. (1959) Anglo-American Folksong Scholarship Since 1898. New Brunswick, N.J.: Rutgers University Press.

WILGUS, D. K. and L. MONTELL (1971) "Beanie Short: A Civil War Chronicle in Legend and Song," in Wayland Hand (ed.) *American Folk Legend.* Berkeley and Los Angeles: University of California.

WILSON, W. (1970) "The Threat of Organized Crime: Highlighting the Challenging New Frontiers in Criminal Law." Notre Dame Lawyer 46.

WILSON, W. (1973) "Folklore and History: Fact Amid the Legends." Utah Historical Quarterly 41.

WILSTACH, F. J. (1926) *Wild Bill Hickok: The Prince of Pistoleers.* Garden City, N.Y.: Garden City.

WINKS, R. W. [ed.] (1968) *The Historian as Detective: Essays on Evidence.* New York: Harper & Row.

WOETZEL, R. K. (1963) "An Overview of Organized Crime: Mores Versus Morality." The Annals 347.

WOOLSTON, H. B. (1969) *Prostitution in the United States: Prior to the Entrance of the United States into the World War.* Montclair, N.J.: Patterson Smith.

WRIGHT, R. M. (1913) *Dodge City, The Cowboy Capital.* Wichita: Wichita Eagle Press.

NAME INDEX

NAME INDEX

SUBJECT INDEX

SUBJECT INDEX

ABOUT THE AUTHORS

JAMES A. INCIARDI is Associate Professor and Director, Division of Criminal Justice, University of Delaware. He received his Ph.D. from New York University and has had some fourteen years experience in the fields of drug abuse and criminal justice. Dr. Inciardi is the editor of *Criminology*, and the author of more than fifty books and articles in the fields of criminology and deviant behavior. His *Careers in Crime* (Rand McNally, 1975) is an historical study of professional theft, and is a clear reflection of his interests in historical criminology.

ALAN A. BLOCK is Assistant Professor of criminology, University of Delaware, Newark. He received his Ph.D. in history from the University of California, Los Angeles in 1975. Among his academic positions has been that of Co-Director, Criminal Justice Program, Alfred University, New York, 1973-1974. Dr. Block is the author of a number of conference papers and articles mainly focusing on the history of organized crime, a subject on which he has conducted extensive research.

LYLE A. HALLOWELL is a historical sociologist who is working toward his Ph.D. at the University of Minnesota, Minneapolis, where he has also been an instructor in elements of criminology and the sociology of law and social control. Among his main research interests are theories for the analysis of folklore data. He has authored a number of articles and papers dealing with the study of folklore and violence.